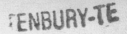

PENGUIN BOOKS

The Penguin German Phrasebook

Jill Norman enjoys exploring language, speaks several
languages and has travelled widely. Jill also created
the Penguin Cookery Library in the 1960s and 1970s,
bringing many first-class authors to the list. She has written
several award-winning books on food and cookery, and is
a leading authority on the use of herbs and spices. She is
the literary trustee of the Elizabeth David estate, and was
Mrs David's publisher for many years.

D1077306

THE PENGUIN
GERMAN
PHRASEBOOK

Fourth Edition

Jill Norman
Ute Hitchin
Renata Henkes

PENGUIN BOOKS

PENGUIN BOOKS

Published by the Penguin Group
Penguin Books Ltd, 80 Strand, London WC2R ORL, England
Penguin Group (USA) Inc., 375 Hudson Street, New York, New York 10014, USA
Penguin Group (Canada), 90 Eglinton Avenue East, Suite 700, Toronto, Ontario, Canada M4P 2Y3
(a division of Pearson Penguin Canada Inc.)
Penguin Ireland, 25 St Stephen's Green, Dublin 2, Ireland (a division of Penguin Books Ltd)
Penguin Group (Australia), 707 Collins Street, Melbourne, Victoria 3008, Australia
(a division of Pearson Australia Group Pty Ltd)
Penguin Books India Pvt Ltd, 11 Community Centre, Panchsheel Park, New Delhi – 110 017, India
Penguin Group (NZ), 67 Apollo Drive, Rosedale, Auckland 0632, New Zealand
(a division of Pearson New Zealand Ltd)
Penguin Books (South Africa) (Pty) Ltd, Block D, Rosebank Office Park, 181 Jan Smuts Avenue,
Parktown North, Gauteng 2193, South Africa

Penguin Books Ltd, Registered Offices: 80 Strand, London WC2R ORL, England

www.penguin.com

First edition 1968
Second edition 1978
Third edition 1988
This revised and updated edition published 2013
001

Set in 9/12pt TheSans and TheSerif
Typeset by Jouve (UK), Milton Keynes
Printed in England by Clays Ltd, St Ives plc

ISBN: 978-0-141-03903-9

www.greenpenguin.co.uk

ALWAYS LEARNING   **PEARSON**

CONTENTS

INTRODUCTION

This series of phrasebooks includes words and phrases essential to travellers of all kinds: the business traveller; the holidaymaker, whether travelling alone, with a group or the family; and the owner of a house, an apartment or a time-share. For easy use the phrases are arranged in sections which deal with specific situations and needs.

The book is designed to help travellers who never had the opportunity to learn German, as well as serving as an invaluable refresher course for those whose knowledge has gone rusty.

Pronunciation is given for each phrase and for all words in the extensive vocabulary. See pp. xi–xiv for the pronunciation guide on which should be read carefully before starting to use this book.

Some of the German phrases are marked with an **asterisk*** – these give an indication of the kind of reply you might get to your question, and of questions you may be asked.

For those who would like to know a little more about the German language the main points of its grammar are covered at the end of the book (pp. 242–62).

PRONUNCIATION

The pronunciation guide is intended for people with no knowledge of German. As far as possible the system is based on English pronunciation. This means that complete accuracy may sometimes be lost for the sake of simplicity, but you should be able to understand German pronunciation, and make yourself understood, if you read this section carefully. Stressed syllables are *in italics*.

Vowels

German vowels are much purer than English ones.

Long **a**	as 'a' in father	symbol **ah**	Abend – *ah*bent
Short **a**	as 'a' in apple	symbol **a**	kalt – kalt
au	as 'ow' in how	symbol **ow**	Ausland – *ows*-lant
ä	as 'ai' in air or 'e' in bed	symbol **ai/ay/e**	Lärm – lairm Nägel – *nay*gul Gepäck – gu*peck*
äu	as 'oy' in boy	symbol **oy**	Gebäude – gu*boy*der
Long **e**	as 'e' in they	symbol **ai/ay**	geht – gait gegen – *gay*gun
Short **e**	as 'e' in bed or 'u' in up	symbol **e/u**	Bett – bet Gesicht – gu*zikht*

e (final)	'e' is pronounced at the end of a word, as 'er' in sister	symbol **er**	Tinte – tinter
e as in 'er'	NB: in most cases the r in 'er' is more pronounced than in English	symbol **air/er**	verlangen – fair*lang*-en
eu	as 'oy' in boy	symbol **oy**	Feuer – *foy*er
ei	as 'i' in fine	symbol **i/y/eye**	ein – ine leisten – *ly*sten Eimer – *eye*mer
i	as 'i' in bit	symbol **i**	Schiff – shif
i	as 'ee' in weed	symbol **ee**	Familie – fa*mee*lyer
ie	as 'ee' in meet	symbol **ee**	Bier – beer
Long **o**	as 'o' in nose	symbol **oh**	sofort – zoh*fort*
Short **o**	as 'o' in not	symbol **o**	von – fon
ö	similar to sound in 'her' and 'first' but made with the lips well rounded	symbol **er**	schön – shern
u	as 'oo' in mood	symbol **oo**	dunkel – *doon*kel
ü	say 'i' as in bit with the lips rounded and pushed forward	symbol **ui**	Büro – bui*roh*

Consonants

b (final)	and before a consonant pronounced as 'p'	symbol **p**	ab – ap
ch and **g** (final)	rather like the sound of 'ch' in Scottish loch or the Welsh 'ch'	symbol **kh**	Buch – bookh fertig – *fair*tikh
chs	as 'x' in six	symbol **ks**	Lachs – laks
d (final)	pronounced as 't'	symbol **t**	Kind – kint
g	hard as 'g' in go, except in some endings	symbol **g**	gut – goot
j	as 'y' in yacht	symbol **y**	ja – yah
kn	in German words which begin kn- the two sounds are pronounced separately, unlike English	symbol **k-n**	Knie – k-nee
qu	two sounds pronounced separately	symbol **k-v**	Qualität – k-vali*tayt*
r	is always guttural and clearly pronounced		
s	before a vowel is pronounced 'z' as in zoo	symbol **z**	Bluse – *bloo*zer

s	at the end of a word is pronounced 's' as in sale	symbol **s/ss**	Hals – hals Nuss – nooss
ß	after long vowels is pronounced 'ss'	symbol **s/ss**	Spaß – shpahs
s	before p or t is pronounced 'sh' as in sheep	symbol **sh**	Stein – shtine Spiel – shpeel
sch	as 'sh' in sheep	symbol **sh**	Schuh – shoo
th	as 't' in tent	symbol **t**	Theater – tay*ahter*
tz	as 'ts' in cuts	symbol **ts**	Netz – nets
v	as 'f' in foot or 'v' in vase	symbol **f** or **v**	viel – feel Vase – *vahzer*
w	usually as 'v' in vase	symbol **v**	Wohnung – *vohnoong*
x	as 'x' in wax	symbol **cks**	Praxis – pracksis
z	as 'ts' in bits	symbol **ts**	zu – tsoo

The German Alphabet

A	ah	H	ha	O	oh	U	oo
B	bay	I	ee	P	pay	V	fow
C	tsay	J	yott	Q	koo	W	vay
D	day	K	kah	R	er	X	iks
E	ay	L	el	S	ess	Y	uipsilon
F	eff	M	em	SS=ß	ess	Z	tset
G	gay	N	en	T	tay		

ESSENTIALS

First Things

Key Phrases		
Yes	**Ja**	Yah
No	**Nein**	Nine
Please	**Bitte**	Bitter
Thank you	**Danke**	Danker
You're welcome	**Bitte sehr**	Bitter zair

Greetings

Key Phrases		
Good morning	**Guten Morgen**	Gooten *morg*un
Good day/afternoon	**Guten Tag**	Gooten tahg
Good day (*south German*)	**Grüß Gott**	Gruis got
Good evening	**Guten Abend**	Gooten *ah*bent
Good night	**Gute Nacht**	Gooter nahkht
Goodbye	**Auf Wiedersehen**	Owf *veeder-zay*en

Goodbye (*informal*)	**Tschüss**	Tshuis
How are you?	**Wie geht es Ihnen?**	Vee gait es eenen
Fine, thank you	**Danke, gut**	Danker goot
See you soon/tomorrow	**Bis bald/morgen**	Bis balt/*morgun*
Have a good journey	**Gute Reise**	Gooter *ryzer*
Have a good time	**Viel Vergnügen/ Viel Spaß**	Feel fairg*nuigun/* Feel shpahs
Good luck/ All the best	**Viel Glück/ Alles Gute**	Feel gluick/ Alles gooter

Polite Phrases

Key Phrases

Sorry	**Verzeihung**	Fair-*tsyoong*
Excuse me	**Entschuldigen Sie bitte**	Ents*hool*digun zee bitter
That's all right (*in reply to* Excuse me)	**Schon gut**	Shohn goot
Is everything all right?	**Alles in Ordnung?**	Alles in *ord*noong
Good/That's fine	**Gut/Das ist gut so**	Goot/Das ist goot zoh
Many thanks for your trouble	**Besten Dank für Ihre Mühe**	Besten dank fuir eerer mui-er

With pleasure	**Gern**	Gairn
Don't worry	**Machen Sie sich keine Sorgen**	Makhen zee zikh kiner *zorg*un
It's a pity	**(Es ist) schade**	(Es ist) *shah*der
It doesn't matter	**(Es) macht nichts**	(Es) makht nikhts
I beg your pardon?	**Wie bitte?**	Vee bitter
Am I disturbing you?	**Störe ich Sie?**	*Shter*-rer ikh zee
I'm sorry to have troubled you	**Es tut mir leid, dass ich Sie belästigt habe**	Es toot meer lite dass ikh zee bu*les*tigt hahber

Language Problems

Key Phrases

Do you speak English?	**Sprechen Sie Englisch?**	*Shprekh*en zee *aing*-lish
Does anybody here speak English?	**Spricht hier irgend jemand Englisch?**	Sprikht heer *eer*gunt yaymant *aing*-lish
I don't speak (much) German	**Ich spreche kein/nur wenig Deutsch**	Ikh *shprekh*er kine/noor *vay*nikh doytsh
Do you understand (me)?	***Verstehen Sie (mich)?**	Fair*shtay*en zee (mikh)
Please speak slowly	**Bitte, sprechen Sie langsam**	Bitter *shprekh*en zee *lang*zam
Please write it down	**Bitte schreiben Sie es auf**	Bitter *shry*ben zee es owf

I'm English/American	**Ich bin Engländer(in)/ Amerikaner(in)**	Ikh bin *aing*-lender(in)/ amairee*kah*nair(in)
I don't understand	**Ich verstehe nicht**	Ikh fair*shtay*er nikht
Would you say that again, please?	**Würden Sie das bitte noch einmal sagen?**	*Vuir*den zee das bitter nokh *ine*-mahl *zah*gun
What does that mean?	**Was bedeutet das?**	Vas bu*doy*tet das
Can you translate this for me?	**Können Sie das für mich übersetzen?**	Kernen zee das fuir mikh *ui*ber-zetsen
What do you call this in German?	**Wie heißt das auf Deutsch?**	Vee hyst das owf doytsh
How do you say that in German?	**Wie sagt man das auf Deutsch?**	Vee zakht man das owf doytsh
Please show me the word in the book	**Können Sie mir das Wort bitte in diesem Buch zeigen?**	Kernen zee meer das vort bitter in deezem bookh *tsy*gun

Questions

Key Phrases

Who?	**Wer?**	Vair
Where is/are ...?	**Wo ist/sind ...?**	Voh ist/zint
When?	**Wann?**	Van
How?	**Wie?**	Vee
How much is/are ...?	**Wie teuer ist/sind ...?/** **Was kostet/kosten ...?**	Vee *toyer* ist/zint/ Vas kostet/kosten
How far?	**Wie weit?**	Vee vite
Why?	**Warum?**	Vah*room*
Is there ...?	**Gibt es ...?**	Geebt es ...

What's that?	**Was ist das?**	Vas ist das
What do you want?	**Was wünschen Sie?**	Vas *vuin*shen zee
What must I do?	**Was muss ich tun?**	Vas mooss ikh toon
Have you ...?	**Haben Sie ...?**	Hahben zee ...
Have you seen ...?	**Haben Sie ... gesehen?**	Hahben zee ... gu*zay*en
May I have ...?	**Darf ich ... haben?**	Darf ikh ... hahben
What's the matter?	**Was ist los?**	Vas ist los
Can I help you?	***Kann ich Ihnen helfen?**	Kan ikh eenen helfen
Can you help me?	**Können Sie mir helfen?**	Kernen zee meer helfen
Can you tell/give/ show me?	**Können Sie mir ... sagen/geben/ zeigen?**	Kernen zee meer ... *zah*gun/*gay*ben/*tsy*gun

Useful Statements

Key Phrases

Here is/are . . .	**Hier ist/sind . . .**	Heer ist/zint . . .
I should like . . .	**Ich möchte . . .**	Ikh *merkh*ter . . .
I want . . .	**Ich will . . .**	Ikh vill
I need . . .	**Ich brauche . . .**	Ikh *browkh*er . . .
I (don't) know	**Ich weiß (nicht)**	Ikh vice (nikht)
It's urgent	**Es ist dringend**	Es ist *dring*-ent

It's cheap	**Es ist billig**	Es ist *bil*likh
It's (too) expensive	**Es ist (zu) teuer**	Es ist (tsoo) *toy*er
That's all	**Das ist alles**	Das ist alles
I didn't know that . . .	**Ich wusste nicht, dass . . .**	Ikh *voos*ter nikht dass . . .
I think so	**Ich glaube**	Ikh *glow*ber
I'm hungry/thirsty	**Ich habe Hunger/ Durst**	Ikh hahber hoong-er/ doorst
I'm tired/ready	**Ich bin müde/ fertig**	Ikh bin *mui*der/ *fair*tikh
I'm in a hurry	**Ich habe es eilig**	Ikh hahber es *eye*likh
Leave me alone	**Lassen Sie mich in Ruhe**	Lassen zee mikh in roo-wer
Go away	**Gehen Sie bitte**	*Gay*en zee bitter
I'm lost	**Ich habe mich verlaufen**	Ikh hahber mikh fair*low*fen

We are looking for . . .	**Wir suchen . . .**	Veer *zookh*en . . .
Just a minute	***Einen Augenblick**	Inen *owg*un-blick
This way, please	***Hier entlang bitte**	Heer ent*lang* bitter
Take a seat	***Nehmen Sie Platz**	*Nay*men zee plats
Come in!	***Herein!**	Hair-*ine*
You are mistaken	**Sie irren sich**	Zee irren zikh
You're right	**Sie haben recht**	Zee hahben rekht
You're wrong	**Das stimmt nicht**	Das shtimt nikht
It's urgent	**Es ist dringend**	Es ist *dring*-ent
It's important	**Es ist wichtig**	Es ist *vikh*tikh

SIGNS AND
PUBLIC NOTICES[1]

Achtung	caution
Aufzug	lift, elevator
Ausgang	exit
Auskunft	information
Ausverkauf	sale
Ausverkauft	sold out, house full
Bank	bank
Berühren verboten	do not touch
Besetzt	occupied, engaged
Bitte klingeln/klopfen	please ring/knock
Damen	ladies
Dolmetscher	interpreter
Drücken	push
Einbahnstraße	one-way street
Eingang	entrance
Eintritt frei	admission free
Es wird gebeten, nicht . . .	you are requested not to . . .

1. See also Road Signs (p. 50) and Signs at Airports and Stations (p. 18).

Frauen	women
Frei	free, vacant
(Fremden-) Führer	guide
Fußgänger	pedestrians
Gefahr	danger
Geöffnet von ... bis ...	open from ... to ...
Geschlossen	closed
Herren	gentlemen
Kasse	checkout, till
Kein Eingang	no entry
Kein Trinkwasser	not for drinking
Keine Zimmer frei	no vacancies
Kein Zutritt	no entry
Männer	men
Nicht ...	do not ...
Notausgang	emergency exit
Offen	open
Polizei	police
Post	post office
Privat	private
Rauchen verboten	no smoking
Rechts halten	keep right
Reserviert	reserved

Schlussverkauf	sale
Stehplätze	standing room
Toilette	lavatory, toilet
Trinkwasser	drinking water
Unbefugten ist das Betreten verboten	trespassers will be prosecuted
Verboten	prohibited
Vorsicht	caution
Warten	wait
Ziehen	pull
Zimmer frei	vacancies
Zimmer zu vermieten	room to let
Zoll	customs
Zutritt verboten	no admission

Abbreviations and Acronyms

AA	**Auswärtiges Amt**	German foreign office
Abf.	**Abfahrt**	departure
ADAC	**Allgemeiner Deutscher Automobil-Club**	German Automobile Association
AG	**Aktien-Gesellschaft**	public company
AOK	**Allgemeine Ortskrankenkasse**	public health insurance

AW	**Antwort**	email, in reply
Betr.	**Betreff**	re, regarding
Bhf	**Bahnhof**	railway station
BRD	**Bundesrepublik Deutschland**	German Federal Republic
b.w.	**bitte wenden**	p.t.o.
DB	**Deutsche Bundesbahn**	German Railways
d.F.	**deutsche Fassung**	German dubbed version
DFB	**Deutscher Fußballbund**	German soccer association
d.h.	**das heißt**	i.e.
DIN	**Deutsche Industrie-Norm**	industrial standard (like BS)
DPD	**Deutscher Paketdienst**	German Parcel Service (a German UPS)
EU	**Europäische Union**	European Union
FU	**Freie Universität Berlin**	Free University Berlin
geb.	**geboren**	born
ggf.	**gegebenfalls**	if applicable
GmbH	**Gesellschaft mit beschränkter Haftung**	limited company
Hbf.	**Hauptbahnhof**	central (main) station
HH	**Hansestadt Hamburg**	Hanseatic (League) Hamburg

HP	**Halbpension**	half board
ICE	**Intercity-Expresszug**	German high-speed train
Ing.	**Ingenieur**	engineer
Inh.	**Inhaber**	owner, proprietor
JH	**Jugendherberge**	youth hostel
jhrl.	**jährlich**	annually
KaDeWe	**Kaufhaus des Westens**	large Berlin department store
Kfm.	**Kaufmann**	businessman, agent
KKW	**Kernkraftwerk**	nuclear power station
Lkw.	**Lastkraftwagen**	lorry, truck
MEZ	**Mitteleuropäische Zeit**	Central European time
mfG	**mit freundlichen Grüßen**	sincerely
MWSt.	**Mehrwertsteuer**	VAT
nachm.	**nachmittags**	in the afternoon
n.Chr.	**nach Christus**	AD
ÖAMTC	**Österreichischer Automobil-Motorrad- und Touring-Club**	Austrian Automobile, Motorcycle and Touring Club
ÖBB	**Österreichische Bundesbahnen**	Austrian Federal Railways
OF	**Originalfassung**	original-language version

OmU	**Originalfassung mit Untertiteln**	original-language version with subtitles
Pkw.	**Personenkraftwagen**	(private) car
Pl.	**Platz**	square
PLZ	**Postleitzahl**	post code
PS	**Pferdestärke**	horsepower
pünktl.	**pünktlich**	on time
SB	**Selbstbedienung**	self-service petrol pumps
S-Bahn	**Schnellbahn, Vorortsbahn**	suburban railway
SBB	**Schweizerische Bundesbahnen**	Swiss Federal Railways
SBB	**Selbstbedienung**	self-service
St.	**Stock**	floor
Std.	**Stunde**	hour
Str.	**Straße**	street
tägl.	**täglich**	daily
TCS	**Touring-Club der Schweiz**	Swiss Touring Club
TH	**Technische Hochschule**	technical college
U	**Umleitung**	detour
U-Bahn	**Untergrundbahn**	underground
usw.	**und so weiter**	etc.
v.Chr.	**vor Christus**	BC

vorm.	**vormittags**	in the morning
VP	**Vollpension**	full board
WEZ	**Westeuropäische Zeit**	West European Time, GMT
z.B.	**zum Beispiel**	e.g.
Zi.	**Zimmer**	room
z.Z.	**zurzeit**	at present
zzgl.	**zuzüglich**	in addition, plus

GETTING AROUND

Arrival

Key Phrases

I've lost my passport. I must have dropped it on the plane	**Ich habe meinen Pass verloren. Er muss im Flugzeug gefallen sein**	Ikh hahber minen pass fair*lohr*en. Er mooss im *floog*-tsoyg gu*fal*-len zine
My luggage has not arrived	**Mein Gepäck ist nicht angekommen**	Mine gu*peck* ist nikht *an*-gu*kommen*
My luggage is damaged	**Mein Gepäck wurde beschädigt**	Mine gu*peck* voorder bu-*shay*dikht
Is there an ATM/ currency exchange office?	**Gibt es hier einen Geldautomaten/ eine Wechselstube?**	Geebt es heer inen gelt-*ow*tohmahten/ ine *veck*sel-*shtoo*ber
Is there a bus/train to the town centre?	**Gibt es einen Bus/Zug zum Stadtzentrum?**	Geebt es inen boos/tsoog tsoom shtat-*tsen*trum
How can I get to...?	**Wie komme ich zum...?**	Vee *kommer* ikh tsoom...

Passports

Your passport, please	*****Ihren Pass bitte**	Eeren pass bitter
Are you together/ with a group?	*****Sind Sie zusammen/ mit einer Gruppe?**	Zint zee tsoo-*zammen*/ mit iner *groo*per

I'm travelling alone	Ich reise allein	Ikh *ryzer* a*line*
I'm travelling with my wife/with my husband/a friend	Ich reise mit meiner Frau/meinem Mann/einem Freund	Ikh *ryzer* mit miner frow/minem man/inem froynd
I'm here on business/ on holiday	Ich bin geschäftlich/ auf Urlaub hier	Ikh bin gu*sheft*likh/ owf *oor*lowp heer
What is your address in …?	*Wie ist Ihre Adresse in …?	Vee ist eerer ad*dresser* in …
How long are you staying here?	*Wie lange bleiben Sie hier?	Vee lang-er *bly*ben zee heer

Customs

Customs	*der Zoll	Tsoll
Nothing to declare	*Zollfreie Waren	Tsoll-*fryer vahren*
Goods to declare	*Zollpflichtige Waren	Tsoll-*pflikh*tigur *vahren*
Which is your luggage?	*Welches ist Ihr Gepäck?	*Velkh*es ist eer gu*peck*
Do you have any more luggage?	*Haben Sie noch mehr Gepäck?	Hahben zee nokh mair gu*peck*
This is (all) my luggage	Das ist (all) mein Gepäck	Das ist (all) mine gu*peck*
Have you anything to declare?	*Haben Sie etwas zu verzollen?	Hahben zee etvas tsoo fair-*tsol*-len

I have only my personal things in it	**Ich habe nur persönliche Sachen darin**	Ikh hahber noor pair*zern*likher zakhen dah*rin*
Open your bag, please	***Öffnen Sie Ihre Tasche bitte**	*Erf*nen zee eerer tasher bitter
May I go through your luggage?	***Darf ich Ihr Gepäck durchsehen?**	Darf ikh eer gu*peck* doorkh-*zayen*

Luggage

My luggage has not arrived	**Mein Gepäck ist nicht angekommen**	Mine gu*peck* ist nikht *an*-guko*mm*en
My luggage is damaged	**Mein Gepäck wurde beschädigt**	Mine gu*peck* voorder bu-*shay*dikht
Our suitcase is missing	**Unser Koffer fehlt**	Oonser koffer failt
Are there any luggage trolleys?	**Gibt es hier Kofferkulis?**	Geebt es heer koffer-koolis
Where is the left-luggage office?	**Wo ist die Gepäckaufbewahrung?**	Voh ist dee gu*peck-owf-*buva*h*roong
Where are the luggage lockers?	**Wo sind die Gepäckschließfächer?**	Voh zint dee gu*peck-shlees*-fekher

Moving on

| Porter! | **Gepäckträger!** | Gu*peck-tray*gur |
| Would you take these bags to a taxi/the bus/the car rental offices | **Bringen Sie bitte diese Taschen zu einem Taxi/ zum Bus/zur Autovermietung** | Bring-en zee bitter deezer tashen tsoo inem taxi/tsoom boos/tsoor *owt*oh-fair*mee*toong |

What's the price for each piece of luggage?	**Wie viel verlangen Sie für jedes Gepäckstück?**	Vee feel fair*lang*-en zee fuir *yay*des gu*peck*-shtuick
I shall take this myself	**Ich nehme dies selbst**	Ikh *nay*mer deez zelbst
That's not mine	**Das gehört mir nicht**	Das g*uhert* meer nikht
How much do I owe you?	**Wie viel schulde ich Ihnen?**	Vee feel *shool*der ikh eenen
Where is the information desk, please?	**Wo ist die Auskunft bitte?**	Voh ist dee *ows*-koonft bitter
Is there an ATM/ currency exchange office?	**Gibt es hier einen Geldautomaten/ eine Wechselstube?**	Geebt es heer inen gelt-*ow*tohmahten/ ine *veck*sel-*shtoo*ber
Is there a bus/train to the town centre?	**Gibt es einen Bus/Zug zum Stadtzentrum?**	Geebt es inen boos/ tsoog tsoom shtat-*tsen*trum
How can I get to …?	**Wie komme ich zum …?**	Vee *kommer* ikh tsoom …

Signs at Airports and Stations

Arrivals	**Ankunft**
Booking Office/Tickets	**Reisezentrum/Fahrkarten**
Buses	**Busse**
Connections	**Verbindungen**

Departures	**Abfahrt**
Exchange	**Geldwechsel, Wechselstube**
Gentlemen	**Herren, Männer**
(Travel) Information	**Reiseauskunft**
Ladies Room	**Damen, Frauen**
Left Luggage	**Gepäckaufbewahrung**
Local Trains	**Nahverkehr**
Lost Property	**Fundbüro**
Luggage Lockers	**Schließfächer**
Main Lines	**Hauptstrecken**
News-stand	**Zeitungskiosk**
Platform	**Gleis, Bahnsteig**
Refreshments/Snack Bar	**Erfrischungen/Imbissstube**
Reservations	**Sitzplatzreservierung**
Smoker	**Raucher**
Suburban Line	**S-Bahn, Vorortsbahn**
Taxi rank	**Taxistand**
Timetables	**Fahrpläne**
Toilets	**Toiletten**
Tourist Office	**Verkehrsamt**
Underground	**U-Bahn**
Waiting Room	**Warteraum**

By Air

Key Phrases

What is the baggage allowance?	**Wie viel Freigepäck ist erlaubt?**	Vee feel *fry-gupeck* ist air*lowbt*
I'd like to change my reservation	**Ich möchte meine Flugreservierung umbuchen**	Ikh *merkh*ter miner floog-rezair*veerung oom-book*hen
Can I check in online?	**Kann ich online einchecken?**	Kan ikh online *ine*-checken
I have only hand luggage	**Ich habe nur Handgepäck**	Ikh hahber noor *hant*-gupeck
The plane has been cancelled	***Der Flug wurde annuliert/ gestrichen**	Dair floog voorder annoo*leert/* gu-*shtrikh*en

Where's the airline office?	**Wo ist das Flugbüro?**	Voh ist das *floog*-buiroh
I'd like to book two seats on the plane to . . .	**Ich möchte zwei Plätze buchen für den Flug nach . . .**	Ikh *merkh*ter tsvy pletser *book*hen fuir den floog nahkh . . .
Is that the cheapest price?	**Ist das der günstigste Preis?**	Ist das der *guin*stikster price
First class	**Erste Klasse**	Airster klasser
Business class	**Business**	Business

Economy	**Economy**	Economy
How long is the flight?	**Wie lange dauert der Flug?**	Vee lang-er dowert dair floog
I'd like an aisle/window seat	**Ich möchte einen Gangplatz/Fensterplatz**	Ikh *merkh*ter inen *gang*-plats/*fenster*-plats
I'd like to order a vegetarian/special meal	**Ich möchte eine vegetarische Mahlzeit/Sondermahlzeit bestellen**	Ikh *merkh*ter iner vegay*tah*risher mahl-tsite/*zonder*-mahl-tsite bu-*shtel*len
Is there a flight to …?	**Gibt es einen Flug nach …?**	Geebt es inen floog nahkh …
What is the flight number?	**Wie ist die Flugnummer?**	Vee ist dee *floog*-noommer
When does the plane leave/arrive?	**Wann startet/landet das Flugzeug?**	Van *shtar*tet/landet das *floog*-tsoyg
When's the next plane?	**Wann fliegt die nächste Maschine?**	Van fleegt dee *naikhs*ter mah*shee*ner
Is there a coach to the airport/town?	**Fährt ein Bus zum Flughafen/in die Stadt?**	Fairt ine boos tsoom *floog*-hahfen/in dee shtat
Which airport does the flight leave from?	**Von welchem Flughafen geht der Flug?**	Fon *velkh*em *floog*-hahfen gait dair floog
Terminal	**der Terminal**	Terminal

Where are the check-in desks for (Lufthansa)?	**Wo sind die Abflugschalter von (Lufthansa)?**	Voh zint dee *ap*-floog-shalter fon (Lufthansa)
When must I check in?	**Wann muss ich einchecken?**	Van mooss ikh *ine*-checken
Please cancel my reservation to …	**Bitte stornieren Sie meine Flugreservierung nach …**	Bitter shtor*neeren* zee miner floog-rezair*veeroong* nahkh
Can I change my flight?	**Kann ich meinen Flug umbuchen?**	Kan ikh minen floog *oom-bookh*en
Will it cost more?	**Kostet das mehr?**	Kostet das mair
I've booked a wheelchair to take me to the plane	**Ich habe einen Rollstuhl zum Flugzeug reserviert**	Ikh hahber inen *rol*-shtool tsoom *floog*-tsoyg rezair*veert*
Can I check in online?	**Kann ich online einchecken?**	Kan ikh online *ine*-checken
I have only hand luggage	**Ich habe nur Handgepäck**	Ikh hahber noor *hant*-gupeck
You will have to pay for excess baggage	***Für Übergepäck müssen Sie eine Gebühr zahlen**	Fuir *uiber*-gupeck *muissen* zee iner gu*buir* tsahlen
The plane leaves from gate …	***Der Flug geht von Flugsteig …**	Dair floog gait fon *floog*-shtyg …
I've lost my boarding card	**Ich habe meine Bordkarte verloren**	Ikh hahber miner *bord*-karter fair*lohren*

| Flight number ... from ... to ... has been delayed | *Flug Nummer ... von ... nach ... hat Verspätung | Floog noommer ... fon ... nahkh ... hat fair*shpay*toong |
| The plane has been cancelled | *Der Flug wurde annuliert/gestrichen | Dair floog voorder annoo*leert*/ gu-*shtrikh*en |

By Boat/Ferry

Key Phrases

Is there a boat/ (car) ferry from here to ...?	Fährt ein Schiff/ eine (Auto-) Fähre von hier nach ...?	Fairt ine shif/ iner (*owt*oh-) fairer fon heer nahkh ...
When does the next boat leave?	Wann fährt das nächste Schiff ab?	Van fairt das *naikh*ster shif ap
I'd like a one way/ return ticket	Ich hätte gern eine einfache Fahrkarte/ Rückfahrkarte	Ikh hetter gairn iner *ine*-fakher fahr-karter/ *ruick*-fahr-karter

Where is the port?	Wo ist der Hafen?	Voh ist dair hahfen
How long does the crossing take?	Wie lange dauert die Fahrt?	Vee lang-er dowert dee fahrt
How often do the boats leave?	Wie oft fährt ein Schiff ab?	Vee oft fairt ine shif ap
Does the boat call at ...?	Legt das Schiff in ... an?	Laigt das shif in ... an

When does the boat leave?	**Wann fährt das Schiff ab?**	Van fairt das shif ap
What does it cost for ...	**Wie viel kostet es für ...**	Vee feel kostet es fuir ...
a bicycle?	**ein Fahrrad?**	ine *fahr*-raht
a caravan?	**ein Wohnmobil?**	ine *vohn*-mobeel
a child?	**ein Kind?**	ine kint
a motorcycle?	**ein Motorrad?**	ine moh*tor*-raht
Can I book a single berth cabin?	**Kann ich eine Einzelkabine buchen?**	Kan ikh iner *ine*-tsel-ka*bee*ner *book*hen
How many berths are there in the cabin?	**Wie viele Betten sind in der Kabine?**	Vee feeler betten zint in dair ka*bee*ner
When must we go on board?	**Wann müssen wir an Bord gehen?**	Van *muis*sen veer an bort *gay*en
When do we dock?	**Wann legen wir an?**	Van *lay*gun veer an
How long do we stay in port?	**Wie lange bleiben wir im Hafen?**	Vee lang-er *bly*ben veer im hahfen
Where are the toilets?	**Wo sind die Toiletten?**	Vo zint dee twah*let*ten
I feel seasick	**Ich bin seekrank**	Ikh bin *zay*-krank
Life jacket	**die Schwimmweste**	*Shvim*-vester
Lifeboat	**das Rettungsboot**	Rettoongs-boht

By Bus/Coach

Key Phrases

Where can I buy a bus ticket?	**Wo kann ich eine Busfahrkarte kaufen?**	Voh kan ikh iner *boos*-fahr-karter *kow*fen
Do I pay the driver?	**Muss ich beim Fahrer zahlen?**	Mooss ikh bime fahrer *tsah*len
When's the next bus?	**Wann fährt der nächste Bus?**	Van fairt dair *naikh*ster boos
Where can I get a bus to …?	**Von wo fährt ein Bus nach …?**	Fon voh fairt ine boos nahkh …
Where do I get off?	**Wo muss ich aussteigen?**	Voh mooss ikh *ows-shty*gun

Where's the bus station?	**Wo ist der Busbahnhof?**	Voh ist der boos-*bahn*-hohf
Bus stop	**Bushaltestelle**	*Boos*-halter-*shtel*ler
Request stop	**Bedarfshaltestelle**	Bu*darfs*-halter-*shtel*ler
Is there a daily/ weekly ticket?	**Gibt es Tageskarten/ Wochenkarten?**	Geebt es *tahg*es-karten/*vokhen*-karten
I'd like to reserve a seat at the front of the coach/bus	**Ich möchte einen Sitzplatz vorne im Bus reservieren**	Ikh *merkh*ter inen sits-plats *for*ner im boos rezair*veer*en
What is the fare?	**Was kostet es?**	Vas kostet es
When does the coach/bus leave?	**Wann fährt der Bus ab?**	Van fairt dair boos ap

When does the coach/bus get to ...?	**Wann kommt der Bus in ... an?**	Van kommt dair boos in ... an
What stops does it make?	**Wo hält der Bus überall?**	Voh hailt dair boos *ui*beral
How long is the journey?	**Wie lange dauert die Fahrt?**	Vee lang-er dowert dee fahrt
How often do the buses run?	**Wie oft fahren die Busse?**	Vee oft fahren dee *boo*sser
What time is the last bus?	**Wann fährt der letzte Bus?**	Van fairt dair *letz*ter boos
Does this bus go to the ...	**Fährt dieser Bus zum ...**	Fairt deezer boos tsoom ...
beach?	**Strand?**	shtrant
station?	**Bahnhof?**	*bahn*-hohf
town centre?	**Stadtzentrum?**	shtat-*tsen*trum
Do you go near ...?	**Fahren Sie in die Nähe von ...?**	Fahren zee in dee *nay*er fon ...
Where can I get a bus to ...?	**Von wo fährt ein Bus nach ...?**	Fon voh fairt ine boos nahkh ...
Which bus goes to ...?	**Welcher Bus fährt nach ...?**	*Velkh*er boos fairt nahkh ...
I'd like to go to ...	**Ich möchte nach ... fahren**	Ikh *merkh*ter nahkh ... fahren
Where do I get off?	**Wo muss ich aussteigen?**	Voh mooss ikh *ows-shty*gun

The tram to ... stops over there	*Die Straßenbahn nach ... hält dort drüben	Dee *shtrahs*en-bahn nahkh ... hailt dort *drui*ben
You must take a number ...	*Sie müssen mit der ... fahren	Zee *muissen* mit dair ... fahren
You get off at the next stop	*Sie müssen an der nächsten Haltestelle aussteigen	Zee *muissen* an dair *naikh*sten halter-*shtel*ler *ows-shty*gun
The trams run every ten minutes/every hour	*Die Straßenbahnen fahren alle zehn Minuten/jede Stunde	Dee *shtrahs*en-bahnen fahren aller tsayn mee*noo*ten/*yay*der *shtoon*der

By Taxi

Key Phrases

Please get me a taxi	Rufen Sie mir bitte ein Taxi	Roofen zee meer bitter ine taxi
Where can I get a taxi?	Wo kann ich ein Taxi bekommen?	Voh kan ikh ine taxi bu*kom*men
Please wait for me	Bitte warten Sie auf mich	Bitter *var*ten zee owf mikh
Stop here	Halten Sie hier	Halten zee heer

| I'd like to book a taxi for tomorrow at ... (*time*) | Ich möchte für morgen um ... Uhr ein Taxi reservieren | Ikh *merkh*ter fuir *mor*gun oom ... oor ine taxi rezair*vee*ren |

Are you free?	**Sind Sie frei?**	Zint zee fry
Please turn on the meter	**Schalten Sie bitte das Taxameter ein**	*Shal*ten zee bitter das taxa*may*ter ine
Please take me	**Bitte fahren Sie mich**	Bitter fahren zee mikh
to the city centre	**ins Stadtzentrum**	ins shtat-*tsen*trum
to the hotel	**zum Hotel**	tsoom hoh*tel*
to the station	**zum Bahnhof**	tsoom *bahn*-hohf
to this address	**zu dieser Adresse**	tsoo deezer ad*ress*er
Can you hurry? I'm late	**Können Sie sich bitte beeilen? Ich habe mich verspätet**	Kernen zee zikh bitter bu-*eye*len? Ikh hahber mikh fair*shpay*tet
Is it far?	**Ist es weit?**	Ist es vite
How much do you charge by the hour/ for the day?	**Wie viel verlangen Sie pro Stunde/ pro Tag?**	Vee feel fairlang-en zee pro *shtoon*der/ pro tahg
How much will you charge to take me to ...?	**Wie viel verlangen Sie für die Fahrt nach ...?**	Vee feel fairlang-en zee fuir dee fahrt nahkh ...
How much is it?	**Wie viel muss ich zahlen?**	Vee feel mooss ikh *tsah*len
That's too much	**Das ist zu viel**	Das ist tsoo feel

By Train

Key Phrases

Where's the railway station/main station?	**Wo ist der Bahnhof/ Hauptbahnhof?**	Voh ist dair *bahn-hohf*/*howpt-bahn-hohf*
What's the cheapest fare to …?	**Wie viel kostet die billigste Fahrkarte nach …?**	Vee feel kostet die *bil*likh-ster fahr-karter nahkh …
Is there a day return?	**Gibt es eine Tagesrückfahrkarte?**	Geebt es iner *tahges-ruick*-fahr-karter
Where do I change?	**Wo muss ich umsteigen?**	Voh mooss ikh *oom-shty*gun
Excuse me, what station is this?	**Entschuldigung, in welchem Bahnhof sind wir hier?**	Ent*shool*digoong, in velkhem *bahn*-hohf zint veer heer

Where is the ticket office?	**Wo ist der Fahrkartenschalter?**	Voh ist dair *fahr*-karten-shalter
Have you a timetable, please?	**Haben Sie einen Fahrplan bitte?**	Hahben zee inen *fahr*-plahn bitter
How much is it first class to …?	**Wie viel kostet es erste Klasse nach …?**	Vee feel kostet es airster klasser nahkh …
A second-class single to …	**Einmal zweiter Klasse nach …**	*Ine*-mahl tsviter klasser nahkh …
Single/One way	**Einfache Fahrt**	*Ine*-fakher fahrt

A return to...	**Eine Rückfahrkarte nach...**	Iner *ruick*-fahr-karter nahkh...
When are you coming back?	**Wann kommen Sie zurück?**	Van *kommen* zee tsoo-*ruick*
What is the child fare?	**Wie viel ist der Kindertarif?**	Vee feel ist der kin-der-tar*eef*
How old is he/she?	***Wie alt ist er/sie?**	Vee alt ist air/zee
How long is this ticket valid?	**Wie lange ist diese Fahrkarte gültig?**	Vee lang-er ist deezer fahr-karter *guil*tikh
Is there a supplementary charge?	**Muss man Zuschlag bezahlen?**	Mooss man tsoo-*shlahg* bu-*tsah*len
Do I need to reserve a seat?	**Muss ich einen Sitzplatz reservieren?**	Mooss ikh inen zits-plats rezair*vee*ren
I'd like a window seat/sleeper	**Ich möchte einen Fensterplatz/ Schlafwagen-Platz**	Ikh *merkh*ter inen *fen*ster-plats/ shlahf-*vah*gun-plats
Is it an express or a local train?	**Ist es ein Schnellzug oder ein Personenzug?**	Ist es ine *shnell*-tsoog ohder ine pair*zohn*en-tsoog?
Is there an earlier/ later train?	**Wann fährt der Zug davor/ danach?**	Van fairt dair tsoog dah*for*/ dah-*nahkh*
Is there a restaurant car on the train?	**Hat der Zug einen Speisewagen?**	Hat dair tsoog inen *shpy*zer-*vah*gun
When does it get to...?	**Wann kommt er in...an?**	Van kommt air in...an
Does the train stop at...?	**Hält der Zug auch in...?**	Hailt dair tsoog owkh in...

| I'd like to make a motorail reservation to... | **Ich möchte den Autozug nach ... reservieren** | Ikh *merkh*ter den *ow*toh-tsoog nahkh ... rezair*vee*ren |
| Where is the motorail loading platform ? | **Wo ist die Laderampe für den Autozug?** | Voh ist dee *lahder*-ramper fuir den *ow*toh-tsoog |

Changing

Is there a through train to ...?	**Fährt ein Zug durch nach ...?**	Fairt ine tsoog doorkh nahkh
Do I have to change?	**Muss ich umsteigen?**	Mooss ikh *oom-shty*gun
Where do I change?	**Wo muss ich umsteigen?**	Voh mooss ikh *oom-shty*gun
Excuse me, what station is this?	**Entschuldigung, in welchem Bahnhof sind wir hier?**	Ent*shool*digoong, in velkhem *bahn*-hohf zint veer heer
Is this where I change for ...?	**Muss ich hier nach ... umsteigen?**	Mooss ikh heer nahkh ... *oom-shty*gun
When is there a connection to ...?	**Wann habe ich Anschluss nach ...?**	Van hahber ikh *an*-shlooss nahkh ...
When does the train from ... get in?	**Wann fährt der Zug von ... ein?**	Van fairt dair tsoog fon ... ine
Is the train late?	**Hat der Zug Verspätung?**	Hat dair tsoog fair*shpay*toong
From which platform does the train to ... leave?	**Von welchem Gleis fährt der Zug nach ...?**	Fon *velkh*em glice fairt dair tsoog nahkh ...
Change at ... and take the local train	***Steigen Sie in ... um und nehmen Sie einen Nahverkehrszug/ Vorortszug**	*Shty*gun zee in ... oom oont *nay*men zee inen nah-fair*kairs*-tsoog/ *for*-orts-tsoog

Departure

When does the train leave?	**Wann fährt der Zug ab?**	Van fairt dair tsoog ap
Which platform does the train to ... leave from?	**Von welchem Bahnsteig fährt der Zug nach ... ab?**	Fon *velkhe*m bahn-shtyg fairt dair tsoog nahkh ... ap
Is this the train for ...?	**Ist dies der Zug nach ...?**	Ist dees dair tsoog nahkh ...
There will be a delay of ...	***Der Zug hat ... Minuten Verspätung**	Dair tsoog hat ... mee*noo*ten fair*shpay*toong

On the train

We have reserved seats	**Wir haben Plätze reserviert**	Veer hahben pletser rezair*veert*
Is this seat free?	**Ist dieser Platz frei?**	Ist deezer plats fry
This seat is taken	**Dieser Platz ist besetzt**	Deezer plats ist bu*zetst*
Dining car	**der Speisewagen**	*Shpyzer-vahgun*
When is the buffet car open?	**Wann ist der Bistrowagen geöffnet?**	Van ist dair bist*roh-vah*gun gu-*erf*net
Where is the sleeping car?	**Wo ist der Schlafwagen?**	Voh ist dair *shlahf-vah*gun
Which is my sleeper?	**Wo ist mein Schlafwagenplatz?**	Voh ist mine *shlahf-vah*gun-plats
Could you wake me at ... please?	**Können Sie mich bitte um ... Uhr wecken?**	Kernen zee mikh bitter oom ... oor vecken

The heating is too high/low	**Die Heizung ist zu warm/kalt**	Dee *hyt*soong ist tsoo varm/kalt
I can't open/close the window	**Ich kann das Fenster nicht öffnen/ schliessen**	Ikh kan das *fen*ster nikht *erf*nen/ *shlees*-sen
What station is this?	**Welcher Bahnhof ist das hier?**	*Velkh*er *bahn*-hohf ist das heer
How long do we stop here?	**Wie lange halten wir hier?**	Vee lang-er halten veer heer

By Underground

Key Phrases

Where is the nearest underground station?	**Wo ist die nächste U-Bahn-Station bitte?**	Voh ist dee *naikh*ster *oo*-bahn-shtats-*yon* bitter
Does this train go to …?	**Fährt dieser Zug nach …?**	Fairt deezer tsoog nahkh …
Have you a map of the underground?	**Haben Sie einen Plan für die U-Bahn?**	Hahben zee inen plahn fuir dee *oo*-bahn

Can I use this ticket on the bus too?	**Ist das Ticket auch im Bus gültig?**	Ist das ticket owkh im boos *guil*tikh
Is there a daily/ weekly ticket?	**Gibt es eine Tages-/ Wochenkarte?**	Geebt es iner *tahg*es-/*vokh*en-karter
Which line goes to …?	**Welche Linie fährt nach …?**	Velkher *leen*-yer fairt nahkh …

Where do I change for ...?	**Wo muss ich umsteigen, um nach ... zu fahren?**	Voh mooss ikh *oom-shty*gun oom nakh ... tsoo fahren
Is the next station ...?	**Ist die nächste Station ...?**	Ist dee *naikh*ster shtats-*yon* ...
What station is this?	**Welche Station ist das hier?**	*Velkh*er shtats-*yon* ist das heer
Have you a map of the underground?	**Haben Sie einen Plan für die U-Bahn?**	Hahben zee inen plahn fuir dee *oo*-bahn

By Car[1]

Key Phrases

Have you a road map, please?	**Haben Sie eine Straßenkarte bitte?**	Hahben zee iner *strahss*en-karter bitter
Where is the nearest car park/garage?	**Wo ist der nächste Parkplatz/die nächste Garage?**	Voh ist dair *naikh*ster *park*-plats/dee naikhster garahjer
May I see your driving licence and passport?	***Kann ich Ihren Führerschein und Pass sehen?**	Kan ikh eeren *fuirer*-shine oont pass *zay*en
I've run out of petrol	**Ich habe trocken gefahren**	Ikh hahber trocken gufahren
I've lost my key	**Ich habe meinen Autoschlüssel verloren**	Ikh haber minen *ow*toh *shluis*sel fair*lohr*en
Can you repair it?	**Können Sie es reparieren?**	Kernen zee es repah*ree*ren

1. See also Directions (p. 52) and Road Signs (p. 50).

(How long) can I park here?	**(Wie lange) kann ich hier parken?**	(Vee lang-er) kan ikh heer parken
Have you any change for the meter, please?	**Haben Sie Kleingeld für die Parkuhr?**	Hahben zee *kline*-gelt fuir dee park-oor
How far is the next petrol station?	**Wie weit ist es bis zur nächsten Tankstelle?**	Vee vite ist es bis tsoor *naikh*sten *tank-shtel*ler
May I see your licence/logbook, please?	***Kann ich bitte Ihren Führerschein/ Kraftfahrzeugschein sehen?**	Kan ikh bitter eeren *fuirer*-shine/kraft-fahr-tsoyg-shine *zayen*
You were speeding	***Sie haben das Tempolimit/die Geschwindigkeit überschritten**	Zee hahben das *tempoh*-limit /dee gu-*shvin*dikh-kite *uiber-shrit*ten
Is this your car?	***Ist das Ihr Wagen/ Auto?**	Ist das eer *vah*gun/*owt*oh
Speed limit	***Geschwindigkeits-grenze**	Gu*shvin*dikh-kites-grentser
Pedestrian precinct	***Fußgängerzone**	*Foos*-geng-er-*tsohn*er

Car rental

| Where can I hire a car? | **Wo kann ich ein Auto mieten?** | Voh kan ikh ine *owt*oh *mee*ten |
| I'd like to hire a small/large car | **Ich möchte einen kleinen/großen Wagen mieten** | Ikh *merkh*ter inen klinen/grohsen *vah*gun *mee*ten |

I'd like an automatic/a manual vehicle	Ich möchte ein Automatikfahrzeug/ ein Fahrzeug mit Schaltgetriebe	Ikh *merkh*ter ine *ow*toh*mah*tik-fahr-tsoyg/ine fahr-tsoyg mit *shalt*-gut*reeb*er
I'd like a car with a sun roof/air conditioning	Ich möchte ein Auto mit Schiebedach/ Klimaanlage	Ikh *merkh*ter ine *ow*toh mit *sheeb*er-dakh/*klee*mah-*an*-lahgur
Does the car have a GPS system/CD player?	Hat das Auto ein GPS-System/einen CD-Spieler?	Hat das *ow*toh ine gay-pay-ess-zist*aim*/ inen tsay-day-*shpeel*er
We've reserved a camper van	Wir haben ein Wohnmobil reserviert	Veer hahben ine *vohn*-mobeel rezair*veert*
Can we rent a baby/child seat?	Können wir einen Baby-/Kindersitz mieten?	Kernen veer inen baby/kin-der-zits *meet*en
What kind of fuel does it take?	Welchen Treibstoff braucht das Auto?	*Velkh*en *tribe*-stoff browkht das *ow*toh
Is there a weekend/midweek rate?	Gibt es einen Wochenend/ Wochenmittetarif?	Geebt es inen *vokh*en-end/*vokh*en-mitter-ta*reef*
I need it for two days/a week	Ich brauche es für zwei Tage/eine Woche	Ikh *browkh*er es fuir tsvy *tah*gur/iner *vokh*er
How much is it by the day/week?	Was kostet es pro Tag/Woche?	Vas kostet es pro tahg/*vokh*er
Does that include unlimited mileage?	Ist unbegrenztes Kilometergeld im Preis einbegriffen?	Ist *oon*-bugrenstes keeloh-*mayter*-gelt im price *ine*-bugriffen
The charge per kilometre is . . .	*Die Gebühr pro Kilometer ist . . .	Dee gu*buir* pro keeloh-*mayter* ist . . .

Would you like full insurance?	*Möchten Sie eine Vollkaskoversicherung?	*Merkh*ten zee iner foll-kaskoh-fairs*ikh*eroong
What is the deposit?	Wie viel muss ich hinterlegen?	Vee feel mooss ikh *hin*ter-*lay*gun
I will pay by credit card	Ich bezahle mit Kreditkarte	Ikh bu-*tsah*ler mit kray*deet*-karter
You have to pay the first ... euros	*Sie müssen die ersten ... Euros selbst bezahlen	Zee *muis*sen dee airsten ... oyrohs zelbst bu-*tsah*len
May I see your driving licence and passport?	*Kann ich Ihren Führerschein und Pass sehen?	Kan ikh eeren *fui*rer-shine oont pass *zay*en
Would you sign here, please?	*Unterschreiben Sie hier, bitte	*Oon*ter-shryben zee heer bitter
Can I return it in ...?	Kann ich ihn in ... zurückbringen?	Kan ikh een in ... tsoo-*ruick*-bring-en
Could you show me the controls/lights, please?	Können Sie mir bitte die Schaltung/Beleuchtung zeigen?	Kernen zee meer bitter dee *shal*toong/bu*loykh*toong *tsy*gun
The car is scratched/dented here	Hier gibt es einen Kratzer/eine Beule	Here geebt es inen *krat*ser/iner *boy*ler

At a garage or petrol station

Fill it up, please	Voll, bitte	Foll bitter
It's a diesel engine	Es ist ein Dieselmotor	Es ist ine *dee*sel-moh*tor*
Please check the oil and water/the battery	Bitte prüfen Sie das Öl und das Wasser/die Batterie	Bitter *prui*fen zee das erl oont das *vas*ser/dee batte*ree*

Could you check the brake/transmission fluid, please?	**Prüfen Sie bitte die Bremsflüssigkeit/ Getriebeflüssigkeit**	Pruifen zee bitter dee *bremz-fluissikh-kite*/ gu*reeber-flui*ssikh-kite
Would you clean the windscreen, please?	**Machen Sie bitte die Windschutzscheibe sauber**	Makhen zee bitter dee *vint*-shoots-*shyber zowber*
The oil needs changing	**Das Öl muss gewechselt werden**	Das erl mooss gu*veck*selt *vair*den
Check the tyre pressure, please	**Prüfen Sie bitte den Reifendruck**	*Pruifen* zee bitter dain *ry*fen-drook
I'd like my car serviced	**Ich möchte mein Auto warten lassen**	Ikh *merkh*ter mine *ow*toh *var*ten lassen
Please wash the car	**Bitte waschen Sie den Wagen**	Bitter vashen zee dain *vah*gun
Can I garage the car here?	**Kann ich den Wagen hier abstellen?**	Kan ikh dain *vah*gun heer *ine*-shtellen
What time does the garage close?	**Wann wird die Garage geschlossen?**	Van veert dee ga*rah*jer gu-*shlos*sen
Where are the toilets?	**Wo sind die Toiletten?**	Voh zint dee twah*let*ten
Please pay at the cash desk	***Zahlen Sie bitte an der Kasse**	*Tsah*len zee bitter an dair kasser
Self-service pumps	**Selbstbedienung (SB)**	Zelbst-bu*dee*noong (ess-bay)

Problems and repairs

| I've run out of petrol | **Ich habe trocken gefahren** | Ikh hahber trocken gufahren |
| I've locked the keys in the car | **Ich habe die Schlüssel im Auto eingeschlossen** | Ikh hahber dee *shlui*ssel im *ow*toh *ine*-gu-*shlos*sen |

I've lost my key	**Ich habe meinen Autoschlüssel verloren**	Ikh haber minen *ow*toh *shluis*sel fair*lohr*en
The lock is broken/jammed	**Das Schloss ist defekt/klemmt**	Das shloss ist *day*fekt/klemt
My car has broken down	**Ich habe eine Autopanne**	Ikh hahber iner *ow*toh-panner
Could you give me a lift to a garage/emergency phone?	**Könnten Sie mich zu einer Garage/einem Notruftelefon bringen?**	Kernten zee mikh tsoo iner ga*rah*jer/inem *noht*-roof-tele*fohn* bring-en
May I use your phone?	**Darf ich Ihr Telefon benutzen?**	Darf ikh eer tele*fohn* bu*noot*sen
Where is there a . . . agent?	**Wo gibt es eine . . . Vertretung?**	Voh geebt es iner . . . fair*tray*toong
Do you have a breakdown service?	**Haben Sie einen Abschleppdienst?**	Hahben zee inen *ap*-shlep-deenst
Is there a mechanic?	**Haben Sie einen Mechaniker?**	Hahben zee inen me*khan*iker
Can you send someone to look at it/tow it away?	**Können Sie jemanden schicken, der sich den Wagen ansieht/der den Wagen abschleppt?**	Kernen zee *yay*manden shicken dair zikh dain *vah*gun anzeet/dair dain *vah*gun *ap*-shlept
It is an automatic	**Er hat ein automatisches Getriebe**	Air hat ine *ow*toh*mah*teeshes gu*tree*ber
Where are you?	***Wo sind Sie?**	Voh zint zee
Where is your car?	***Wo ist Ihr Wagen?**	Voh ist eer *vah*gun

I am on the road from ... to ... near kilometre post ...	**Ich bin auf der Straße von ... nach ... in der Nähe von Kilometerstein ...**	Ikh bin owf dair *shtrah*ser fon ... nahkh ... in der *nay*er fon ... keeloh-*may*ter-shtine ...
How long will you be?	**Wie lange wird es dauern?**	Vee lang-er veert es *dow*ern
This tyre is flat; can you mend it?	**Dieser Reifen ist platt; können Sie ihn reparieren?**	Deezer *ry*fen ist plat; kernen zee een repah*ree*ren
The exhaust is broken	**Der Auspuff ist kaputt**	Dair *ows*-poof ist kah*poot*
The windscreen wipers do not work	**Die Scheibenwischer funktionieren nicht**	Dee *shy*ben-visher foonkts-yon*ee*ren nikht
The valve/radiator is leaking	**Das Schlauchventil/ der Kühler ist undicht**	Das *shlowkh*-fen*teel*/dair *kui*ler ist *oon*dikht
The battery is flat; it needs charging	**Die Batterie ist leer; sie muss aufgeladen werden**	Dee batt*eree* ist lair; zee mooss *owf*-gu*lah*den *vair*den
My car won't start	**Mein Wagen springt nicht an**	Mine *vah*gun shpringt nikht an
It's not running properly	**Er läuft nicht richtig**	Air loyft nikht *rikh*-tikh
The engine is overheating/firing badly	**Der Motor läuft sich heiß/hat Fehlzündung**	Dair moh*tor* loyft zikh hice/hat *fail-tsuin*doong
There's a petrol/oil leak	**Ich verliere Benzin/ Öl**	Ikh fair-*leer*er ben*tseen*/erl
There's a smell of petrol/rubber	**Es riecht nach Benzin/Gummi**	Es reekht nahkh ben*tseen*/*goom*mee

There's a rattle/squeak	**Es klappert/quietscht**	Es *klap*pert/k-veetsht
Something is wrong	**Etwas funktioniert nicht**	Etvas foonkts-yon*eert* nikht
with my car	**an meinem Wagen**	an minem *vah*gun
with the brakes	**an der Bremse**	an dair *brem*zer
with the clutch	**an der Kupplung**	an dair kooploong
with the engine	**an dem Motor**	an daim moh*tor*
with the gearbox	**am Getriebe**	am gu*tree*ber
with the lights	**an dem Licht**	an daim likht
with the steering	**an der Steuerung**	an dair *shtoye*roong
I've got electrical/ mechanical trouble	**Der Wagen hat einen elektrischen/ mechanischen Defekt**	Dair *vah*gun hat inen el*ek*trishen/ mekh*ah*nishen *day*fekt
The carburettor needs adjusting	**Der Vergaser muss eingestellt werden**	Dair fair-*gah*zer mooss *ine*-gu-*shtelt* vair*den*
Can you repair it?	**Können Sie es reparieren?**	Kernen zee es repah*ree*ren
How long will it take to repair?	**Wie lange wird die Reparatur dauern?**	Vee lang-er veert die repahrah*toor* dow*ern*
What will it cost?	**Wie teuer ist es?**	Vee *toy*er ist es
When can I pick the car up?	**Wann kann ich den Wagen abholen?**	Van kan ikh dain *vah*gun *ap*-hohlen
I need it	**Ich brauche ihn**	Ikh *browkher* een
as soon as possible	**so bald wie möglich**	zo balt vee *merk*likh
in the morning	**am Morgen**	am *mor*gun
in three hours	**in drei Stunden**	in dry *shtoon*den

It will take two days	*Es dauert zwei Tage	Es *dowert* tsvy *tahgur*
We can repair it temporarily	*Wir können es vorübergehend reparieren	Veer kernen es *for-uiber-gay*ent repah*reeren*
We haven't the right spares	*Wir haben nicht die richtigen Ersatzteile	Veer hahben nikht dee *rikh*-tigun airzats-*tyler*
We have to send for the spares	*Wir müssen uns die Ersatzteile schicken lassen	Veer *muissen* oons dee airzats-*tyler* shicken lassen
You will need a new ...	*Sie brauchen ein (eine, einen) neues (neue, neuen) ...	Zee *browkh*en ine (iner, inen) *noyes* (*noyer*, *noyen*) ...
Could I have an itemized bill, please?	Geben Sie mir bitte eine Rechnung mit Einzelangaben	*Gay*ben zee meer bitter iner *rekh*noong mit *ine*-tsel-an*gahb*en

Parts of a car and other useful words

accelerate (to)	beschleunigen	bu-*shloy*nigun
accelerator	das Gaspedal	gas-pe*dahl*
aerial	die Antenne	*an-ten*ner
air pump	die Luftpumpe	looft-*poom*per
alarm	die Alarmanlage	alarm-*an*-lahgur
alternator	die Lichtmaschine	likht-ma*sheen*er
anti-freeze	der Frostschutz	frost-shoots
automatic transmission	das Automatikgetriebe	*ow*tohmahtik-gut*reeb*er
axle	die Achse	*ag*ser

battery	**die Batterie**	batter*ee*
bonnet	**die Motorhaube**	moh*tor-how*ber
boot/trunk	**der Gepäckraum**	gu*peck*-rowm
brake	**die Bremse**	*bremzer*
brake lining	**der Bremsbelag**	bremz-bu*lahg*
breakdown	**die Panne**	panner
bulb	**die Glühbirne**	*glui-beer*ner
bumper	**die Stoßstange**	shtos-shtang-er
carburettor	**der Vergaser**	fair*gah*ser
clutch	**die Kupplung**	kooploong
cooling system	**die Kühlanlage**	kuil-*an*-lahgur
crankshaft	**die Kurbelwelle**	koorbel-veller
cylinder	**der Zylinder**	tseelinder
differential gear	**das Ausgleichgetriebe**	*ows*-glykh-gu*tree*ber
dipstick	**der Ölmesser**	erl-messer
distilled water	**das destillierte Wasser**	desti*leer*ter *vas*ser
distributor	**der Verteiler**	fair*ty*ler
door	**die Tür**	tuir
door handle	**der Türgriff**	tuir-griff
drive (to)	**fahren**	fahren
dynamo	**der Dynamo**	duinah*moh*
engine	**der Motor**	moh*tor*
exhaust	**der Auspuff**	*ows*-poof

fan	**der Autokühler**	*ow*toh-*kui*ler
fanbelt	**der Ventilatorriemen**	fentee*lator-reemen*
(oil) filter	**der (Öl-) Filter**	(erl-) filter
foglamp	**die Nebellampe**	*nay*bul-*lam*per
fusebox	**die Sicherungsdose**	*zikh*eroongs-*dohzer*
gasket	**der Dichtungsring**	*dikh*toongs-ring
gears	**die Gänge**	*gaing*-er
gearbox	**das Getriebe**	gu*treeber*
gear lever	**der Schalthebel**	shalt-*hay*bel
grease (to)	**schmieren**	*shmee*ren
handbrake	**die Handbremse**	hant-*bremz*er
heater	**die Heizung**	*hyt*soong
horn	**die Hupe**	hooper
hose	**der Schlauch**	shlowkh
ignition	**die Zündung**	tsuindoong
ignition key	**der Zündschlüssel**	tsuind-*shluiss*el
indicator	**der Winker**	vinker
jack	**der Wagenheber**	*vah*gun-*hay*ber
lights	**die Scheinwerfer**	*shine-vairf*er
headlights	**die Scheinwerfer**	*shine-vairf*er
parking lights	**das Parklicht**	park-likht
rear lights	**das Schlusslicht**	schlooss-likht
reversing lights	**das Rückfahrlicht**	*ruick*fahr-likht
side lights	**das Standlicht**	shtand-likht

lock/catch	**das Schloss**	shloss
mirror	**der Spiegel**	*shpee*gul
number plate	**das Nummernschild**	noomern-shilt
nut	**die Mutter**	mootter
oil	**das Öl**	erl
pedal	**das Pedal**	pe*dahl*
petrol	**das Benzin**	ben*tseen*
petrol can	**der Benzinkanister**	ben*tseen*-kanister
propeller shaft	**die Gelenkwelle**	gu*lenk*-veller
piston	**der Kolben**	kolben
plug	**die Zündkerze**	tsuint-*kair*tser
points	**die Kontakte**	kon*tak*ter
(fuel/water) pump	**die (Benzin-/Wasser-) Pumpe**	(ben*tseen*-/*vas*ser-) *poom*per
puncture	**die Reifenpanne**	*ry*fen-panner
radiator	**der Kühler**	*kui*ler
rear axle	**die Hinterachse**	*hinter-ag*ser
rear-view mirror	**der Rückspiegel**	*ruick-shpee*gul
reverse (to)	**rückwärts fahren**	*ruick*vairts fahren
reverse gear	**der Rückwärtsgang**	*ruick*vairts-gang
roof	**das Dach**	dakh
screwdriver	**der Schraubenzieher**	*shrow*ben-tsee-yer
seat	**der Sitz**	zits
seatbelt	**der Sicherheitsgurt**	*zikher*-hites-goort

shock absorber	**der Stoßdämpfer**	*shtohs*-daimpfer
silencer	**der Auspufftopf**	*ows*-poof-topf
spanner	**der Schraubenschlüssel**	*shrow*ben-*shlui*ssel
spares	**die Ersatzteile**	airzats-*ty*ler
spark plug	**die Zündkerze**	tsuint-*kair*tser
speed	**die Geschwindigkeit**	gu-*shvin*dikh-kite
speedometer	**der Zähler**	*tsay*ler
spring	**die Feder**	*fay*der
stall (to)	**stehenbleiben**	*shtayen*-*bly*ben
starter	**der Anlasser, Starter**	*an*lasser, *shtar*ter
steering	**die Steuerung**	*shtoye*roong
steering wheel	**das Steuerrad**	*shtoyer*-raht
sunroof	**das Schiebedach**	*sheeb*er-dakh
suspension	**die Federung**	*fay*deroong
(petrol) tank	**der (Benzin-) Tank**	(bent*seen*-) tank
tappets	**die Stössel**	*shter*sel
transmission	**die Kraftübertragung**	*kraft-ui*ber-trahgoong
(spare) tyre	**der (Ersatz-) Reifen**	(airzats-) *ry*fen
valve	**das Schlauchventil**	*shlowkh*-fen*teel*
warning light	**das Warnlicht**	varn-likht
wheel	**das Rad**	raht
back	**Hinterrad**	*hint*er-raht
front	**Vorderrad**	*ford*er-raht
spare	**Ersatzrad**	airzats-raht

window	**das Fenster**	*fen*ster
windscreen	**die Windschutzscheibe**	*vint*-shoots-*shy*ber
windscreen washers	**die Scheibenwaschanlage**	*shy*ben-*vash-an*-lahgur
windscreen wiper	**der Scheibenwischer**	*shy*ben-visher

By Bike or Moped[1]

Key Phrases

Where can I hire a . . .	**Wo kann ich ein . . . mieten?**	Voh kan ikh ine . . . *mee*ten
bicycle?	**Fahrrad**	*fahr*-raht
moped?	**Moped**	*moh*pet
motorbike?	**Motorrad**	*moh*tor-raht
mountain bike?	**Mountain-Bike**	mountain bike
Is it obligatory to wear a helmet?	**Ist es Pflicht, einen Helm zu tragen?**	Ist es pflikht inen helm tsoo *trah*gun
Do you repair bicycles?	**Reparieren Sie Fahrräder?**	Raypah*reer*en zee *fahr*-raider

What does it cost per day/week?	**Wie viel kostet es pro Tag/Woche?**	Vee feel kostet es pro tahg/*vokh*er
I'd like a lock please	**Ich hätte gern ein Schloss**	Ikh hetter gairn ine shloss
Where is the cycle shop?	**Wo ist das Fahrradgeschäft?**	Voh ist das *fahr*-raht-gu-*sheft*

1. See also Directions (p. 52) and Road Signs (p. 50).

Do you repair bicycles?	**Reparieren Sie Fahrräder?**	Raypah*reeren* zee *fahr*-raider
The brake isn't working	**Die Bremse funktioniert nicht**	Dee *brem*zer foonkts-yone*eert* nikht
The tyre is punctured	**Ich habe einen Platten**	Ikh hahber inen platten
The gears need adjusting	**Die Gänge müssten neu eingestellt werden**	Dee geng-er *muis*sten noy *ine*-gu-*shtelt vair*den
The saddle is too high	**Der Sattel ist zu hoch**	Dair zattel ist tsoo hohkh
Could you straighten the wheel?	**Könnten Sie die Räder gerade richten?**	Kernten zee dee *ray*der gu*rah*der rikhten
The handlebar is loose	**Der Lenker ist lose**	Dair lenker ist *loh*ser
Could you lend me a spanner?	**Könnten Sie mir einen Schraubenschlüssel leihen?**	Kernten zee meer inen *shrow*ben-*shluis*sel *ly*-en
Can I take my bike on the boat/train?	**Kann ich mein Fahrrad auf das Schiff/in den Zug nehmen?**	Kan ikh mine *fahr*-raht owf das shif/in den tsoog *nay*men

Parts of a bicycle and other useful words

basket	**der Korb**	korb
bell	**die Klingel**	kling-el
brake, front	**die Vorderbremse**	*forder-brem*zer
brake, rear	**die Rückbremse**	*ruick-brem*zer
brake cable	**das Bremskabel**	bremz-*kah*bel

brake lever	**der Bremsheber**	bremz-*hay*ber
bulb	**die Glühbirne**	*glui-beer*ner
chain	**die Kette**	ketter
chain guard	**der Kettenschutz**	ketten-shoots
child's seat	**der Kindersitz**	kin-der-zits
dynamo	**das Dynamo**	duinah*moh*
fork	**die Gabel**	*gah*bul
frame	**das Gestell**	gu-*shtel*
gear cable	**der Schaltzug**	shalt-tsoog
gear lever	**der Schalthebel**	shalt-*hay*bel
gears	**die Gänge**	gaing-er
handlebar	**das Lenkrad**	lenk-raht
helmet	**der Helm**	helm
high-visibility jacket	**die Leucht-Jacke**	loykht-*yack*er
inner tube	**der Schlauch**	shlaukh
light, front	**das Vorderlicht**	*forder*-likht
light, rear	**das Rücklicht**	*ruick*-likht
mudguard	**das Schutzblech**	shoots-blekh
panniers	**die Fahrradtasche**	*fahr*-raht-tasher
pedal	**das Pedal**	pe*dahl*
pump	**die Pumpe**	*poom*per
puncture	**der platte Reifen**	platter *ry*fen
puncture repair kit	**das Flickzeug**	flick-tsoyg
reflector	**der Reflektor**	reflek*tor*

rim	**die Felge**	felgur
saddle	**der Sattel**	zattel
spoke	**die Speiche**	*shpykh*er
suspension	**die Aufhängung**	*owf*-heng-oong
tyre	**der Reifen**	*ry*fen
valve	**das Ventil**	fen*teel*
wheel	**das Rad**	raht

Road Signs

Ausfahrt (für Lkws)	exit (for lorries)
Bahnübergang	level crossing
Blaue Zone	restricted parking
Busspur	bus lane
Durchgangsverkehr	through traffic
Einbahnstraße	one-way street/system
Eingeschränktes Parken	restricted parking
Einordnen	get in lane
Gefahr	danger
Geschwindigkeitsgrenze	speed limit
Halt!	stop!
Keine Durchfahrt	no through road
Keine Zufahrt	no entry
Kurven	bends, curves
Langsam (fahren)	(go) slow
Lawinengefahr	avalanche area

Licht einschalten	lights on
Maut	toll
Maximalgeschwindigkeit	maximum speed
Nicht überholen	overtaking prohibited
Nur für Fußgänger	pedestrians only
Parken nur mit Parkscheiben	parking disc required
Parken verboten	no parking
Rechts fahren/bleiben	keep right
Sackgasse	dead end
Scheinwerfer einschalten	headlights on
Schlechte Fahrbahn	bad surface
Seitenstreifen nicht befahrbar	soft verges closed to traffic
Steinschlag	falling stones
Steiler Hang	steep hill
Straße gesperrt	road blocked
Straßenbau	roadworks ahead
Straßenglätte	slippery surface
Umgehungsstraße	ring road
Umleitung	diversion
Unebene Fahrbahn	uneven surface
Verkehrsampeln	traffic lights
Vorfahrt beachten	give way
Vorsicht	caution
Vorsicht Splitt	loose chippings
Zoll	customs

DIRECTIONS

Key Phrases

Where is . . . ?	**Wo ist . . . ?**	Voh ist . . .
How do I get to . . . ?	**Wie komme ich nach . . . ?**	Vee *komm*er ikh nahkh
How many kilometres?	**Wie viel Kilometer?**	Vee feel keeloh-*mayt*er
Please show me on the map	**Bitte, zeigen Sie mir auf der Karte**	Bitter *tsyg*un zee meer owf dair karter
You are going the wrong way	***Sie fahren in die falsche Richtung**	Zee fahren in dee falsher *rikh*toong

Excuse me, could you tell me . . .	**Entschuldigen Sie bitte, können Sie mir sagen . . .**	Ent*shool*digun zee bitter, kernen zee meer *zahg*un . . .
How far is it to . . . ?	**Wie weit ist es nach . . . ?**	Vee vite ist es nahkh
How do we get on to the motorway to . . . ?	**Wie kommen wir auf die Autobahn nach . . . ?**	Vee *komm*en veer owf dee *owt*oh-bahn nahkh
Which is the best road to . . . ?	**Welches ist die beste Straße nach . . . ?**	*Velkh*es ist dee bester *shtrahs*ser nahkh
Is there a scenic route to . . . ?	**Gibt es eine malerische Straße nach . . . ?**	Geebt es iner *mahl*erishe *shtrahs*ser nahkh . . .
Where does this road lead to?	**Wohin führt diese Straße?**	Voh-hin fuirt deezer *shtrah*ser

Is it a good road?	**Ist die Straße gut?**	Ist die *shtrahss*er goot
Is it a motorway?	**Ist es eine Autobahn?**	Ist es iner *owt*oh-bahn
Is there a toll?	**Gibt es eine Maut?**	Geebt es iner mowt
Is there any danger of snowdrifts?	**Besteht Gefahr von Schneewehen?**	Bu-*stayt* gu*fahr* fon shnay-*vay*en
Is the tunnel/pass open?	**Ist der Tunnel/Pass offen?**	Ist dair *toon*el/pass offen
Will we get to . . . by evening?	**Werden wir bis zum Abend in . . . sein?**	*Vair*den veer bis tsoom *ahb*ent in . . . zine
Where are we now?	**Wo sind wir jetzt?**	Voh zint veer yetst
What is the name of this place?	**Wie heißt dieser Ort?**	Vee hyst deezer ort
I'm lost	**Ich habe mich verlaufen**	Ikh haber mikh fair*low*fen
It's that way	***Da entlang**	Dah ent*lang*
It isn't far	***Es ist nicht weit**	Es ist nikht vite
It's on the square	***Es ist an dem Platz**	Es ist an daim plats
It's at the end of this street	***Es ist am Ende der Straße**	Es ist am ender der *shtrahss*er
There is a bank in the pedestrian area	***Es gibt eine Bank in der Fußgängerzone**	Es geebt iner bank in der *foos*-geng-er-*tsohn*er
Follow this road for five kilometres	***Fahren Sie auf dieser Straße fünf Kilometer**	Fahren zee owf deezer *shtrahss*er fuinf keeloh-*mayt*er
Keep straight on	***Fahren Sie geradeaus**	Fahren zee gu*rahd*er-*ows*

Turn right at the crossroads	*Biegen Sie an der Kreuzung nach rechts ab	*Bee*gun zee an dair *kroyt*soong nahkh rekhts ap
Take the second road on the left	*Biegen Sie in die zweite Straße links ein	*Bee*gun zee in dee tsviter *shtrahs*ser links ine
Turn right at the traffic-lights	*Biegen Sie an der Verkehrsampel rechts ab	*Bee*gun zee an dair fair*kairs*-ampel rekhts ap
Turn left after the bridge	*Biegen Sie hinter der Brücke links ab	*Bee*gun zee *hint*er dair *bruick*er links ap
The best road is the 35	*Am besten fahren Sie die fünfunddreißig	Am besten fahren zee dee fuinf-oont-*dry*sikh
Take the 35 to ... and ask again	*Fahren Sie auf der fünfunddreißig bis ... und fragen Sie dann wieder	Fahren zee owf dair fuinf-oont-*dry*sikh bis ... oont *frah*gun zee dan *veeder*
Take junction 10/the exit for ...	*Nehmen Sie die Anschluss-Stelle zehn/die Ausfahrt nach ...	*Nay*men zee dee *an*-shlooss-*shtel*ler tsayn/dee *ows*-fahrt nahkh ...
You are going the wrong way	*Sie fahren in die falsche Richtung	Zee fahren in dee falsher *rikh*toong
One-way system	Einbahnstraße	*Ine*-bahn-*shtrahs*ser
North	Norden	Norden
South	Süden	Zuiden
East	Osten	Osten
West	Westen	Vesten

ACCOMMODATION[1]

B&B	**Fremdenzimmer/ Zimmer mit Frühstück/ Pension**	Fremden-tsimmer/ Tsimmer mit *frui-*shtuick/pens-*yon*
Campsite	**der Campingplatz**	Camping-plats
Cottage	**das Landhaus**	Land-hows
Country inn	**der Gasthof auf dem Land**	Gast-hohf owf daim lant
Guest-house	**das Gasthaus**	Gast-hows
Youth hostel	**die Jugendherberge**	*Yoogunt-hair*bairgur
Rooms to let/ vacancies	***Zimmer zu vermieten/ Zimmer frei**	Tsimmer tsoo fair*meeten/* Tsimmer fry
No vacancies	***Keine Zimmer frei**	Kiner tsimmer fry
No camping	***Zelten verboten**	*Tsel*ten fair*bohten*
Can you show me on the map where the hotel is?	**Können Sie mir auf der Landkarte zeigen, wo das Hotel ist?**	Kernen zee meer owf dair *lant*-karter *tsy*gun voh das hoh*tel* ist
Is it in the centre?	**Ist es im Zentrum?**	Ist es im *tsen*trum

1. Every German city has a *Verkehrsamt* or *Touristeninformation*. It gives information about entertainment and has a list of hotels and rooms, a *Hotel- und Zimmernachweis* or *Zimmervermittlung*. It will recommend a hotel or guest-house, give you the price and the address, and direct you there.

| Is it near a bus stop? | **Ist es in der Nähe einer Bushaltestelle?** | Ist es in der *nay*er iner *boos*-halter-*shtel*ler |
| Is it on a train/metro route? | **Ist es auf einer Zug-/U-Bahnlinie?** | Ist es owf iner tsoog-/*oo*-bahn-*leen*-yer |

Check In

Key Phrases

Do you have a room for the night?	**Haben Sie ein Zimmer für heute Nacht?**	Hahben zee ine tsimmer fuir *hoy*ter nahkht
Does the hotel have wi-fi?	**Hat das Hotel Wi-fi?**	Hat das hoh*tel* wi-fi
I've reserved a room; my name is . . .	**Ich habe ein Zimmer reserviert; mein Name ist . . .**	Ikh hahber ine tsimmer rezair*veert*; mine *nah*mer ist . . .
Is there a lift/ elevator?	**Gibt es einen Fahrstuhl?**	Geebt es inen fahr-shtool
How much is the room per night?	**Wie viel kostet das Zimmer pro Nacht?**	Vee feel kostet das tsimmer pro nahkht

Can you suggest . . .	**Kennen Sie . . .**	Kennen zee . . .
a moderately priced hotel?	**ein Mittelklasse-Hotel?**	ine mittel-klasser hohtel
an inexpensive hotel?	**ein günstiges Hotel?**	ine *guin*stiges hoh*tel*
another good hotel?	**ein anderes gutes Hotel?**	ine *anderes gootes hohtel*

Is there an internet connection in the rooms?	**Haben die Zimmer Internet-Anschluss?**	Hahben dee tsimmer internet-*an*-shlooss
Yes, it's free/it costs … euros per hour	***Ja, das ist kostenlos/ das kostet … Euros pro Stunde**	Yah, das ist *kosten*-los/ das kostet … *oy*rohs pro *shtoon*der
Does the hotel have a business centre?	**Hat das Hotel Konferenzräume?**	Hat das hoh*tel* konfe*rence-roy*mer
Is there a spa/fitness centre?	**Gibt es einen Wellness-/ Fitnessbereich?**	Geebt es inen wellness-/ fitness-bu-*rykh*
Does the hotel have a swimming pool/a private beach?	**Hat das Hotel ein Schwimmbad/einen Privatstrand?**	Hat das hoh*tel* ine *shvim*-baht/inen pri*vaht*-shtrand
I'd like a single room with a shower	**Ich möchte ein Einzelzimmer mit Dusche**	Ikh *merkh*te ine *ine*-tsel-tsimmer mit *doosh*er
I'd like a room with a double bed and a bathroom	**Ich möchte ein Doppelzimmer mit Bad**	Ikh *merkh*ter ine doppel-tsimmer mit baht
I'd like a family room/ adjoining rooms	**Ich möchte ein Familienzimmer/ Nebenzimmer**	Ikh *merkh*ter ine fa*meel*-yen-tsimmer/*nay*ben-tsimmer
Have you a room with twin beds/a king-size bed?	**Haben Sie ein Zweibettzimmer/ein Zimmer mit einem großen Doppelbett?**	Hahben zee ine tsvy-bet-tsimmer/ine tsimmer mit inen grohsen doppel-bet
How long will you be staying?	***Wie lange bleiben Sie?**	Vee lang-er *bly*ben zee
Is it for one night only?	***Ist es nur für eine Nacht?**	Ist es noor fuir ine nahkht

I'd like a room	**Ich möchte ein Zimmer**	Ikh *merkh*ter ine tsimmer
for a week	**für eine Woche**	fuir iner *vokh*er
for two or three days	**für zwei oder drei Tage**	fuir tsvy ohder dry *tahg*ur
until Friday	**bis Freitag**	bis *fry*-tahg
What floor is the room on?	**In welchem Stock ist das Zimmer?**	In *velkh*em shtock ist das tsimmer
Is there a lift/ elevator?	**Gibt es einen Fahrstuhl?**	Geebt es inen fahr-shtool
Are there facilities for the disabled?	**Gibt es Einrichtungen für Behinderte?**	Geebt es *ine-rikh*toong-en fuir bu*hind*erter
Have you a room on the first floor?	**Haben Sie ein Zimmer im ersten Stock?**	Hahben zee ine tsimmer im airsten shtok
May I see the room?	**Kann ich bitte das Zimmer sehen?**	Kan ikh bitter das tsimmer *zay*en
I'll take this room	**Ich nehme dieses Zimmer**	Ikh *nay*mer deezez tsimmer
I don't like this room	**Dieses Zimmer gefällt mir nicht**	Deezez tsimmer gu*felt* meer nikht
Have you another one?	**Haben Sie ein anderes?**	Hahben zee ine *and*eres
I'd like a quiet room	**Ich möchte ein ruhiges Zimmer**	Ikh *merkh*ter ine roo-iges tsimmer

There's too much noise	**Hier ist zu viel Lärm**	Heer ist tsoo feel lairm
I'd like a room with a balcony	**Ich möchte ein Zimmer mit Balkon**	Ikh *merkh*ter ine tsimmer mit balkohn
Have you a room looking on to the street?	**Haben Sie ein Zimmer zur Straßenseite?**	Hahben zee ine tsimmer tsoor *shtrahs*sen-ziter
Have you a room	**Haben Sie ein Zimmer**	Hahben zee ine tsimmer
near the swimming pool?	**neben dem Schwimmbad?**	*nay*ben dem *shvim*baht
overlooking the sea?	**mit Blick auf das Meer?**	mit blik owf das mair
We've only a double/twin-bedded room	***Wir haben nur ein Doppel-/Zweibettzimmer**	Veer hahben noor ine doppel-/*tsvy*-bet-tsimmer
This is the only room vacant	***Dies ist das einzige freie Zimmer**	Deez ist das *ine*-tsigur *fry*er tsimmer
We shall have another room tomorrow	***Morgen wird ein anderes Zimmer frei**	*Mor*gun veert ine *an*deres tsimmer fry
The room is only available tonight	***Das Zimmer ist nur für heute Nacht frei**	Das tsimmer ist noor fuir *hoy*ter nahkht fry
How much is the room per night?	**Wie viel kostet das Zimmer pro Nacht?**	Vee feel kostet das tsimmer pro nahkht
Have you nothing cheaper?	**Haben Sie nichts Billigeres?**	Hahben zee nikhts *bil*ligures

What do we pay for the child(ren)?	**Was müssen wir für das Kind (die Kinder) bezahlen?**	Vas *muis*sen veer fuir das kint (dee kin-der) bu-*tsah*len
Could you put a cot in the room?	**Könnten Sie ein Kinderbett ins Zimmer stellen?**	Kernten zee ine kin-der-bet ins tsimmer *shtel*len
Is the service (and tax)[1] included?	**Ist Bedienung (und Kurtaxe) einbegriffen?**	Ist bu*dee*noong (oont koor-takser) *ine*-bugriffen
Is breakfast included?	**Ist das Frühstück einbegriffen?**	Ist das *frui*-shtuick *ine*-bugriffen
How much is the room with full board/ without meals?	**Wie viel kostet das Zimmer mit Vollpension/ohne Mahlzeiten?**	Vee feel kostet das tsimmer mit foll-pens-*yon*/ohner mahl-tsiten
Do you have a weekly rate?	**Haben Sie einen festen Preis pro Woche?**	Hahben zee inen festen price pro *vokh*er
It's too expensive	**Das ist mir zu teuer**	Das ist meer tsoo *toy*er
Would you fill in the registration form, please?	***Füllen Sie bitte dieses Anmeldeformular aus**	*Fuil*len zee bitter deezez *an*-melder-formoo*lar* ows
Could I have your passport, please?	***Könnte ich bitte Ihren Pass haben?**	Kernte ikh bitter eeren pass hahben
Surname/First name	***Familienname/ Vorname**	Fa*meel*-yen-*nah*mer/ *for*-nahmer
Address	***Adresse**	Ad*dress*er

1. In health resorts only.

Date and place of birth	***Geburtsdatum und -ort**	G*uboorts*-dahtoom oont -ort
Passport number	***Passnummer**	Pass-noommer
What is your car registration number?	***Wie ist Ihr Kfz-Kennzeichen?**	Vee ist eer kah-ef-tset-*kenn-tsykh*en

Check Out

Key Phrases

Can you have my bill ready?	**Können Sie bitte meine Rechnung fertig machen?**	Kernen zee bitter miner *rekh*noong *fair*tikh makhen
There is a mistake on the bill	**Es gibt einen Fehler mit der Rechnung**	Es geebt inen failer mit der *rekh*noong
Please store the luggage. I will be back at . . .	**Können Sie bitte mein Gepäck aufbewahren. Ich komme am . . . zurück**	Kernen zee bitter mine g*upeck owf*-buvahren. Ikh *komm*er um . . . tsoo-*ruick*

I'd like to leave tomorrow	**Ich möchte morgen abfahren**	Ikh *merkh*ter *mor*gun *ap*-fahren
How would you like to pay?	***Wie möchten Sie bezahlen?**	Vee *merkh*ten zee bu-*tsah*len
I'll pay by credit card	**Ich zahle mit Kreditkarte**	Ikh *tsah*ler mit kray*deet*-karter
I shall be coming back on . . . Can I book a room?	**Ich komme am . . . zurück. Kann ich ein Zimmer reservieren?**	Ikh *komm*er am . . . tsoo-*ruick*. Kan ikh ine tsimmer rezairv*ee*ren

Could you have my luggage brought down?	**Können Sie bitte mein Gepäck runterbringen lassen?**	Kernen zee bitter mine gu*peck roon*ter-bring-en lassen
Please order a taxi for me	**Bitte bestellen Sie mir ein Taxi**	Bitter bu-*shtell*en zee meer ine taxi
Thank you for a pleasant stay	**Vielen Dank für den angenehmen Aufenthalt**	Feelen dank fuir dain *an*-gu*nay*men *ow*fent-halt

Problems and Complaints

The air conditioning/television doesn't work	**Die Klimaanlage/Der Fernsehapparat funktioniert nicht**	Dee *klee*mah-*an*-lahgur/der fairnzay-appar*aht* foonkts-yon*eert* nikht
There are no towels in my room	**In meinem Zimmer sind keine Handtücher**	In minem tsimmer zint kiner hant-*tuikh*er
There's no soap	**Es gibt keine Seife**	Es geebt kiner *zy*fer
There's no (hot) water	**Es gibt kein (heißes) Wasser**	Es geebt kine (hices) *vass*er
There's no plug in my washbasin	**Mein Waschbecken hat keinen Stopfen**	Mine *vash*-becken hat kinen shtopfen
There's no toilet paper in the lavatory	**Im WC ist kein Toilettenpapier**	Im vay-tsay ist kine twah*letten*-pa*peer*
The lavatory won't flush	**Die Toilettenspülung ist defekt**	Dee twah*letten*-shpuiloong ist *day*fekt

The toilet is blocked	**Die Toilette ist verstopft**	Dee twah*letter* ist fair*shtopft*
The shower doesn't work/is flooded	**Die Dusche funktioniert nicht/ steht unter Wasser**	Dee *doo*sher foonkts-yon*eert* nikht/shtayt *oon*ter *vasser*
The bidet leaks	**Das Bidet ist undicht**	Das bidet ist *oon*dikht
The light doesn't work	**Die Lampe funktioniert nicht**	Dee *lamper* foonkts-yon*eert* nikht
The light bulb is broken	**Die Glühbirne ist kaputt**	Dee *glui-beer*ner ist kah*poot*
The blind is stuck	**Das Rollo klemmt**	Das rol-*loh* klemmt
The curtains won't close	**Die Vorhänge schließen nicht**	Dee *for*-heng-er *shlee*ssen nikht

Hotels

In your room

Chambermaid	**das Zimmermädchen**	Tsimmer-*mayt*-khen
Room service	**die Zimmerbedienung**	Tsimmer-bu*dee*noong
I'd like breakfast in my room, please	**Ich möchte bitte Frühstück in meinem Zimmer haben**	Ikh *merkh*ter bitter *frui*-shtuick in minem tsimmer hahben
Can I have more hangers, please?	**Kann ich bitte mehr Kleiderbügel haben?**	Kan ikh bitter mair *klyder*-*bui*gul hahben
Is there a socket for an electric razor?	**Gibt es eine Steckdose für Rasierapparate?**	Geebt es iner *shteck-doh*zer fuir rahzeer-appa*rah*ter

Where is the bathroom?	**Wo ist das Badezimmer?**	Voh ist das *bah*der-tsimmer
Where is the lavatory?	**Wo ist die Toilette?**	Voh ist dee twah*lett*er
Is there a shower?	**Gibt es eine Dusche?**	Geebt es iner *doo*sher
May I have another blanket/pillow?	**Kann ich bitte noch eine Decke/noch ein Kopfkissen haben?**	Kan ikh bitter nokh einer decker/nokh ine kopf-kissen hahben
These sheets are dirty	**Diese Bettlaken sind schmutzig**	Deezer *bet*-lahken zint *shmoot*sikh
I can't open my window; please open it	**Ich kann mein Fenster nicht aufmachen; bitte öffnen Sie es für mich**	Ikh kan mine *fen*ster nikht *owf*-makhen; bitter *erf*nen zee es fuir mikh
It's too hot/cold	**Es ist zu heiß/kalt**	Es ist tsoo hice/kalt
Can the heating be turned up?	**Kann die Heizung weiter/etwas mehr aufgedreht werden?**	Kan dee *hyt*soong viter/etvas mair *owf*-gu*drayt vair*den
Can the heating be turned down?	**Kann die Heizung etwas mehr abgedreht werden?**	Kan dee *hyt*soong etvas mair *ap*-gu*drayt vair*den
Come in	**Herein**	Hair-*ine*
Put it on the table, please	**Stellen Sie es bitte auf den Tisch**	*Shtel*len zee es bitter owf dain tish
Have you a needle and thread?	**Haben Sie Nadel und Faden?**	Hahben zee *nah*del oont *fah*den
Do you have an iron and ironing board?	**Haben Sie ein Bügeleisen und Bügelbrett?**	Hahben zee ine *bui*gul-eye-zen oont *bui*gul-bret

I'd like these shoes cleaned	**Lassen Sie bitte diese Schuhe putzen**	Lassen zee bitter deezer shoo-wer *poot*sen
I'd like this dress cleaned	**Lassen Sie bitte dieses Kleid reinigen**	Lassen zee bitter deesez klite *ry*nigun
I'd like this suit pressed	**Lassen Sie bitte diesen Anzug bügeln**	Lassen zee bitter deezen antsoog *bui*geln
When will it be ready?	**Wann wird er fertig sein?**	Van veert air *fair*tikh zine
It will be ready tomorrow	***Es wird morgen fertig sein**	Es veert *mor*gun *fair*tikh zine

Other services

My key, please	**Meinen Schlüssel bitte**	Minen *shluis*sel bitter
A second key, please	**Einen zweiten Schlüssel bitte**	Inen tsviten *shluis*sel bitter
I've lost my key	**Ich habe meinen Schlüssel verloren**	Ikh hahber minen shluissel fair*lohr*en
Do you have a map of the town/ an entertainment guide?	**Haben Sie einen Stadtplan/ein Veranstaltungs-programm?**	Hahben zee inen shtat-plahn/ine fair*an*shtaltoongs-pro*gram*
Could you put this in your safe?	**Könnten Sie dies in Ihren Tresor/ Safe legen?**	Kernten zee deez in eeren tray*zohr*/safe *lay*gun
Are there any letters for me?	**Sind Briefe für mich da?**	Zint *bree*fer fuir mikh dah
Is there any message for me?	**Ist eine Nachricht für mich da?**	Ist iner nahkh-rikht fuir mikh dah

What is the international dialing code?	**Wie ist die internationale Vorwahlnummer?**	Vee ist dee internats-yon*ah*ler *for*-vahl-noommer
Could you send a fax for me please?	**Könnten Sie bitte ein Fax für mich senden?**	Kernten zee bitter ine fax fuir mikh zenden
Is there a computer for guests to use?	**Gibt es für Gäste einen Computer/ Rechner?**	Geebt es fuir gaister inen computer/*rekh*ner
Is there a charge for this?	**Kostet das etwas?**	Kostet das etvas
Do I need a password?	**Brauche ich ein Kennwort?**	*Browkh*er ikh ine ken-vort
There's a lady/ gentleman to see you	***Eine Dame/ein Herr möchte Sie sprechen**	Iner dahmer/ine hair *merkh*ter zee *shprekh*en
Please ask her/him to come up	**Bitten Sie sie/ihn heraufzukommen**	Bitten zee zee/een hair*owf*-tsoo-*kom*men
I'm coming down	**Ich komme hinunter**	Ikh *kom*mer hinoonter
Have you any	**Haben Sie**	Hahben zee
envelopes?	**Umschläge?**	*oom*-shlaygur
stamps?	**Briefmarken?**	*breef*-marken
writing paper?	**Schreibpapier?**	*shribe*-papeer
Please send the chambermaid/the waiter	**Schicken Sie mir bitte das Zimmermädchen/ den Kellner**	Shicken zee meer bitter das tsimmer-*mayt*-khen/ dain *kell*ner
I need a guide/an interpreter	**Ich brauche einen Fremdenführer/ einen Dolmetscher**	Ikh *browkh*er inen fremden-*fuir*er/inen *dol*metsher

Does the hotel have a babysitting service?	**Hat das Hotel einen Babysitter-Dienst?**	Hat das hoh*tel* inen babysitter-deenst
Where is the dining room?	**Wo ist der Speisesaal?**	Voh ist dair *shpy*zer-zahl
What time is breakfast/lunch/dinner served?	**Wann wird das Frühstück/Mittagessen/Abendessen serviert?**	Van veert das *frui*-shtuick/*mit*-tahg-essen/*ahb*ent-essen sair*veert*
Is there a garage?	**Gibt es eine Garage?**	Geebt es iner ga*rah*jer
Where can I park the car?	**Wo kann ich mein Auto parken?**	Voh kan ikh mine *ow*toh parken
Is the hotel open all night?	**Ist das Hotel die ganze Nacht offen?**	Ist das hoh*tel* dee gantser nahkht offen
What time does it close?	**Wann wird es abgeschlossen?**	Van veert es *ap*-gu-*shlo*ssen
Please wake me at …	**Bitte wecken Sie mich um …**	Bitter vecken zee mikh oom …

Hostels

How long is the walk to the youth hostel?	**Wie lange geht man zur Jugendherberge?**	Vee lang-er gait man tsoor *yoo*gunt-*hair*bairgur
Do you have a room/bed for the night?	**Haben Sie ein Zimmer/Bett für heute Nacht frei?**	Hahben zee ine tsimmer/bet fuir *hoy*ter nahkht fry
How many days can we stay?	**Wie viele Tage können wir bleiben?**	Vee feeler *tah*gur kernen veer *bly*ben
Here is my membership card	**Hier ist meine Mitgliedskarte**	Heer ist miner *mit*-gleets-karter

Do you serve meals?	**Kann man bei Ihnen essen?**	Kan man by eenen essen
Can I use the kitchen?	**Kann ich die Küche benutzen?**	Kan ikh dee *kuikh*er bu*noot*sen
Is there somewhere cheap to eat nearby?	**Kann man hier in der Nähe billig essen?**	Kan man heer in dair *nay*er *bil*likh essen
Can I rent sheets/a sleeping bag?	**Kann ich Bettlaken/ einen Schlafsack mieten?**	Kan ikh *bet*-lahken/ inen *shlahf*-zak *mee*ten
Does the hostel have an internet connection?	**Gibt es in der Herberge Internetanschluss?**	Geebt es in dair *hair*bairgur internet-*an*-shlooss

Camping

Key Phrases

Is there a camp site near here?	**Gibt es einen Campingplatz in der Nähe?**	Geebt es inen camping-plats in dair *nay*er
May we camp here/ in your field?	**Dürfen wir hier/auf Ihrem Feld zelten?**	*Duir*fen veer heer/owf eerem felt *tsel*ten
Is this drinking water?	**Ist dies Trinkwasser?**	Ist deez *trink*-vasser

| Is this an authorized camp site? | **Ist das Zelten hier erlaubt?** | Ist das *tsel*ten heer air*lowbt* |
| Can we hire a tent? | **Können wir ein Zelt mieten?** | Kernen veer ine tselt *mee*ten |

Can we park our caravan here?	**Können wir unseren Wohnwagen hier parken?**	Kernen veer oonzeren *vohn-vah*gun heer parken
Are lavatories/ showers provided?	**Gibt es Toiletten/ Duschen?**	Geebt es twah*letten*/ *doo*shen
What does it cost per person/day/ week?	**Was kostet es pro Person/Tag/ Woche?**	Vas kostet es pro pair*zohn*/tahg/ *vok*her
Where are the shops?	**Wo sind die Geschäfte?**	Voh sind dee gu-*shef*ter
Is there	**Gibt es**	Geebt es
a launderette?	**einen Waschsalon?**	inen *vash*-salon
a playground?	**einen Spielplatz?**	inen *shpeel*-plats
a restaurant?	**ein Restaurant?**	ine restor-*rant*
a swimming pool?	**Schwimmbad?**	ine *shvim*-baht
My camping gas has run out	**Ich habe kein Campinggas mehr**	Ikh haber kine camping-gahs mair
Where can I buy butane gas?	**Wo kann ich Butangas kaufen?**	Voh kan ikh boo*tahn*-gahs *kow*fen
May we light a fire?	**Dürfen wir ein Feuer anzünden?**	*Duir*fen veer ine *foyer* an-tsuinden
Where do I get rid of rubbish?	**Wo kann ich den Abfall hintun?**	Voh kan ikh den *ap*-fal hintoon
Should we sort the rubbish (for recycling)?	**Sollten wir den Abfall (zum Recyclen) trennen?**	Zollten veer den *ap*-fal (tsoom recyclen) trennen

Where can I wash up/wash clothes?	**Wo kann ich das Geschirr spülen/ Wäsche machen?**	Voh kan ikh das gu-*sheer shpui*len/*vesh*er makhen
Is there somewhere to dry clothes?	**Kann ich die Wäsche irgendwo trocknen?**	Kan ikh dee *vesh*er *eer*gunt-voh trocknen
I'm afraid the campsite is full	***Leider ist der Campingplatz voll**	Dair camping-plats ist *ly*der foll

APARTMENTS AND VILLAS

Key Phrases

Please could you show us around?	**Könnten Sie einen Rundgang mit uns machen?**	*Kern*ten zee inen *roond*-gang mit oons *makh*en
How does the heating/hot water work?	**Wie funktioniert die Heizung/das heiße Wasser?**	Vee foonkts-yon*eert* dee *hyt*soong/das hicer *vass*er
Please could you show me how this works?	**Könnten Sie mir bitte zeigen, wie das funktioniert?**	Kernten zee mir bitter *tsyg*un vee das foonkts-yon*eert*
Which days does the maid come?	**An welchen Tagen kommt das Zimmermädchen?**	An *velkh*en *tahg*un kommt das tsimmer-*mayt*-khen
When is the rubbish collected?	**Wann wird der Müll abgeholt?**	Van veert dair muill *ap*-guhohlt
Please could you give me another set of keys?	**Könnten Sie mir bitte noch einen Satz Schlüssel geben?**	Kernten zee meer bitter nokh inen zats *shluiss*el *gay*ben

We have rented an apartment/villa	**Wir haben eine Ferienwohnung/ Villa gemietet**	Veer hahben iner *fairee*-yen-*voh*noong/ vee*lah* gu*mee*tet
Here is our reservation	**Hier ist unsere Reservierung**	Heer ist oonzerer rezair*vee*roong
Is the cost of electricity/of the gas cylinder/of the maid included?	**Sind die Kosten für Strom/Gas/das Zimmermädchen inklusive?**	Zint dee kosten fuir shtrohm/gahs/das tsimmer-*mayt*-khen inkloo*see*ver
Where is	**Wo ist**	Voh ist
the electricity mains switch?	**der Hauptstromschalter?**	dair *howpt*-shtrohm-shalter
the fuse box?	**der Sicherungskasten?**	dair *zikh*eroongs-kasten
the light switch?	**der Lichtschalter?**	dair *likht*-shalter
the socket?	**die Steckdose?**	dee *shteck-doh*zer
the water mains stopcock?	**der Absperrhahn für das Wasser?**	dair *ap*-shpair-hahn fuir das *vass*er
Is there a spare gas cylinder?	**Gibt es eine Reserve-Gasflasche?**	Geebt es iner rezairver-*gahs-flash*er
Are gas cylinders delivered?	**Können Gasflaschen geliefert werden?**	Kernen *gahs-flash*en gu*lee*efert *vair*den
Which days does the maid come?	**An welchen Tagen kommt das Zimmermädchen?**	An *velkh*en *tah*gun kommt das tsimmer-*mayt*-khen
For how long?	**Für wie lange?**	Fuir vee lang-er
When is the rubbish collected?	**Wann wird der Müll abgeholt?**	Van veert dair muill *ap*-guhohlt

Should we sort the rubbish for recycling?	**Sollten wir den Müll für das Recycling sortieren?**	Zolten veer den muill fuir das recycling zorteeren
The rubbish hasn't been collected	**Der Müll ist nicht abgeholt worden**	Dair muill ist nikht ap-guhohlt vorden
Where can we buy logs for the fire?	**Wo können wir Feuerholz kaufen?**	Voh kernen veer foyer-holts kowfen
Is there a barbecue?	**Gibt es einen Grill?**	Geebt es inen grill
Please could you give me another set of keys?	**Könnten Sie mir bitte noch einen Satz Schlüssel geben?**	Kernten zee meer bitter nokh inen zats shluissel gayben
Does someone come to service the swimming pool?	**Kommt jemand, um den Swimming Pool instand zu halten?**	Kommt yaymant oom dain swimming pool inshtant tsoo halten
Is there an inventory?	**Gibt es ein Inventar?**	Geebt es ine inventahr
This was broken when we arrived	**Das war bei unserer Ankunft schon defekt**	Das vahr by oonzerer ankoonft shohn dayfekt
We have replaced the broken . . .	**Wir haben die kaputte . . . ersetzt**	Veer hahben dee kahpooter . . . airzetst
Here is the bill	**Hier ist die Rechnung**	Heer ist dee rekhnoong
Please return my deposit against damage	**Geben Sie mir bitte die Kaution zurück**	Gayben zee meer bitter dee kowts-yon tsoo-ruick

Cleaning and Maintenance[1]

Where is a DIY centre/hardware shop?	**Wo gibt es einen Heimwerkermarkt/ein Eisenwarengeschäft?**	Voh geebt es inen hime-verker*markt*/ine *eyezen*-vahren-gu-*sheft*
all-purpose cleaner	**der Universalreiniger**	oonivair*sahl*-rynigur
bleach	**das Bleichmittel**	*blykh*-mittel
bracket	**der Befestigungsarm**	bu*festi*goongs-*arm*
broom	**der Besen**	*bay*zen
brush	**die Bürste**	*buir*ster
bucket	**der Eimer**	*eye*mer
butane gas	**das Butangas**	bootahn-*gahs*
charcoal	**die Holzkohle**	*holts*-kohler
clothes line	**die Wäscheleine**	*vesh*er-liner
clothes pegs	**die Wäscheklammern**	*vesh*er-klam*mern*
detergent	**das Reinigungsmittel**	*ry*nigungs-mittel
dustbin	**der Mülleimer**	*muill-eye*mer
dustpan	**die Handschaufel**	*hant-show*fel
fire extinguisher	**der Feuerlöscher**	*foyer-ler*sher
hammer	**der Hammer**	*hah*mer
mop	**der Mopp**	mop
nails	**die Nägel**	*nay*gul
paint	**die Farbe**	*far*ber

1. See also Hardware and Outdoors (p. 189).

paint brush	**der Pinsel**	*pin*zel
plastic	**das Plastik**	*plastik*
pliers	**die Zange**	*tsang*-er
rubbish sacks	**die Müllsäcke**	*muill*-zecker
saw	**die Säge**	*zay*gur
screwdriver	**der Schraubenzieher**	*shrow*ben-tsee-yer
screws	**die Schrauben**	*shrow*ben
spanner	**der Schraubenschlüssel**	*shrow*ben-*shluiss*el
stainless steel	**der Edelstahl**	*ay*del-shtahl
vacuum cleaner	**der Staubsauger**	*shtowp-zow*gur
washing powder	**der Waschpulver**	*vash*-poolfer
washing-up liquid	**das Spülmittel**	*shpuil*-mittel
wire	**der Draht**	draht
wood	**das Holz**	holts

Furniture and Fittings

armchair	**der Sessel**	*zess*el
barbecue	**der Grill**	grill
bath	**das Bad**	baht
bed	**das Bett**	bet
(woollen) blanket	**die (Woll-) Decke**	*(voll-) deck*er
bolt (for door)	**der Bolzen**	boltsen

central heating	die Zentralheizung	tsen*trahl hyt*soong
chair	der Stuhl	shtool
clock	die Uhr	oor
cooker	der Herd	hairt
cupboard	der Schrank	shrank
curtains	die Vorhänge	*for*-heng-er
cushions	die Kissen	kissen
deckchair	der Liegestuhl	*leeg*ur-shtool
dishwasher	der Geschirrspüler	gu-*sheer-shpui*ler
doorbell	die Türklingel	*tuir*-kling-el
doorknob	die Türknauf	*tuir*-k-nowf
hinge	das Scharnier	shar*neer*
hob	das Kochfeld	*kokh*-felt
immersion heater	die Tauchheizung	*towkh*-hyt*soong
iron	das Bügeleisen	*bui*gul-*eyezen*
lamp	die Lampe	*lamper*
lampshade	der Lampenschirm	*lam*pen-sheerm
light bulb	die Glühbirne	*glui-beer*ner
lock	das Schloss	shloss
mattress	die Matratze	matratser
mirror	der Spiegel	*shpee*gul
oven	der Ofen	ohfen
padlock	das Vorhängeschloss	*for*-heng-er-shloss

pillow	das Kissen	kissen
pipe	das Rohr	rohr
plug (electric)	der Stecker	*shteck*er
plug (bath)	der Badewannenstopfen	*bah*der-vannen-shtopfen
radio	das Radio	*rah*deeyoh
refrigerator	der Kühlschrank	*kuil*-shrank
sheet	das Bettlaken	*bet*-lahken
shelf	das Regal	ray*gahl*
shower	die Dusche	*doo*sher
sink	das Spülbecken	*shpuil*-becken
sofa	das Sofa	*zoh*fa
stool	der Hocker	hocker
sun-lounger	der Faulenzer	*fow*lentser
table	der Tisch	tish
tap	der Wasserhahn	*vasser*-hahn
television	der Fernsehapparat	*fairn*-zay-appa*raht*
toilet	die Toilette	twah*letter*
towel	das Handtuch	hant-tookh
washbasin	das Waschbecken	*vash*-becken
washing machine	die Waschmaschine	*vash*-masheener
window latch	der Fensterriegel	*fenster-reeg*ul
window sill	das Fensterbrett	*fen*ster-bret

Kitchen Equipment

bottle opener	**der Flaschenöffner**	*flash*en-*erf*ner
bowl	**die Schale**	*shah*ler
can opener	**der Büchsenöffner**	*buiks*en-*erf*ner
candle	**die Kerze**	*kair*tser
chopping board	**das Schneidebrett**	*shny*der-bret
coffee pot	**die Kaffeekanne**	kaf*fay*-*ka*nner
colander	**das Küchensieb**	*kuikh*en-zeeb
coolbag	**die Kühltasche**	*kuil*-tasher
corkscrew	**der Korkenzieher**	*korken*-tsee-yer
cup	**die Tasse**	*tas*ser
fork	**die Gabel**	*gah*bul
frying pan	**die Bratpfanne**	*braht*-pfanner
glass	**das Glas**	glahs
grill	**der Grill**	grill
ice tray	**die Eiswürfelschale**	*ice-vuir*fel-*shah*ler
kettle	**der Wasserkocher**	*vasser*-kokher
knife	**das Messer**	*mess*er
matches	**die Streichhölzer**	*shtrykh-herl*tser
microwave	**die Mikrowelle**	*meek*roh-veller
pan with lid	**der Kochtopf mit Deckel**	kokh-topf mit deckel
plate	**der Teller**	teller

scissors	**die Schere**	*shay*rer
sieve	**das Sieb**	zeep
spoon	**der Löffel**	*ler*fel
tea towel	**das Geschirrtuch**	gu-*shir*-tookh
torch	**die Taschenlampe**	*tashen-lamper*

Parts of a House and Grounds

balcony	**der Balkon**	bal*kohn*
bathroom	**das Badezimmer**	*bah*der-tsimmer
bedroom	**das Schlafzimmer**	*shlahf*-tsimmer
ceiling	**die Decke**	*deck*er
chimney	**der Schornstein**	*shorn*-shtine
corridor	**der Korridor, Flur**	*korreedor*, floo-er
door	**die Tür**	tuir
fence	**der Zaun**	tsown
fireplace	**der Kamin**	ka*meen*
floor	**der Boden**	*bohd*en
garage	**die Garage**	ga*rah*jer
garden	**der Garten**	garten
gate	**das Tor**	tohr
hall	**der Eingang**	*ine*-gang
kitchen	**die Küche**	*kuikh*er
living room	**das Wohnzimmer**	*vohn*-tsimmer

patio	**der Patio, die Veranda**	*pah*-tee-oh, vairan*dah*
roof	**das Dach**	dakh
shutters	**die Fensterläden**	*fen*ster-*lay*den
stairs	**die Treppen**	*treppen*
swimming pool	**das Schwimmbad**	*shvim*-baht
terrace	**die Terrasse**	tair*rasser*
wall	**die Wand**	vant
window	**das Fenster**	*fen*ster

Problems

The drain is blocked	**Der Abfluss ist verstopft**	Dair *ap*-flooss ist fair-*shtopft*
The pipe/sink is blocked	**Das Rohr/ Spülbecken ist verstopft**	Das rohr/*shpuil*-becken ist fair-*shtopft*
The toilet doesn't flush	**Die Toilettenspülung funktioniert nicht**	Dee twah*letten*-*shpui*loong foonkts-yon*eert* nikht
There's no water	**Es kommt kein Wasser**	Es kommt kine *vasser*
We can't turn the water off	**Wir können das Wasser nicht abstellen**	Veer kernen das *vasser* nikht *ap-shtel*len
We can't turn the shower on	**Wir können die Dusche nicht anstellen**	Veer kernen dee *doo*sher nikht *an-shtel*len

There is a leak (water, gas)	**Es gibt eine undichte Stelle; das Wasser/ Gas kommt raus**	Es geebt iner *oon*dikhter *sht*eller, das *v*asser/gahs kommt rows
There is a broken window	**Ein Fenster ist kaputt**	Ine *fen*ster ist kah*poot*
The shutters won't close	**Die Fensterläden schließen nicht**	Dee *fen*ster-*lay*den *shlees*sen nikht
The window won't open/shut	**Das Fenster lässt sich nicht öffnen/ schließen**	Das *fen*ster lest zikh nikht *erf*nen/*shlees*sen
The electricity has gone off	**Der Strom ist ausgefallen**	Dair shtrohm ist *ows*-gufal-len
The heating/cooker/ refrigerator doesn't work	**Die Heizung/ Der Herd/Der Kühlschrank ist ausgegangen**	Dee *hyt*soong/Dair hairt/ Dee kühl-shrank ist *ows*-gugangen
The boiler doesn't work	**Der Boiler funktioniert nicht**	Dair boiler foonkts-yon*eert* nikht
The lock is stuck	**Das Schloss klemmt**	Das shloss klemmt
This is broken	**Das ist kaputt**	Das ist kah*poot*
This needs repairing	**Es muss repariert werden**	Es mooss repah*reert* *vair*den
The apartment/villa has been burgled	**In die Wohnung/ Villa ist eingebrochen worden**	In dee *voh*noong/ *vee*lah ist *ine*-gu*brok*hen vorden

COMMUNICATIONS

Key Phrases

Is there an internet café near here?	**Gibt es in der Nähe ein Internet-Café?**	Geebt es in dair *nayer* ine internet-café
Do I need a password?	**Brauche ich ein Kennwort?**	*Browkh*er ikh ine ken-vort
Can I print this?	**Kann ich das ausdrucken?**	Kan ikh das *ows*-drooken
What is your email address?	**Wie ist Ihre E-Mail-Adresse?**	Vee ist eerer email-ad*ress*er
Where's the nearest post office?	**Wo ist die nächste Post?**	Voh ist dee *naikh*ster post
I'd like to get a local SIM card for this phone	**Ich möchte für dieses Telefon eine lokale SIM-Karte kaufen**	Ikh merkhter fuir deezez tele*fohn* iner loh-*kah*ler zeem-karter *kow*fen

Email and Internet

Does this café have wi-fi?	**Hat dieses Café Wi-fi?**	Hat deezez café wee-fee
Is there a connection fee?	**Gibt es eine Anschlussgebühr?**	Geebt es iner *an*-shlooss-gu*buir*

Can I access the internet?	**Gibt es Internetzugang?**	Geebt es internet-*tsoo*gang
Can I check my emails?	**Kann ich meine E-Mails lesen?**	Kan ikh miner emails *lay*zen
Can I use any computer?	**Kann ich alle Computer benutzen?**	Kan ikh aller computer bu*noo*tsen
How much does it cost for an hour/half an hour?	**Wie viel kostet es pro Stunde/halbe Stunde?**	Vee feel kostet es pro *shtoon*der/halber *shtoon*der
How do I turn on the computer?	**Wie mache ich den Computer an?**	Vee makher ikh dain computer an
How do I log on/off?	**Wie logge ich mich ein/ aus?**	Vee loggur ikh mikh ine/ows
The computer doesn't respond	**Der Computer reagiert nicht**	Dair computer ray-ah-*geert* nikht
The computer has frozen	**Der Computer ist erstarrt**	Dair computer ist air*shtarrt*
Can you change this to an English keyboard?	**Können Sie eine englische Tastatur einrichten?**	Kernen zee iner *aing*-lisher tasta*toor ine*-rikhten
Where is the @/ at sign on the keyboard?	**Wo ist das @/ at-Zeichen auf der Tastatur?**	Voh ist das @/ at-tsykhen owf dair tasta*toor*
My email address is …	**Meine E-Mail-Adresse ist …**	Miner email-ad*dress*er ist …

Did you get my email?	**Haben Sie meine E-Mail bekommen?**	Hahben zee miner email bu*kommen*
Email me please	**Können Sie mir eine E-Mail senden?**	Kernen zee meer iner email zenden
Do you have a website?	**Haben Sie eine Webseite?**	Hahben zee iner *veb*-ziter

Faxing and Copying

Can I send a fax?	**Kann ich ein Fax senden?**	Kan ikh ine fax zenden
Can I receive a fax here?	**Kann ich hier ein Fax empfangen?**	Kan ikh heer ine *fax* emp-*fang*-en
How much does it cost per page?	**Wie viel kostet es pro Seite?**	Vee feel kostet es pro *ziter*
Do you have a fax machine?	**Haben Sie ein Faxgerät?**	Hahben zee ine *fax*-gurait
What is your fax number?	**Wie ist Ihre Fax-Nummer?**	Vee ist eerer *fax*-noommer
Please resend your fax	**Senden Sie das Fax bitte noch einmal**	Zenden zee das fax bitter nokh *ine*-mahl
Can I make photocopies here?	**Kann ich hier Fotokopien machen?**	Kan ikh bitter fohtoh-ko*pee*-yen makhen
Can you scan this for me?	**Können Sie das für mich scannen?**	Kernen zee das fuir mikh scannen

Post

Where's the main post office?	**Wo ist die Hauptpost?**	Voh ist dee *howpt*-post
Where's the nearest post office?	**Wo ist die nächste Post?**	Voh ist dee *naikh*ster post
What time does the post office open/close?	**Wann macht die Post auf/zu?**	Van makht dee post owf/tsoo
Where's the post box?	**Wo ist der Briefkasten?**	Voh ist dair *breef*-kasten
Which counter do I go to for stamps/poste restante?	**An welchem Schalter bekomme ich Briefmarken/postlagernd?**	An *velkh*em shalter bukommer ikh *breef*-marken/post-lah*gairnt*
How much is a postcard to Britain?	**Wie teuer ist eine Postkarte nach Großbritannien?**	Vee *toyer* ist iner *post*-karter nahhk grohs-brit*an*-yen
How much is airmail to the USA?	**Wie teuer ist Luftpost in die USA?**	Vee *toyer* ist looft-post in dee oo-ess-ah
How much is it to send a letter surface mail to the USA?	**Wie teuer ist ein Brief per Schiffpost in die USA?**	Vee *toyer* ist ine breef pair *shif*-post in dee oo-ess-ah
It's inland	**Es ist fürs Inland**	Es ist fuirs *in*lant
Give me three ...-euro stamps, please	**Geben Sie mir bitte drei Briefmarken zu ... Euros**	*Gay*ben zee meer bitter dry *breef*-marken tsoo ... *oy*rohs
I'd like to send this letter express	**Ich möchte diesen Brief per Eilpost senden**	Ikh *merkh*ter deezen breef pair *ile*-post zenden

I'd like to register this letter	**Ich möchte diesen Brief einschreiben**	Ikh *merkh*ter deezen breef *ine*-shryben
I want to send a parcel	**Ich möchte ein Päckchen senden**	Ikh *merkh*ter ine *peck*-khen zenden
Are there any letters for me?	**Sind Briefe für mich da?**	Zeend *bree*fer fuir mikh dah
What is your name?	***Wie ist Ihr Name?**	Vee ist eer *nah*mer
Have you any means of identification?	***Können Sie sich identifizieren/ ausweisen?**	Kernen zee zikh *ee*dentifee-*tseer*en/ *ows*-vizen

Telephones, Mobiles and SMS

Do you have a mobile/cell phone?	**Haben Sie ein Handy (Mobiltelefon)?**	Hahben zee ine handy (mo*beel*-tele*fohn*)
What is your mobile/ cell number?	**Wie ist Ihre Handy- (Mobiltelefon-) Nummer?**	Vee ist eerer handy- (mo*beel*-tele*fohn*-) noommer
My mobile/cell phone doesn't work here	**Mein Handy (Mobiltelefon) funktioniert hier nicht**	Mine handy (mo*beel*-tele*fohn*) foonkts-yon*eert* heer nikht
I'd like to get a local SIM card for this phone	**Ich möchte für dieses Telefon eine lokale SIM-Karte kaufen**	Ikh *merkh*ter fuir deezez tele*fohn* iner loh-*kahler* zeem-karter *kow*fen
Can you give me his mobile/cell number?	**Können Sie mir seine Handy- (Mobiltelefon-) Nummer geben?**	Kernen zee meer ziner handy- (mo*beel*-tele*fohn*-) noommer *gay*ben

I'll send you a text/SMS	**Ich sende Ihnen eine Textnachricht/SMS**	Ikh zender eenen iner *text*-nahkh-rikht/ ess-em-ess
Where's the nearest phone box?	**Wo ist die nächste Telefonzelle?**	Voh ist dee *naikh*ster tele*fohn*-tseller
I want to make a phone call	**Ich möchte telefonieren**	Ikh merkhter telefoh*neeren*
May I use your phone?	**Kann ich Ihr Telefon benutzen?**	Kan ikh eer tele*fohn* bu*noot*sen
Do you have a telephone directory for ...?	**Haben Sie ein Telefonbuch für ...?**	Hahben zee ine tele*fohn*-bookh fuir ...
Could you give me the number for international directory enquiries?	**Haben Sie die Nummer für die internationale Auskunft?**	Hahben zee dee noommer fuir dee internats-yon-*ahler* *ows*-koonft
What is the international access code?	**Wie ist die Vorwahl für internationale Gespräche?**	Vee ist dee *for*-vahl fuir internats-yon-*ahler* gu-*shpraikh*er
What is the country/ area code for ...?	**Wie ist die Landes-/ Ortsvorwahl für ...?**	Vee ist dee *landes*-/ orts-*for*-vahl
Can I dial international direct?	**Kann ich für ein Auslandsgespräch direkt wählen?**	Kan ikh fuir ine *ows*-lands-gu-*shpraikh* dee*rekt vay*len
Please get me ...	**Bitte verbinden Sie mich mit ...**	Bitter fair*bin*-den zee mikh mit ...
I'd like to telephone England	**Ich möchte nach England telefonieren**	Ikh *merkh*ter nahkh *aing*-lant telefoh*neeren*

I was cut off; can you reconnect me?	**Ich wurde unterbrochen; können Sie mich wieder verbinden?**	Ikh voorder *oon*ter-*brokh*en; kernen zee mikh *vee*der fair*bin*-den
The line is engaged	***Die Leitung ist besetzt**	Dee *ly*toong ist bu*zetst*
There's no reply	***Es meldet sich niemand**	Es meldet zikh *nee*mant
You have the wrong number	***Sie sind falsch verbunden**	Zee zint falsh fair*boon*den

On the phone

Hello	**Hallo**	Hallo
I want extension . . .	**Apparat . . . bitte**	Appa*raht* . . . bitter
May I speak to . . .	**Kann ich bitte . . . sprechen**	Kan ikh bitter . . . *shprekh*en
Speaking	**Am Apparat**	Am appa*raht*
Who's speaking?	***Wer spricht da?**	Vair shprikht dah
Hold the line, please	***Bleiben Sie bitte am Apparat**	*Bly*ben zee bitter am appa*raht*
He's not here	***Er ist nicht hier**	Air ist nikht heer
When will he be back?	**Wann kommt er zurück?**	Van kommt air tsoo-*ruick*
Will you take a message?	**Würden Sie bitte etwas ausrichten?**	*Vuir*den zee bitter etvas *ows*-rikhten
Tell him that . . . phoned	**Sagen Sie ihm bitte, dass . . . angerufen hat**	*Zah*gun zee eem bitter dass . . . *an*-guroofen hat

I'll ring again later	**Ich rufe später wieder an**	Ikh roofer *shpay*ter *vee*der an
Please ask him to phone me	**Bitten Sie ihn, mich anzurufen**	*Bit*ten zee een mikh *ant*soo-roofen
Please repeat that	**Könnten Sie das bitte wiederholen?**	Kernten zee das bitter *veeder-hohl*en
Please speak slowly	**Könnten Sie bitte langsamer sprechen?**	Kernten zee bitter *lang*zamer *shprekh*en
What's your number?	***Wie ist Ihre Nummer?**	Vee ist eerer noommer
My number is . . .	**Meine Nummer ist . . .**	Miner noommer ist . . .
I can't hear/don't understand you	**Ich kann Sie nicht hören/verstehen**	Ikh kan zee nikht her-ren/fair*shtay*en

DISABLED TRAVELLERS

Key Phrases

Is there a disabled parking area?	**Gibt es Parkplätze für Behinderte?**	Geebt es *park*-pletser fuir bu*hind*erter
Are there facilities for the disabled?	**Gibt es Einrichtungen für Behinderte?**	Geebt es *ine-rikh*toong-en fuir bu*hind*erter
I'd like to reserve a wheelchair please	**Ich möchte bitte einen Rollstuhl reservieren**	Ikh merkhter bitter inen *rol*-shtool rezair*vee*ren
I need a bedroom on the ground floor/ near the lift	**Ich brauche ein Zimmer im Erdgeschoss/neben dem Aufzug**	Ikh *browkh*er ine tsimmer im *aird*-gu-shoss/*nay*ben daim *owf*-tsoog
Do the buses take wheelchairs?	**Können die Busse Rollstühle mitnehmen?**	Kernen dee *boos*ser *rol*-shtui*ler *mit-nay*men

Access

Can we borrow/hire a wheelchair/mobility scooter?	**Können wir einen Rollstuhl/ Elektroroller mieten?**	Kernen veer inen *rol*-shtool/*elektro-rol*-ler *mee*ten

I want to book a wheelchair from the check-in desk to the plane	**Ich möchte bitte einen Rollstuhl vom Check-In-Schalter bis zum Flugzeug reservieren**	Ikh *merkh*ter bitter inen *rol*-shtool fom check-in-shalter bis tsoom *floog*-tsoyg rezair*vee*ren
Is it possible to visit the old town/the site in a wheelchair?	**Kann man die Altstadt/die Stätte mit einem Rollstuhl besichtigen?**	Kan man dee alt shtat/die shtetter mit inem *rol*-shtool bu*zikh*tigun
Is there wheelchair access to the gallery/concert hall/theatre?	**Hat die Galerie/die Konzerthalle/das Theater Rollstuhl-Zugang?**	Hat dee galai*ree*/dee kon*tsairt*-haller/das tay*ah*ter *rol*-shtool *tsoo*gang
Are the paths in the garden/park suitable for wheelchairs?	**Sind die Wege im Garten/Park für Rollstühle geeignet?**	Zint dee *vay*gur im garten/park fuir *rol*-shtui*l*er gu-*ike*-net
Is there a wheelchair ramp?	**Gibt es eine Rollstuhlrampe?**	Geebt es iner *rol*-shtool-*ramp*er
Are there seats reserved for the disabled?	**Sind Plätze für Behinderte reserviert?**	Zint dee pletzer fuir bu-*hind*erter rezair*veert*
Is there a table with place for a wheelchair?	**Gibt es einen Tisch mit Platz für einen Rollstuhl?**	Geebt es inen tish mit plats fuir inen *rol*-shtool
Are mobility scooters allowed inside?	**Darf man Elektroroller mit hinein nehmen?**	Darf man e*lek*tro-rol-er mit hin-*ine nay*men
Where is the lift?	**Wo ist der Aufzug?**	Voh ist dair *owf*-tsoog
Are there disabled toilets?	**Gibt es Behinderten-Toiletten?**	Geebt es bu*hind*erten twah*let*ten

Is there a reduction for the disabled?	**Gibt es eine Ermäßigung für Behinderte?**	Geebt es iner air*messi*goong fuir bu*hind*erter
Are guide dogs allowed?	**Sind Blindenhunde gestattet?**	Zint blin-den-*hoon*der gu-*shtat*tet
I can't walk far	**Ich kann nicht weit gehen**	Ikh kan nikht vite *gay*en
I can't climb stairs	**Ich kann keine Treppen steigen**	Ikh kan kiner *trep*pen *shty*gun
Is the bathroom equipped for the disabled?	**Ist das Badezimmer behindertengerecht?**	Ist das *bahd*er-tsimmer bu-*hind*erten-gu*rekht*

Assistance

Please could you hold the door open?	**Würden Sie bitte die Tür aufhalten?**	*Vuir*den zee bitter dee tuir *owf*-halten
Can you help me?	**Können Sie mir helfen?**	Kernen zee meer helfen
I am deaf; please speak louder	**Ich bin schwerhörig; sprechen Sie bitte lauter**	Ikh bin *shvair*-herikh; *shprekh*en zee bitter *low*ter
Could you help me cross the road, please?	**Könnten Sie mir bitte über die Straße helfen?**	Kernten zee meer bitter *uiber* dee *shtrahs*ser helfen

Travel

Do the buses take wheelchairs?	**Können die Busse Rollstühle mitnehmen?**	Kernen dee *boos*ser *rol-shtui*ler *mit-nay*men
Can I get onto the train/plane with a mobility scooter?	**Kann ich mit dem Elektroroller in den Zug/das Flugzeug einsteigen?**	Kan ikh mit daim *elektro-rol*-ler in den tsoog/das *floog*-tsoyg *ine-shty*gun
Could you order a taxi that will take a wheelchair please?	**Bestellen Sie bitte ein Taxi, das einen Rollstuhl mitnehmen kann**	Bu-*shtel*len zee bitter ine taxi das inen *rol*-shtool *mit-nay*men kan

EATING OUT

Key Phrases

Can you suggest a good/cheap/vegetarian restaurant?	**Können Sie ein gutes/billiges/vegetarisches Restaurant vorschlagen?**	Kernen zee ine gootes/*bil*liges/vegay*tah*rishes restor-*rant* for-*shlah*gun
I've reserved a table; my name is …	**Ich habe einen Tisch reserviert; mein Name ist …**	Ikh hahber inen tish rezair*veert*; mine *nah*mer ist
May I see the menu/the wine list, please?	**Darf ich bitte die Speisekarte/Weinkarte sehen?**	Darf ikh bitter dee *shpy*zer-karter/*vine*-karter *zay*en
Is there a set menu?	**Gibt es ein Tagesmenü?**	Geebt es ine *tah*ges-menui
What is your dish of the day?	**Was ist Ihre Tagesspezialität?**	Vas ist eerer *tah*ges-shpay-tsee-yali*tayt*
It was very good	**Das war sehr gut**	Das var zehr goot
The bill, please	**Die Rechnung bitte/Ich möchte zahlen**	Dee *rekh*noong bitter/Ikh *merkh*ter *tsah*len
Does it include service?	**Ist Bedienung einbegriffen?**	Ist bu*dee*noong *ine*-bugriffen

I'd like to book a table for four at one o'clock	**Ich möchte einen Tisch für vier Personen für ein Uhr bestellen**	Ikh *merkh*ter inen tish fuir feer pair*zohn*en fuir ine oor bu-*shtel*len
We did not make a reservation	**Wir haben keinen Tisch reserviert**	Veer hahben kinen tish rezair*veert*
Do you have a table for three?	**Haben Sie einen Tisch für drei Personen?**	Hahben zee inen tish fuir dry pair*zohn*en
We'd like a table where there is room for a wheelchair	**Wir möchten einen Tisch, wo es Platz für einen Rollstuhl gibt**	Veer *merkh*ten inen tish voh es plats fuir inen *rol*-shtool geebt
Do you have a high chair?	**Haben Sie einen Hochstuhl?**	Hahben zee inen hohkh-shtool
Is there a table	**Haben Sie einen Tisch**	Hahben zee inen tish
by the window?	**beim Fenster?**	bime *fen*ster
in the corner?	**in der Ecke?**	in dair ecker
on the terrace?	**auf der Terrasse?**	owf dair tair*rass*er
This way, please	***Hier entlang bitte**	Heer ent*lang* bitter
We shall have a table free in half an hour	***In einer halben Stunde haben wir einen Tisch frei**	In iner *hal*ben *shtoon*der hahben veer inen tish fry
We don't serve lunch until half past twelve	***Das Mittagessen wird erst um halb eins serviert**	Das *mit*-tahg-essen veert airst oom halp ines zair*veert*

We don't serve dinner until eight o'clock	*Das Abendessen wird erst um acht Uhr serviert	Das *ahb*ent-essen veert airst oom akht oor zair*veert*
Sorry, the kitchen is closed	*Die Küche ist leider geschlossen	Dee *kuik*her ist *lyd*er gu-*shloss*en
We stop serving at ten o'clock	*Wir servieren nur bis zehn Uhr	Veer zair*veer*en noor bis tsayn oor
Where are the toilets?	Wo sind die Toiletten?	Voh zind dee twah*letter*
The toilets are downstairs	*Die Toiletten sind unten	Dee twah*lett*en zint oonten
We are in a hurry	Wir haben es eilig	Veer hahben es *eye*likh
Do you serve snacks?	Servieren Sie einen Imbiss?	Zair*veer*en zee inen *imbiss*
I am a vegetarian	Ich bin Vegetarier	Ikh bin vegay*tah*ree-yer
I am allergic to wheat/nuts	Ich habe eine Weizen-/ Nussallergie	Ikh hahber iner *vytsen*-/ *nooss*-allair*ghee*
I am allergic to dairy products	Ich habe eine Allergie gegen Milchprodukte	Ikh hahber iner allair*ghee gay*gun milkh-pro*dook*ter

Ordering

| Cover charge | *Gedeck | Gu*deck* |
| Service and VAT included | *(Unsere Preise sind) Endpreise | (Oonzerer *pry*zer zint) *ent-pry*zer |

Service and VAT not included	*Bedienung und Mehrwertsteuer nicht einbegriffen	Bu*dee*noong oont *mair*-vairt-*shtoy*er nikht *ine*-bugriffen
Service charge	*Bedienungsgeld	Bu*dee*noongs-gelt
Waiter/Waitress (*addressing*)	Ober/Frau Ober	Ohber/Frow ohber
May I see the menu/ the wine list, please?	Darf ich bitte die Speisekarte/ Weinkarte sehen?	Darf ikh bitter dee *shpy*zer-karter/ *vine*-karter *zay*en
Is there a set menu?	Gibt es ein Tagesmenü?	Geebt es ine *tah*ges-menui
I'll have the twenty-five-euro menu/ today's special menu, please	Ich hätte gern das fünfundzwanzig Euro-Menü/das Tagesmenü	Ikh hetter gairn das fuinf-oont-*tsvan*-tsikh *oyroh*-menui/das *tah*ges-menui
As the first course/ main course/ side dish	Als erster Gang/ Hauptgang/ Beilage	Als airster gang/ *howpt*-gang/ *by-lah*gur
I'd like something light	Ich möchte eine leichte Kost	Ikh *merkh*ter iner *lykh*ter kost
Do you have a children's menu?	Haben Sie ein Kindermenü?	Hahben zee ine kin-der-menui
What is your dish of the day?	Was ist Ihre Tagesspezialität?	Vas ist eerer *tah*ges-shpay-tsee-yali*tayt*
What do you recommend?	Was empfehlen Sie?	Vas emp*fay*len zee
Can you tell me what this is?	Können Sie mir sagen, was dies ist?	Kernen zee meer *zah*gun vas deez ist

What is the speciality of the restaurant/of the region?	Was ist die Spezialität dieses Restaurants/dieser Gegend?	Vas ist dee shpay-tsee-yali*tayt* deezez restor-*rants*/deezair *gay*gunt
Do you have any vegetarian dishes?	Haben Sie vegetarische Gerichte?	Hahben zee vegay*tah*-risher gu*rikh*ter
Would you like to try ...?	*Möchten Sie ... probieren?	*Merkh*ten zee ... proh*bee*ren
There's no more ...	*... sind (ist) nicht mehr da	... zint (ist) nikht mair dah
I'd like ...	Ich möchte ...	Ikh *merkh*te ...
May I have peas instead of beans?	Darf ich Erbsen statt Bohnen haben?	Darf ikh *airp*zen shtat *boh*nen hahben
Is it hot or cold?	Ist es warm oder kalt?	Ist es varm ohder kalt
Without sauce/oil, please	Ohne Sauce/Öl bitte	*Ohner soh*ser/erl bitter
Some more bread, please	Noch etwas Brot bitte	Nokh etvas broht bitter
A little more ...	Etwas mehr ...	Etvas mair ...
Salt and pepper/ napkins, please	Salz und Pfeffer/ Servietten bitte	Salts oont pfeffer/ zairvee-*yet*ten bitter
How would you like it cooked?	Wie soll es gekocht werden?	Vee zoll es gu*kokht* verden
Rare/medium/well done	Rot/rosa/ durchgebraten	Roht/roza/ doorkh-gu*brah*ten

Would you like a dessert?	**Möchten Sie einen Nachtisch/Nachspeise?**	*Merkh*ten zee inen *nahkh*-tish/*nahkh-shpy*zer
Something to drink?	**Etwas zu trinken?**	*Et*vas tsoo *trinken*
The wine list, please	**Die Weinkarte bitte**	Dee *vine*-karter bitter
A (half) bottle of the local wine please	**Eine (halbe) Flasche vom hiesigen Wein**	Iner (halber) *flash*er fom *heezi*gun vine

Paying

The bill, please	**Die Rechnung bitte/ Ich möchte zahlen**	Dee *rekh*noong bitter/Ikh *merkh*ter *tsah*len
Does it include service?	**Ist Bedienung einbegriffen?**	Ist bu*dee*noong *ine*-bugriffen
Please check the bill; I don't think it's correct	**Bitte prüfen Sie die Rechnung; ich glaube, sie stimmt nicht**	Bitter *prui*fen zee dee *rekh*noong; ikh *glow*ber zee shtimmt nikht
What is this amount for?	**Wofür ist dieser Betrag?**	Voh-*fuir* ist deezer bu*trahg*
I didn't have soup	**Ich habe keine Suppe gehabt**	Ikh hahber kiner *zoop*per guhapt
I had chicken not beef	**Ich hatte Huhn, kein Rindfleisch**	Ikh hatter hoohn, kine *rint*-flysh
May we have separate bills?	**Können wir bitte getrennte Rechnungen haben?**	Kernen veer bitter gu*trenn*ter *rekh*noong-en hahben
Do you take credit cards?	**Nehmen Sie Kreditkarten?**	*Nay*men zee kray*deet*-karten
Keep the change	**Das ist gut so**	Das ist goot zoh

Compliments

It was very good	**Das war sehr gut**	Das var zehr goot
We enjoyed it, thank you	**Es hat uns sehr gut geschmeckt, danke**	Es hat oons zair goot gu-*shmeckt* danker
The food was delicious	**Das Essen war köstlich**	Das essen var *kerst*likh
Especially ...	**Besonders ...**	Bu*zonders* ...

Complaints

We've been waiting a long time for our drinks	**Wir warten schon lange auf unsere Getränke**	Veer *varten* shohn lang-er owf oonserer gu*trenker*
Why is the food taking so long?	**Warum müssen wir so lange auf unser Essen warten?**	*Vah*room *muissen* veer zoh lang-er owf oonzer essen *varten*
This isn't what I ordered; I'd like ...	**Das habe ich nicht bestellt; ich möchte ...**	Das hahber ikh nikht bu-*shtellt*; ikh *merkh*ter ...
This is bad	**Dies ist schlecht**	Deez ist shlekht
This is uncooked/overcooked	**Dies ist nicht gar/zu lange gekocht**	Deez ist nikht gahr/tsoo lang-er gu*kokht*
This is stale	**Dies ist alt/schal**	Deez ist alt/shahl
This is too cold/salty	**Dies ist zu kalt/salzig**	Deez ist tsoo kalt/*zal*-tsikh

| This plate/knife/spoon/glass is not clean | **Dieser Teller/Dieses Messer/Dieser Löffel/Dieses Glas ist nicht sauber** | Deezer *teller*/Deezez *messer*/Deezer *lerfel*/Deezez glahs ist nikht *zowber* |
| I'm sorry; I will bring you another | ***Tut mir leid; ich bringe ein anderes** | Toot meer lite; ikh bring-er ine *anderes* |

Breakfast and Tea[1]

Café	**das Café, Kaffeehaus**	Café, Kaf*fay*-hows
Tearoom	**die Teestube**	*Tay*-shtoober
Breakfast	**das Frühstück**	*Frui*-shtuick
A white coffee, please	**Eine Tasse Milchkaffee bitte**	Iner tasser *milkh*-kaf*fay* bitter
Black coffee (with cream)	**Schwarzen Kaffee (mit Sahne)**	*Shvar*tsen kaf*fay* (mit *zah*ner)
I'd like a decaffeinated coffee/hot chocolate	**Ich hätte gern einen entkoffeinierten Kaffee/eine heiße Schokolade**	Ikh hetter gairn inen ent-koffer-ee*nee*erten kaf*fay*/iner hicer shohko*lah*der
I would like tea with milk/lemon	**Ich möchte Tee mit Milch/Zitrone**	Ikh *merkh*ter tay mit milkh/tsee*troh*ner
Do you have sweeteners?	**Haben Sie Süßstoff?**	Hahben zee *zuis*-shtof
May we have some sugar, please?	**Können wir bitte etwas Zucker haben?**	*Kern*en veer bitter etvas *tsoo*ker hahben

1. Don't forget to go into a café or *Konditorei*, particularly in Austria. Try one of the wide selection of *Torten*, a pastry speciality, with names like *Sachertorte*, *Kaffeecremetorte*, *Linzertorte*, *Imperialtorte*.

A roll and butter, please	Ein Brötchen und Butter bitte	Ine *brert*-khen oont *boot*ter bitter
Toast	Toast	Tohst
More butter, please	Etwas mehr Butter bitte	Etvas mair *boot*ter bitter
Have you some marmalade/jam/honey?	Haben Sie Orangenmarmelade/Marmelade/Honig?	Hahben zee *oran*jen-marmer*lahder*/marmer*lahder*/*hoh*nikh
I would like a soft-/hard-boiled egg	Ich möchte ein weich/hart gekochtes Ei	Ikh *merkh*ter ine vykh/hart gu*kokh*tes eye
Fried eggs	Gebratene Eier	Gu*brah*tener eyer
Scrambled eggs	Rühreier	*Ruir*-eyer
What fruit juices do you have?	Was für Obstsäfte haben Sie?	Vas fuir *ohpst*-zefter hahben zee
Orange/Tomato/Blackcurrant juice	der Apfelsinensaft (Orangensaft)/Tomatensaft/Johannisbeersaft	Apfel*zeenen*-zaft (*oran*jenzaft)/toh*mahten*-zaft/yoh-*hannis*bair-zaft
Help yourselves at the buffet	*Bedienen Sie sich bitte am Büffet	Bu*deenen* zee zikh am *bui*-fay
fresh fruit	frisches Obst	frishes ohpst
ham	der Schinken	*shinken*
cheese	der Käse	*kayzer*
yoghurt	der Joghurt	yoh-*goort*

pastry[1]	**das Gebäck**	gu*beck*
tart/layer cake	**die Torte**	torter
cake	**der Kuchen**	kookhen
iced coffee	**der Eiskaffee**	ice-kaf*fay*
iced tea	**der Eistee**	ice-tay
China tea	**chinesischer Tee**	khee-*nay*-zisher-tay
Indian tea	**indischer Tee**	*in*disher tay
green tea	**grüner Tee**	*gru*iner tay
tea with nothing added	**tee ohne alles**	tee ohner alles
camomile tea	**der Kamillentee**	kah*meel*len-tay
herbal tea	**der Kräutertee**	*kroy*ter-tay
mint tea	**der Pfefferminztee**	*pfef*fer-mints-tay

Drinks[2]

Bar	**die Bar, Schenke, Theke, der Ausschank**	Bar, shenker, t*ay*ker, *ows*-shank
What will you have to drink?	**Was möchten Sie trinken?**	Vas *merkh*ten zee trinken
A (half) bottle of the local wine, please	**Eine (halbe) Flasche vom hiesigen Wein bitte**	Iner (halber) *flash*er fom *hee*zigun vine bitter
I'd like to see the wine list	**Ich möchte die Weinkarte sehen**	Ikh *merkh*ter dee *vine*-karter *zay*en

1. For names of cakes and pastries, see pp. 121–2.
2. For the names of beverages, see pp. 125–7.

Do you serve wine by the glass?[1]	**Haben Sie offenen Wein?**	Hahben zee *off*enen vine
Carafe/Glass	**die Karaffe/das Glas**	Ka*raff*er/Glahs
Bottle	**die Flasche**	*Flasher*
Two glasses of beer, please	**Zwei Gläser Bier bitte**	Tsvy *glay*zer beer bitter
A large/small beer	**Ein großes/kleines Bier**	Ine grohses/kline-es beer
Do you have draught beer?	**Haben Sie Bier vom Fass?**	Hahben zee beer fom fass
Light/Dark beer	**Helles/Dunkles Bier**	Helles/Doonkles beer
Two more beers	**Noch zwei Bier**	Nokh tsvy beer
Neat/On the rocks	**Pur/Mit Eis**	Poor/Mit ice
With (soda) water	**Mit (Soda-) Wasser**	Mit (zoh*dah*-) *vass*er
Mineral water (with/ without gas)	**das Mineralwasser (mit/ohne Kohlensäure)**	Minair*ahl*-*vass*er (mit/*ohner kohl* en-*zoyr*er)
Tap water	**das Leitungswasser**	*Ly*toongs-*vass*er
Ice cubes	**die Eiswürfel**	Ice-*vuir*fel
Cheers!	**Prost!**	Prohst
I'd like a soft drink with ice	**Ich hätte gern ein alkoholfreies Getränk mit Eis**	Ikh hetter gairn ine *al*kohol-fry-es gu*trenk* mit ice
Apple juice	**der Apfelsaft**	*Ap*fel-zaft
Blackcurrant juice	**der Johannisbeersaft**	Yoh-*hann*isbair-zaft
Fruit juice	**der Fruchtsaft**	*Frookht*-zaft

1. Usually open wine is sold by the *Viertel*, a glass holding a quarter litre (250ml).

What smoothies do you have?	**Welche Smoothies haben Sie?**	*Velkher* smoothies hahben zee
I'd like a glass of water, please	**Ich möchte bitte ein Glas Wasser**	Ikh *merkh*te bitter ine glahs *vas*ser
The same again, please	**Noch einmal dasselbe bitte**	Nokh *ine*-mahl das-*zel*ber bitter
Three black coffees and one with cream	**Dreimal schwarzen Kaffee und einen mit Sahne**	*Dry*-mahl *shvart*sen kaf*fay* oont inen mit *zah*ner
A decaffeinated coffee	**Einen entkoffeinierten Kaffee**	Inen ent-koffer-ee*neer*ten kaf*fay*
Tea with milk/lemon	**Tee mit Milch/Zitrone**	Tay mit milkh/tsee*troh*ner

Quick Meals

What is there to eat?	**Was kann man hier essen?**	Vas kan man heer *ess*en
We are in a hurry; what can you suggest that won't take long?	**Wir sind in Eile; was empfehlen Sie, was schnell geht?**	Weer zint in *eye*-ler; vas emp*fay*len zee vas shnell gait
I only want a snack	**Ich möchte nur einen Imbiss**	Ikh *merkh*ter noor inen *im*biss
Is it to eat here or to take away?	***Ist das zum hier essen oder zum Mitnehmen?**	Ist das tsoom heer essen ohder tsoom *mit-nay*men
May I have a sandwich, please?	**Kann ich bitte ein belegtes Brot haben?**	Kan ikh bitter ine bu*laig*tes broht hahben

What sandwiches do you have?	**Welche Sandwiches haben Sie?**	*Velkher* sandwiches hahben zee
cheese	**Käse**	*Kay*zer
cooked ham	**Gekochter Schinken**	Gu*kokh*ter *shin*ken
cured ham	**Marinierter Schinken**	Mari*nee*rter *shin*ken
salami	**Salami**	Za*lah*mee
tuna	**Thunfisch**	Toon-*fish*
toasted ham and cheese	**Gegrillter Schinken und Käse**	Gu*grill*ter *shin*ken oont *kay*zer
I'd like a . . . sandwich with/without butter	**Ich möchte einen . . . Sandwich mit/ohne Butter**	Ikh *merkh*ter inen sandwich mit/ohner *boot*ter
I'm sorry, we've run out	***Tut mir leid, wir haben keine mehr**	Toot meer *lite*, veer hahben kiner mair
What are those things over there?	**Was ist das dort?**	Vas ist das dort
What are they made of?	**Woraus ist es gemacht?**	Voh-*rows* ist es gu*makht*
What is in them?	**Was ist da drin?**	Vas ist dah drin
I'll have one of these, please	**Eins davon bitte**	Ines dah-*fon* bitter
I'd like a pancake, please	**Ich hätte gern einen Pfannkuchen bitte**	Ikh hetter gairn inen pfann-*kookh*en bitter
A plain omelette	**Ein Omelett natur**	Ine ome*lett* na*toor*

A cheese omelette	**Ein Käseomelett**	Ine *kayzer*-omelett
chips	**die Pommes frites**	pomm fritt
biscuits	**die Kekse**	*kayk*-zer
bread	**das Brot**	broht
butter	**die Butter**	*boot*ter
cheese	**der Käse**	*kayzer*
chocolate bar	**die Tafel Schokolade**	*tah*fel shohko*lah*der
egg(s)	**das Ei (die Eier)**	eye (eyer)
ham	**der Schinken**	*shinken*
ice cream (*flavours*: p. 121)	**das Eis**	ice
meatballs/croquettes	**die Frikadellen**	freekah*dellen*
meat/fruit pie	**die Fleischpastete/ Obstkuchen**	*flysh*-past*ai*ter/ *ohbst*-kookhen
pancakes	**die Pfannkuchen, Palatschinken**	pfann-*kookh*en, pa*laht*-shinken
roll	**das Brötchen**	*brert*khen
salad	**der Salat**	za*laht*
sausage (roll)	**die Wurst (-pastete)**	voorst (-past*ai*ter)
snack	**der Imbiss**	*imbiss*
snack bar	**der Schnellimbiss**	*shnell-im*biss
soup	**die Suppe**	*zoop*er
tomato	**die Tomate**	toh*mah*ter
waffles	**die Waffel**	vaffel

Restaurant Vocabulary

bill	**die Rechnung**	*rekh*noong
bowl	**die Schüssel**	*shui*ssel
bread	**das Brot**	broht
butter	**die Butter**	*boo*tter
course (dish)	**der Gang**	gang
cream	**die Sahne**	*zah*ner
cup	**die Tasse**	tasser
dessert	**der Nachtisch, die Nachspeise**	*nahkh*-tish, *nahkh*-shpyzer
dressing	**die Salatsoße**	za*laht*-zohser
dish of the day	**das Tagesgericht**	*tah*ges-gurikht
first course/starter	**der erste Gang/die Vorspeise**	airster gang/*for*-shpyzer
fork	**die Gabel**	*gah*bul
glass	**das Glas**	glahs
head waiter	**der Oberkellner**	*ohber-kell*ner
hungry (to be)	**Hunger haben/ hungrig sein**	hoong-er hahben/ hoongrikh zine
knife	**das Messer**	messer
light (easily digested) meals	**die Schonkost**	shohn-kost
menu	**die Speisekarte**	*shpy*zer-karter

mustard	**der Senf**	zenf
napkin	**die Serviette**	zairvee-*yet*ter
oil	**das Öl**	erl
pepper	**der Pfeffer**	pfeffer
pickles	**die Pickles**	pickles
plate	**der Teller**	*tell*er
salt	**das Salz**	zalts
sauce	**die Sauce**	*zoh*ser
saucer	**die Untertasse**	*oon*ter-*tas*ser
service	**die Bedienung**	bu*dee*noong
set menu	**das Menü**	me*nui*
spoon	**der Löffel**	*ler*fel
straw	**der Strohhalm**	*shtroh*-halm
sugar	**der Zucker**	*tsoo*ker
sweetener	**der Süßstoff**	*suis*-shtof
table	**der Tisch**	tish
tablecloth	**das Tischtuch**	*tish*-tookh
thirsty (to be)	**Durst haben/ durstig sein**	doorst hahben/ *doors*tikh zine
tip	**das Trinkgeld**	*trink*-gelt
toilets	**die Toiletten**	twah*let*ten
toothpick	**der Zahnstocher**	*tsahn*-shtokher
tomato sauce	**die Tomatensoße**	to*mahten*-*zoh*ser

vegetarian	**der Vegetarier**	vegay*tah*ree-yer
vinegar	**der Essig**	*essikh*
waiter	**der Kellner**	*kellner*
waitress	**die Kellnerin**	*kellnerin*
water	**das Wasser**	*vasser*

THE MENU

Vorspeisen / Starters

Artischocken / artichokes

Austern / oysters

Gänseleberpastete / goose liver paté

geräucherter Lachs / smoked salmon

Königinpastete / pastry filled with meat ragoût

Matjesfilet ('Hausfrauenart') / herring fillet (with apple and sour cream)

(geeiste) Melone / (iced) melon

Ölsardinen (mit Brot) / tinned sardines (with bread)

Räucheraal / smoked eel

Rollmops / rollmops

russische Eier / hard-boiled eggs with caviare, capers and mayonnaise

(Westfälischer) Schinken / cured ham

Schinkenwurst / ham sausage

(Weinberg-) Schnecken / snails

Spargelspitzen / asparagus tips

Stangenspargel mit Kräutersauce / asparagus with herb sauce

Strammer Max / ryebread, raw ham and fried egg

Wurstplatte / assorted sliced sausage

Suppen / Soups

Aalsuppe / eel soup

Bohnensuppe / bean soup

Erbsensuppe / pea soup

Gaisburger Marsch / vegetable soup with dumplings

Gemüsesuppe / vegetable soup

Gulaschsuppe / beef and paprika soup

Hühnerbrühe / chicken broth

Kartoffelsuppe / potato soup

Kirschkaltschale / cold cherry soup

Kraftbrühe mit Ei/Magen / bouillon with egg/tripe

Leberknödelsuppe / clear soup with liver dumplings

Linsensuppe / lentil soup

Mandelsuppe / almond and cream soup

Nudelsuppe / noodle soup

Ochsenschwanzsuppe / oxtail soup

Tomatensuppe / tomato soup

Zwiebelsuppe / onion soup

Fisch / Fish

Aal / eel

Aal grün mit Dillsauce / fresh eel with dill sauce

Austern / oysters

Barsch / perch

Forelle / trout

Garnele / shrimp

Hecht / pike

Heilbutt / halibut

Hering / herring

Hummer / lobster

Kabeljau / cod

Karpfen / carp

Krabben / small shrimps

Krebs / crab

Lachs, Salm / salmon

Makrele / mackerel

Muscheln / mussels

Rotbarsch / redfish

Sardellen / anchovies

Schellfisch / haddock

Scholle / plaice

Seebarsch / bass

Seezunge / sole

Steinbutt / turbot

Thunfisch / tuna

Zander / pike-perch

Fleisch / Meat

Lamm/Hammel: / lamb/mutton:

   Hammelbraten/Lammbraten / roast mutton/lamb

   Hammelragout / mutton stew

   Lammskeule / roast leg of lamb

Kalb: / veal:

   Kalbsbrust / breast of veal

   Kalbshaxe / roast knuckle of veal

   Kalbskoteletts / veal cutlets, chops

   Kalbsvögel / veal roulade

(Wiener) Schnitzel / (fried) escalope of veal

Rind: / beef:

   deutsches Beefsteak / minced beef, hamburger

   gekochte Rinderbrust / boiled brisket of beef

   Gulasch / goulash

   Rinderbraten / roast beef

   Rinderfilet / fillet of beef

   Rindsrouladen / stuffed beef

   Rinderschmorbraten / braised beef

   Sauerbraten / braised pickled beef

   Stroganoff / beef fillet with mushrooms and cream

Schweinefleisch: / pork:

   Eisbein / pickled pork knuckle

   (Kasseler) Rippchen / (smoked) pork chop

   Schweinebraten / roast pork

   Schweinefilet / loin of pork

   Spanferkel / suckling pig

Würste und Innereien / Sausages and Offal

Aufschnitt / cold cuts

Blutwurst / black pudding

Bockwurst / spiced, smoked sausage

Bratwurst / frying sausage

Knackwurst / frankfurter

Nürnberger Würstchen / small spiced sausages

Pinkel / smoked sausage with onions

Weißwurst / veal sausage

Fleischkloß / meatball

Frikadelle / meatball, croquette

Hirn / brains

Kalbsbries: / sweetbreads

   (*north German*: **Kalbsmilcher**)

Leber / liver

Nieren / kidneys

Ochsenschwanz / oxtail

Schinken / ham (smoked raw)

   gekochter Schinken / cooked ham

Schlachtplatte / mixed cold meats

Speck / bacon

Zunge / tongue

Wild und Geflügel / Game and Poultry

Ente / duck

Fasan / pheasant

Gans / goose

Hähnchen/Huhn am Spieß / roast chicken

Hase / hare

Hasenpfeffer / jugged hare

Hirsch / venison

Huhn / chicken

Kaninchen / rabbit

Rebhuhn / partridge

Reh (braten) / (roast) venison

Rehrücken / saddle of venison

Taube / pigeon

Truthahn/Pute / turkey

Gemüse und Salate /
Vegetables and Salads

Blumenkohl / cauliflower

Bohnen: / beans:

   grüne Bohnen / green beans

   Stangenbohnen / runner beans

   weiße Bohnen / haricot beans

Brunnenkresse / watercress

Champignons / mushrooms

Edelpilze / (best varieties of wild) mushrooms

Erbsen / peas

Grüner Salat / lettuce

Grünkohl / kale

Gurke: / cucumber:

   Gewürzgurken / pickled cucumbers

Himmel und Erde / potato and apple

Kartoffeln: / potatoes:

   Bratkartoffeln / fried potatoes

   Kartoffelklöße / potato dumplings

   Kartoffelpüree / mashed potatoes

   Kartoffelsalat / potato salad

   Pommes frites / chips

   Rösti / hashed brown potatoes

   Salzkartoffeln / boiled potatoes

Kastanien / chestnuts

Knoblauch / garlic

(Weiß-, Rot-) Kohl / (white, red) cabbage

Kopfsalat / round lettuce

Kürbis / pumpkin, marrow

Lauch, Porree / leeks

Meerrettich / horse radish

Möhren, Karotten / carrots

Paprika (-schoten) / peppers

Pfifferlinge / chanterelles

Pilze / mushrooms

Reis / rice

Rettich / radish

Rosenkohl / Brussels sprouts

Rote Beete / beetroot

Rüben / swedes

Salat / lettuce, salad

Sauerkraut / pickled cabbage

Schwarzwurzeln / black salsify

Sellerie / celery

Spargel / asparagus

Spinat / spinach

Steinpilze / porcini/ceps

Tomaten / tomatoes

Weiße Rübe / turnip

Wirsingkohl / savoy cabbage

Zwiebeln / onions

Knödel und Nudeln /
Dumplings and Noodles

Leberknödel / liver dumplings

Kartoffelknödel / potato dumplings

Klöße / dumplings

Kräuterklöße / herb dumplings

Maultasche / Swabian ravioli

Nockerl / dumpling

Nudeln / noodles

Spätzle / short German noodles

Eier / Eggs

gekochtes Ei (weich, hart) / boiled egg (soft, hard)

Omelett: / omelette:

    mit Kräutern / with herbs

    mit Pilzen / with mushrooms

Bauernomelett / omelette with diced bacon and onion

Rührei / scrambled eggs

russische Eier / hard-boiled eggs with caviar, capers and mayonnaise

Spiegeleier / fried eggs

verlorene Eier / poached eggs

Käse / Cheese

Allgäuer, Bengkäse / Bavarián mountain cheeses

Käseteller / cheese board

Kümmelkäse / cheese with caraway seed

Rahmkäse, Sahnekäse / cream cheese

Räucherkäse / smoked cheese

Schmelzkäse / cheese spread

Thüringer Käse, Harzkäse / sausage-shaped cheeses made from curd

Nachspeisen und Kuchen /
Desserts and Cakes

Apfelkuchen / apple cake

Apfelstrudel / flaky pastry stuffed with apple, nuts and spices

Auflauf / soufflé

Eis (Speiseeis): / ice cream:

   Erdbeer- / strawberry

   gemischtes / mixed

   Mokka- / coffee

   Nuss- / nut

   Schokoladen- / chocolate

   Vanille- / vanilla

Eisbecher / ice cream with fresh fruit

frisches Obst / fresh fruit

Fruchttörtchen / small fruit tart

Kaiserschmarren / shredded pancake with raisins and syrup

Käsetorte / cheesecake

Keks / biscuit

Krapfen / doughnuts

Kuchen / cake

Lebkuchen / spiced cake or biscuits, gingerbread

Linzer Torte / cake spread with jam, topped with whipped cream

Makronen / macaroons

Mohrenkopf / pastry filled with cream, topped with chocolate

Mokka-Torte / coffee cake

Nusstorte / nut cake

Obstkompott / stewed fruit

Obstkuchen / fruit tart

Obstsalat / fruit salad

Palatschinken / pancakes filled with soft cheese and nuts or with jam

Pfannkuchen / pancakes, doughnuts, fritters

Pflaumenkuchen / plum cake

rote Grütze / raspberries or redcurrants cooked with semolina, served with cream

Sacher Torte / chocolate cake spread with jam and chocolate icing

Sandtorte / Madeira cake

Schlagsahne / whipped cream

Stollen / Christmas bread with dried fruit and marzipan

Streuselkuchen / cake made with fresh fruit and topped with crumble

Torte / tart, flat cake

Obst und Nüsse /
Fruit and Nuts

Ananas / pineapple

Apfel / apple

Apfelsine / orange

Aprikose / apricot

Banane / banana

Birne / pear

Brombeere / blackberry

Erdbeere / strawberry

Feige / fig

Haselnuss / hazelnut

Himbeere / raspberry

Johannisbeere (rot) / redcurrant

Johannisbeere (schwarz) / blackcurrant

Kirsche / cherry

Mandarine / mandarin, tangerine

Mandel / almond

Melone / melon

Pampelmuse / grapefruit

Pfirsich / peach

Pflaume / plum

Reineclaude / greengage

Stachelbeere / gooseberry

(Wein-) Traube / grape

Walnuss / walnut

Wassermelone / water melon

Zitrone / lemon

Zwetsche / plum

Some Cooking Methods

Fleisch: / meat:

    durchgebraten / well done

    rosa / medium

    rot / rare

gebacken / baked

gebraten / roast

(in der Pfanne) gebraten / fried

gedämpft / steamed, stewed

gefüllt / stuffed

gegrillt / grilled

gekocht / boiled

geräuchert / smoked

gerieben / grated

geschmort / braised, stewed

geschwenkt / sautéed

mariniert / marinated

...püree / creamed ...

roh / raw

Sauces and Garnishes

Butter- / Buttered ...

grüne Sauce / mayonnaise (or vinaigrette with chopped egg) with mixed green herbs

holländisch / with mayonnaise

Holstein / topped with fried egg, garnished with anchovy

nach Jägerart / sautéed with mushrooms, in wine sauce

Kräuter (-butter) / herb (butter)

Petersilien- / parsleyed ...

Sahne-/Rahm- / ... and cream

Senf- / mustard ...

Sülz- / ... in aspic

Getränke / Drinks

Alkohol / alcohol

Apfelwein / cider

Bier (hell/dunkel): / beer (light/dark):

   Berliner Weiße / cloudy wheat beer served with flavoured syrups

   Bockbier / dark, strong beer

   Hefeweizen / cloudy wheat beer

   Malzbier / malt beer

   Märzen / strong beer

   Weizenbier / wheat beer

Bowle / fruit cup

Cognac / brandy

(Himbeer-) Geist / (raspberry) eau de vie

Glühwein / mulled wine

Kaffee: / coffee:

   Kaffee Hag (koffeinfrei) / dacaffeinated

   Milchkaffee / white

   mit Sahne / with cream

   schwarzer / black

Kirschwasser / kirsch

Likör / liqueur

Limonade / lemonade

Milch / milk

Mineralwasser / mineral water

Obstler / fruit eau de vie

Orangeade / orangeade

Pilsener / lager

Portwein / port

Rum / rum

(Frucht-/Obst-) Saft / (fruit) juice

  Ananas- / pineapple

  Apfel- / apple

  Apfelsinen-/Orangen- / orange

  Johannisbeer- / blackcurrant

  Tomaten- / tomato

Sekt / sparkling wine

Schnaps / grain spirit

Sodawasser / soda water

Tee / tea

Wasser / water

Wein: / wine:

  offen / open, by the glass

  rot / red

  süß / sweet

  trocken / dry

  weiß / white

Weinbrand / brandy

Wermut / vermouth

Zwetschenwasser / plum eau de vie

EMERGENCIES[1]

Key Phrases		
Emergency numbers:	**Notrufnummern:**	*Noht*-roof-noommern:
110 police	**die Polizei**	Pohli*tsy*
112 ambulance (service)	**der Rettungsdienst**	*Ret*toongs-deenst
112 fire brigade	**die Feuerwehr**	*Foyer*-vair
Help!	**Hilfe!**	Hilfer
Danger!	**Gefahr!**	*Gu*fahr
Where's the police station?	**Wo ist die Polizeiwache?**	Voh ist dee pohli*tsy*-vakher
Call a doctor	**Rufen Sie einen Arzt**	Roofen zee inen artst
Call an ambulance	**Rufen Sie einen Krankenwagen**	Roofen zee inen *kranken*-*vahg*un
Where is the nearest A&E hospital?	**Wo ist das nächste Krankenhaus mit Notaufnahme?**	Voh ist das *naikh*ster *kranken*-hows mit *noht*-owf-*nah*mer
Fire brigade	**die Feuerwehr**	*Foyer*-vair
My son/daughter is lost	**Mein Sohn/Meine Tochter wird vermisst**	Mine zohn/Miner *tokh*ter veert fair*mist*

1. For car breakdown, see By Car, p. 34. For problems with a house rental, see Apartments and Villas, p. 71.

Call the police	**Rufen Sie die Polizei**	Roofen zee dee pohli*tsy*
Where is the British consulate?	**Wo ist das britische Konsulat?**	Voh ist das *bri*tisher konzoo*laht*
Please let the consulate know	**Bitte benachrichtigen Sie das Konsulat**	Bitter bu*nahkh-rikh*tigun zee das konzoo*laht*
I want to speak to someone from the embassy	**Ich möchte mit jemand von der Botschaft sprechen**	Ikh *merkh*ter mit *yay*mant von dair *boht*-shaft *shprekh*en
I want a lawyer who speaks English	**Ich möchte einen Anwalt, der Englisch spricht**	Ikh *merkh*ter inen anvalt dair *aing*-lish shprikht
It's urgent	**Es ist dringend**	Es ist *dring*-ent
Can you help me?	**Können Sie mir helfen?**	Kernen zee meer helfen

Accidents[1]

Call a doctor	**Rufen Sie einen Arzt**	Roofen zee inen artst
Call an ambulance	**Rufen Sie einen Krankenwagen**	Roofen zee inen *kran*ken-*vahg*un
Where is the nearest A&E hospital?	**Wo ist das nächste Krankenhaus mit Notaufnahme?**	Voh ist das *naikh*ster *kran*ken-hows mit *noht*-owf-*nahm*er
Paramedics	**die Rettungssanitäter**	*Ret*toongs-zani*tay*ter
Fire brigade	**die Feuerwehr**	*Foyer*-vair

1. See also Doctor (p. 141).

Lifeguard	**der Rettungsschwimmer**	*Ret*toongs-*shvim*mer
There has been an accident	**Es gab einen Unfall**	Es gahb inen *oon*fal
Is anyone hurt?	**Ist jemand verletzt?**	Ist *yay*mant fair*letst*
Do you need help?	**Brauchen Sie Hilfe?**	*Browkh*en zee hilfer
Emergency exit	**der Notausgang**	*Noht-ows*-gang
Fire extinguisher	**der Feuerlöscher**	*Foyer-lersh*er
He's badly hurt	**Er ist schwer verletzt**	Er ist shvair fair*letst*
He has fainted	**Er ist ohnmächtig geworden**	Er ist *ohn*-mekhtikh guvorden
He's losing blood	**Er verliert Blut**	Er fair*leert* bloot
Please get some water/a blanket/some bandages	**Bitte holen Sie etwas Wasser/eine Decke/Verbandszeug**	Bitter hohlen zee etvas *vasser*/ iner decker/ fair*bant*-tsoyg
I've broken my glasses	**Meine Brille ist kaputt**	Miner *bril*ler ist kah*poot*
I can't see	**Ich kann nichts sehen**	Ikh kan nikhts *zay*en
A child has fallen in the water	**Ein Kind ist ins Wasser gefallen**	Ine kint ist ins *vasser* gu*fal*-len
A woman is drowning	**Eine Frau ist am Ertrinken**	Iner frow ist am air*trinken*
She can't swim	**Sie kann nicht schwimmen**	Zee kan nikht *shvim*men
There's a fire	**Es gibt ein Feuer**	Es geebt ine *foyer*
I had an accident	**Ich hatte einen Unfall**	Ikh hatter inen *oon*fal

The other driver hit my car	**Der andere Fahrer ist gegen mein Auto gefahren**	Dair *anderer* fahrer ist *gay*gun mine *owt*oh gufahren
It was my/his fault	**Es war mein/sein Fehler**	Es var *mine/sine* failer
I didn't understand the sign	**Ich habe das Schild nicht verstanden**	Ikh hahber das shilt nikht fair-*shtan*den
May I see your ...	***Ich möchte Ihren ...**	Ikh *merkh*ter eeren ...
driving licence?	**Führerschein sehen?**	*fuirer*-shine *zay*en
insurance certificate?	**Versicherungsschein sehen**	fair-*zikh*eroongs-shine *zay*en
vehicle registration papers?	**Kraftfahrzeugbrief sehen**	*kraft*-fahr-tsoyg-breef *zay*en
Apply to the insurance company	***Wenden Sie sich an die Versicherungs- gesellschaft**	Venden zee zikh an dee fair-*zikh*eroongs- guze*l*shaft
What are the name and address of the owner?	**Wie ist der Name und die Adresse des Besitzers?**	Vee ist dair *nah*mer oont dee a*dress*er des buz*it*sers
Are you willing to act as a witness?	**Sind Sie bereit, als Zeuge aufzutreten?**	Zint zee bu*rite* als *tsoy*ger owf-tsoo*tray*ten
Can I have your name and address, please?	**Ihren Namen und Ihre Adresse, bitte**	Eeren *nah*men oont eerer a*dress*er bitter
You must make a statement	***Sie müssen eine Aussage machen**	Zee *muiss*en iner *ows-zah*gur makhen
I want a copy of the police report	**Ich möchte eine Kopie des Polizeiberichts**	Ikh *merkh*ter iner ko*pee* des pohli*tsy*-burikhts

| You were speeding | *Sie haben das Tempolimit überschritten | Zee haben das *tempoh-limit uiber-shritten* |
| How much is the fine? | Wie viel ist die Strafgebühr? | Vee *feel* ist dee *strahf-gubuir* |

Lost Property

My luggage is missing	Mein Gepäck fehlt	Mine gu*peck* failt
Has my luggage been found yet?	Ist mein Gepäck schon gefunden worden?	Ist mine gu*peck* shohn gu*foon*den vorden
My luggage has been damaged/broken into	Mein Gepäck ist beschädigt worden/ In mein Gepäck wurde eingebrochen	Mine gu*peck* ist bu-*shay*dikht vorden/ In mine gu*peck* voorder *ine*-gu*brokh*en
I have lost	Ich habe ... verloren	Ikh hahber fair*lohr*en
my camcorder	meinen Camcorder	minen camcorder
my credit card	meine Kreditkarte	miner kray*deet*-karter
my luggage	mein Gepäck	mine gu*peck*
my keys	meine Schlüssel	miner *shluiss*el
my mobile phone	mein Handy	mine handy
my passport	meinen Pass	minen pass
I've locked myself out	Ich habe mich ausgeschlossen	Ikh hahber mikh *ows*-gu-*shloss*en

Where is the lost property office?	**Wo ist das Fundbüro?**	Voh ist das *foond*-buiroh
I found this in the street	**Ich habe dies auf der Straße gefunden**	Ikh hahber dees owf dair *shtrahs*ser gu*foon*den

Missing Persons

My son/daughter is lost	**Mein Sohn/Meine Tochter wird vermisst**	Mine zohn/Miner *tokh*ter veert fair*mist*
He is . . . years old, and wearing a blue shirt and shorts	**Er ist . . . Jahre alt, und trägt ein blaues Hemd und Shorts**	Er ist . . . *yahr*er alt, und traigt ine *blou*wes hemt und shorts
This is his photo	**Das ist sein Foto**	Das ist zine fohtoh
Could you help me find him?	**Könnten Sie mir helfen, ihn zu finden?**	Kernten zee meer *hel*fen, een tsoo fin-den
Have you seen a small girl with brown curly hair?	**Haben Sie ein kleines Mädchen mit braunen, lockigen Haaren gesehen?**	Hahben zee ine klines *mayt*-khen mit *brow*nen, lockigun hahren gu*zay*en
I've lost my wife	**Ich habe meine Frau verloren**	Ikh hahber miner frow fair*lohr*en
Could you please ask for . . . over the loudspeaker?	**Könnten Sie bitte über die Sprechanlage nach . . . fragen?**	Kernten zee bitter *ui*ber dee shprekh-*an*-lahgur nahkh . . . *frah*gun

Theft

I've been robbed/ mugged	**Ich bin überfallen/ ausgeraubt worden**	Ikh bin *uiber-fal*-len/ *ows-gurowbt* vorden
Did you have any jewellery/valuables on you?	**Hatten Sie Schmuck/ Wertgegenstände bei sich?**	Hatten zee shmook/*vairt-gaygun-*shtender by zikh
Were there any witnesses?	***Gab es Zeugen?**	Gab es *tsoy*gun
My bag/wallet has been stolen	**Man hat mir meine Tasche/Brieftasche gestohlen**	Man hat meer miner tasher/*breef*-tasher gu-*shtoh*len
Some things have been stolen from our car	**Einige Sachen wurden aus unserem Wagen gestohlen**	*Ine*-igur zakhen voorden ows oonzerem *vahg*un gu-*shtoh*len
It was stolen from our room	**Es wurde aus unserem Zimmer gestohlen**	Es voorder ows oonzerem tsimmer gu-*shtoh*len

ENTERTAINMENT[1]

Key Phrases		
Is there an entertainment guide?	**Gibt es ein Veranstaltungs- programm?**	Geebt es ine fair*an*-shtaltoongs-pro*gram*
What is there for children?	**Was kann man hier mit Kindern machen?**	Vas kan man heer mit kin-dern makhen
Do you have a programme for the festival?	**Haben Sie ein Programm für das Festival?**	Hahben zee ine pro*gram* fuir das festi*val*
The cheapest seats, please	**Die billigsten Plätze bitte**	Dee *bil*likh-sten *plet*ser bitter

What is there to do/ see here?	**Was kann man hier machen/besichtigen?**	Vas kan man here makhen/bu-*zikh*tigun
Is the circus on?	**Findet der Zirkus statt?**	Fin-det dair *tseer*koos shtatt
Is there a son et lumière show at the castle?	**Gibt es eine Ton- und Lichtshow im Schloss?**	Geebt es iner *tohn*- oont *likht*-show im shloss
What time is the firework display?	**Wann ist das Feuerwerk?**	Van ist das *foyer*-verk
How far is it to the amusement park?	**Wie weit ist es zum Vergnügungspark?**	Vee vite ist es tsoom fair*gnui*goongs-park
Is there a casino?	**Gibt es ein Kasino?**	Geebt es ine kazee*noh*

1. See also Going Out (pp. 159–62).

Booking Tickets

I'd like two seats for tonight/for the matinee tomorrow	**Ich möchte zwei Plätze für heute Abend/für die Matinee-Vorstellung morgen**	Ikh *merkh*ter tsvy *plet*ser fuir *hoy*ter *ah*bent/ fuir dee matee*nay-for-shtel*loong *mor*gun
I'd like to book seats for Thursday	**Ich möchte Plätze für Donnerstag reservieren**	Ikh *merkh*ter *plet*ser fuir *donn*ers-tahg rezairvee*ren*
I'd like seats	**Ich möchte Plätze**	Ikh *merkh*ter *plet*ser
in the circle	**im ersten Rang**	im *airs*ten rang
in the gallery	**in der Galerie**	in dair gala*iree*
in the stalls	**im Parkett**	im par*ket*
I'd like a seat at the front	**Ich möchte einen Platz in den vorderen Reihen**	Ikh *merkh*te inen plats in dain forderen *rye*-en
The cheapest seats, please	**Die billigsten Plätze bitte**	Dee *bill*ikh-sten *plet*ser bitter
Are there any concessions?	**Gibt es Ermäßigungen?**	Geebt es air*mess*igoong-en
Are they good seats?	**Sind es gute Plätze?**	Zint es gooter *plet*ser
Where are these seats?	**Wo sind diese Plätze?**	Voh zint deezer *plet*ser
This is your seat	***Hier ist Ihr Platz**	Heer ist eer plats
That performance is sold out	***Die Vorstellung ist ausverkauft**	Dee *for-shtel*loong ist *ows*-fair*kowft*
Everything is sold out	***Alles ist ausverkauft**	Alles ist *ows*-fair*kowft*

| Standing room only | *Es gibt nur Stehplätze | Es geebt noor *shtay*-pletser |
| Pick the tickets up before the performance | *Holen Sie bitte die Tickets vor der Vorstellung ab | Hohlen zee bitter dee tickets for dair *for-shtel*loong ab |

Cinema, Theatre and Live Music

Chamber music	die Kammermusik	Kammer-moo*zeek*
Film	der Film	Film
Modern dance	der moderne Tanz	Mo*dair*ner tants
Opera	die Oper	*Ohper*
Play	das Theater	Tay*ahter*
Recital	der Liederabend	*Leeder-ahbent*
What's on at the theatre/cinema?	Was wird im Theater/im Kino gespielt?	Vas veert im tay*ahter*/*keeno* gu-*shpeelt*
Is it the original version?	Ist es die Originalversion?	Ist es dee orighee*nahl*-fairz-*yon*
Are there subtitles?	Gibt es Untertitel?	Geebt es *oonter-teetel*
Is it dubbed?	Ist es die Synchronfassung?	Ist es dee zuin*krohn*-fassoong
Is there a concert on?	Gibt es ein Konzert?	Geebt es ine kont*sairt*
Is there a support band?	Gibt es eine Vorgruppe?	Geebt es iner *for*-grupper

What time does the main band start?	**Wann beginnt die Hauptgruppe?**	Van buginnt dee *howpt*-grupper
Who is	**Wer**	Vair
acting?	**spielt?**	shpeelt
conducting?	**dirigiert?**	diri*geert*
directing?	**führt Regie?**	fuirt re*jee*
singing?	**singt?**	zingt
When does the ballet start?	**Wann beginnt das Ballett?**	Van buginnt das ba*let*
What time does the performance end?	**Wann ist die Vorstellung zu Ende?**	Van ist dee *for-shtel*loong tsoo *ender*
A programme, please	**Ein Programm bitte**	Ine pro*gram* bitter
Where is the cloakroom?	**Wo ist die Garderobe?**	Voh ist dee garder-*rohb*er

Clubs and Discos

Can you recommend a good show/a disco?	**Können Sie eine gute Veranstaltung/ eine Diskothek empfehlen?**	Kernen zee iner gooter fairan-shtaltoong/iner diskoh-*taik* emp*fay*len
What's the best nightclub?	**Welches ist der beste Nachtklub?**	*Velkh*es ist dair bester *nahkht*-kloob
Is there a jazz club here?	**Gibt es hier einen Jazzclub?**	Geebt es here inen *jazz*-kloob
Where can we go dancing?	**Wo können wir tanzen gehen?**	Voh kernen veer *tant*sen *gay*en
Would you like to dance?	**Möchten Sie tanzen?**	*Merkh*ten zee *tant*sen

HEALTH

Dentist

Key Phrases		
I need to see a dentist	**Ich muss zum Zahnarzt**	Ikh mooss tsoom *tsahn*-artst
Can you recommend one?	**Können Sie einen empfehlen?**	Kernen zee inen emp*fay*len
I have toothache	**Ich habe Zahnschmerzen**	Ikh hahber *tsahn-shmair*tsen
Can you do it now?	**Können Sie es jetzt machen?**	Kernen zee es yetst makhen
Can you fix it (temporarily)?	**Können Sie sie (vorläufig) reparieren?**	Kernen zee zee (*for-loy*fikh) repah*ree*ren

Can I make an appointment?	**Kann ich mich anmelden?**	Kan ikh mikh *an*-melden
As soon as possible, please	**So bald wie möglich bitte**	Zo balt vee *merk*likh bitter
This tooth hurts	**Dieser Zahn tut weh**	Deezair tsahn toot vay

I've lost a filling	Ich habe eine Füllung/Plombe verloren	Ikh hahber iner *fuil*loong/*plomb*er fair*lohr*en
Can you fill it?	Können Sie ihn füllen/plombieren?	Kernen zee een fuillen/plom*beer*en
I do not want the tooth taken out	Ziehen Sie den Zahn bitte nicht raus	*Tsee*-yen zee dain tsahn bitter nikht
Please give me an injection first	Bitte geben Sie mir zuerst eine Spritze/örtliche Betäubung	Bitter *gay*ben zee meer tsoo-airst iner *shprits*er/*ert*likher butoyboong
My gums are swollen/keep bleeding	Mein Zahnfleisch ist geschwollen/blutet immer	Mine *tsahn*-flysh ist gu-*shvoll*en/*bloo*tet immer
I have broken/chipped my dentures	Meine Zahnprothese ist zerbrochen/angeschlagen	Miner *tsahn*-protayzer ist tsair*brokh*en *an*-gu-*shlah*gun
You're hurting me	Sie tun mir weh	Zee toon meer vay
Please rinse your mouth	*Bitte spülen Sie den Mund aus	Bitter *shpui*len zee dayn moot ows
I will X-ray your teeth	*Ich werde Ihre Zähne röntgen	Ikh vairder eerer *tsayner rernt*-gun
You have an abscess	*Sie haben ein Geschwür/einen Abszess	Zee hahben ine gu-*shvuir*/inen *aps*-tsess
The nerve is exposed	*Der Nerv ist bloßgelegt	Dair nairf ist *blohs*-gu*laygt*

This tooth can't be saved	***Dieser Zahn ist nicht zu retten**	*Dee*zair tsahn ist nikht tsoo *ret*ten
How much do I owe you?	**Wie viel schulde ich Ihnen?**	Vee feel *shool*der ikh eenen
When should I come again?	**Wann soll ich wiederkommen?**	Van zoll ikh *veeder-kommen*

Doctor

Key Phrases

I must see a doctor. Can you recommend one?	**Ich muss zum Arzt. Können Sie mir einen empfehlen?**	Ikh mooss tsoom artst. Kernen zee meer inen emp*fay*len
Please call a doctor	**Bitte, rufen Sie einen Arzt**	Bitter roofen zee inen artst
I suffer from . . . Here is a list of my medication	**Ich leide an . . . Hier ist eine Liste meiner Medikamente**	Ikh *lyder* an . . . Heer ist iner lister miner medikah*menter*
I have a heart condition	**Ich habe Herzprobleme**	Ikh hahber *hairts-*prob*lay*mer
I am diabetic	**Ich bin Diabetiker**	Ikh bin dee-ah-*bay*tiker
I suffer from asthma	**Ich leide an Asthma**	Ikh *lyder* an *ast*mah
I've had a high temperature since yesterday	**Ich habe seit gestern Fieber**	Ikh hahber zite *ge*stern *fee*ber
My stomach is upset	**Ich habe Magenbeschwerden**	Ikh hahber *mah*gun-bu-*shvair*den

Is there a doctor's surgery nearby?	**Gibt es hier in der Nähe eine Arztpraxis?**	Geebt es heer in dair *nay*er iner *artst*-pracksis
When can the doctor come?	**Wann kann der Arzt kommen?**	Van kan dair artst *kommen*
Does the doctor speak English?	**Spricht der Arzt Englisch?**	Sprikht dair artst *aing*-lish
Can I make an appointment for as soon as possible?	**Kann ich bitte so bald wie möglich einen Termin haben?**	Kan ikh bitter zo balt vee *merk*likh inen ter*meen* hahben
I'd like to find a paediatrician	**Ich brauche einen Kinderarzt**	Ikh *browkh*er inen kin-der-artst

Medication

I take daily medication for ...	**Ich nehme täglich Medikamente für ...**	Ikh nay*mer* *tayg*likh medikah*men*ter fuir ...
I suffer from ... Here is a list of my medication	**Ich leide an ... Hier ist eine Liste meiner Medikamente**	Ikh *lyd*er an ... Heer ist iner lister miner medikah*men*ter
This is a copy of my UK prescription. Could you please prescribe ... for me?	**Hier ist das Rezept mit den Medikamenten, die ich in England nehme. Könnten Sie mir bitte ... verschreiben**	Heer ist das ray*tsept* mit den medikah*men*ten dee ikh in *aing*-lant *nay*mer. Kernten zee meer bitter ... fair*shry*ben

Symptoms and conditions

I am ill	**Ich bin krank**	Ikh bin krank
I have high/low blood pressure	**Ich habe hohen/ niedrigen Blutdruck**	Ikh hahber *hoh-*en/*need*rigun *bloot-*drook
I have a heart condition	**Ich habe Herzprobleme**	Ikh hahber *hairts-*prob*lay*mer
I am diabetic	**Ich bin Diabetiker**	Ikh bin dee-ah-*bay*tiker
I suffer from asthma	**Ich leide an Asthma**	Ikh *ly*der an *ast*mah
I've had a high temperature since yesterday	**Ich habe seit gestern Fieber**	Ikh hahber zite *ges*tern *fee*ber
I've a pain in my right arm	**Ich habe Schmerzen im rechten Arm**	Ikh hahber *shmair*tsen im *rekh*ten arm
My wrist hurts	**Mein Handgelenk tut mir weh**	Mine *hant-*gulenk toot meer vay
I think I've sprained my ankle/broken my ankle	**Ich glaube, ich habe mir den Fuß verstaucht/den Knöchel gebrochen**	Ikh *glow*ber ikh hahber meer den foos fair-*shtowkht/*dain k-*nerkh*el gu*brokh*en
I fell down and hurt my back	**Ich bin hingefallen und habe mir den Rücken verletzt**	Ikh bin hin-gu*fal-*len oont hahber meer dain *ruicken* fairletst
My foot is swollen	**Mein Fuß ist geschwollen**	Mine foos ist gu-*shvol*len
I've burned/cut/ bruised myself	**Ich habe mich verbrannt/ geschnitten/ gestoßen (gequetscht)**	Ikh hahber mikh fair*brant*/gu-*shnit*ten/ gu-*shtohs*sen (gu-*k-vetsht*)

I think it is infected	**Ich glaube, es ist entzündet**	Ikh *glow*ber es hat zikh ent-*suin*det
I've developed a rash/ an inflammation	**Ich habe einen Ausschlag/eine Entzündung**	Ikh hahber inen *ows*-shlahg/iner ent-*suin*doong
My stomach is upset	**Ich habe Magenbeschwerden**	Ikh hahber *mahg*un-bu-*shvair*den
My appetite's gone	**Ich habe den Appetit verloren**	Ikh hahber dain appe*teet* fair*lohr*en
I've got indigestion	**Ich habe eine Magenverstimmung**	Ikh hahber iner *mahg*un-fair*shtimm*oong
I have diarrhoea	**Ich habe Durchfall**	Ich hahbe *doorkh*-fal
I think I've got food poisoning	**Ich glaube, ich habe eine Lebensmittelver- giftung**	Ikh *glow*ber ikh hahber iner *lay*bens-mittel- fair*gift*oong
I can't eat/sleep	**Ich kann nicht essen/nicht schlafen**	Ikh kan nikht essen/ shlahfen
My nose keeps bleeding	**Meine Nase blutet immer**	Miner *nahz*er *bloo*tet *imm*er
I have difficulty in breathing	**Ich habe Schwierigkeiten beim Atmen**	Ikh hahber shveerikh- kiten bime *aht*men
I feel dizzy/sick	**Mir ist schwindlig/ schlecht**	Meer ist *shvind*likh/ shlekht
I feel shivery	**Mich fröstelt**	Mikh *frer*stelt
I keep vomiting	**Ich muss mich immer übergeben**	Ikh mooss mikh *immer* uiber-*gay*ben
I think I've caught 'flu	**Ich glaube, ich habe Grippe**	Ikh *glow*ber ikh hahber *gripp*er

I've got a cold	**Ich habe eine Erkältung**	Ikh hahber iner air*kel*toong
I've had it since yesterday/for a few hours	**Ich habe es seit gestern/ein paar Stunden**	Ikh hahber es zite *gestern*/ine pahr *shtoonden*
abscess	**das Geschwür, der Abszess**	gu-*shvuir*, *aps*-tsess
ache	**der Schmerz**	shmairts
allergy	**die Allergie**	allair*ghee*
appendicitis	**die Blinddarm-Entzündung**	*blint*-darm-ent-*tsuind*oong
asthma	**das Asthma**	*ast*mah
blister	**die Blase**	*blah*zer
boil	**der Furunkel**	foo*roon*kel
bruise	**die Quetschung**	k-*vets*hoong
burn	**die Brandwunde**	*brant*-voonder
cardiac condition	**der Herzfehler**	*hairts*-failer
chill, cold	**die Erkältung**	air*kel*toong
constipation	**die Verstopfung**	fair*shtop*foong
cough	**der Husten**	hoosten
cramp	**der Krampf**	krampf
diabetic	**zuckerkrank**	*tsook*er-krank
diarrhoea	**der Durchfall**	*doorkh*fal
earache	**die Ohrenschmerzen**	ohren-*shmairts*en
epilepsy	**die Epilepsie**	epilep*see*
fever	**das Fieber**	*feeber*

food poisoning	die Lebensmittel-Vergiftung	*lay*bens-mittel-fair*gift*oong
fracture	der Bruch	brookh
hay-fever	der Heuschnupfen	*hoy*-shnoopfen
headache	die Kopfschmerzen	*kopf-shmair*tsen
heart attack	der Herzinfarkt	*hairts*-infarkt
high blood pressure	hoher Blutdruck	*hoh*-er *bloot*-drook
ill, sick	krank	krank
illness	die Krankheit	*krank*-hite
indigestion	die Verdauungsstörung	fair*dowoongs-shter*-roong
infection	die Ansteckung	*an*-shteckoong
influenza	die Grippe	*gripp*er
insomnia	die Schlaflosigkeit	*shlahf*-lohsikh-kite
itch	das Jucken	yooken
nausea	die Übelkeit	*uibel*-kite
pain	der Schmerz	shmairts
rheumatism	der Rheumatismus	*roo*-matizmoos
sore throat	die Halsschmerzen	*hals-shmair*tsen
sprain	die Verstauchung	fair-*shtowkho*ong
stomach ache	die Magenschmerzen	*mahg*un-*shmair*tsen
sunburn	der Sonnenbrand	*zonnen*-brant
sunstroke	der Sonnenstich	*zonnen*-shtikh
tonsillitis	die Mandelentzündung	mandel-ent-*tsuin*doong

toothache	**die Zahnschmerzen**	*tsahn-shmair*tsen
ulcer	**das Geschwür**	gu-*shvuir*
wound	**die Wunde**	*voon*der

Diagnosis and treatment

Where does it hurt?	***Wo tut es weh?**	Voh toot es vay
Have you a pain here?	***Haben Sie hier Schmerzen?**	Hahben zee heer *shmair*tsen
How long have you had the pain?	***Seit wann haben Sie die Schmerzen?**	Zite van hahben zee dee *shmair*tsen
Does that hurt?	***Tut das weh?**	Toot das vay
A lot?	***Sehr?**	Zair
A little?	***Ein wenig?**	Ine *vay*nikh
Open your mouth	***Machen Sie den Mund auf**	Makhen zee dain moont owf
Put out your tongue	***Stecken Sie die Zunge raus**	*Shteck*en zee dee tsoong-er rows
Breathe in/out	***Atmen Sie ein/aus**	Ahtmen zee ine/ows
You're hurting me	**Sie tun mir weh**	Zee toon meer vay
Please lie down	***Legen Sie sich bitte hin**	*Lay*gun zee zikh bitter hin
I will need a urine specimen	***Ich brauche eine Urinprobe**	Ikh *browkh*er iner *ooreen-proh*ber
You must have a blood test	***Wir müssen einen Bluttest machen**	Veer *muiss*en inen *bloot*-test makhen
What medicines have you been taking?	***Welche Medikamente haben Sie eingenommen?**	*Velkh*er medikah*men*ter hahben zee *ine*-gunommen

I am pregnant	**Ich bin schwanger**	Ikh bin *shvang*-er
I am allergic to . . .	**Ich bin allergisch gegen . . .**	Ikh bin al*lair*gish *gay*gun . . .
I'll give you	***Ich gebe Ihnen**	Ikh *gay*ber eenen
an antibiotic	**ein Antibiotikum**	ine antee-bee*oh*teekoom
a sedative	**ein Beruhigungsmittel**	ine bu*roo*-igoongs-mittel
some medicine	**Arznei/Medizin**	arts*ny*/maydit*seen*
some pills	**Pillen**	pillen
Take this prescription to the chemist's	***Bringen Sie dieses Rezept in die Apotheke**	Bring-en zee deezes ray*tsept* in dee apoh*tayker*
Take this three times a day	***Nehmen Sie dies dreimal täglich ein**	*Nay*men zee dees dry-mahl *tay*glikh ine
I'll give you an injection	***Ich gebe Ihnen eine Spritze**	Ikh gayber eenen iner *shprit*ser
I'll put you on a diet	***Ich werde Sie auf Diät setzen**	Ikh *vair*der zee owf dee-*yet* zetsen
You must be X-rayed	***Sie müssen geröntgt werden**	Zee muissen gu-*rerngt* *vair*den
You must go to hospital	***Sie müssen ins Krankenhaus**	Zee muissen ins *kran*ken-hows
You've pulled a muscle	***Sie haben eine Muskelzerrung**	Zee hahben iner *moos*kel-tserroong
You have a fracture/sprain	***Sie haben einen Knochenbruch/eine Verstauchung**	Zee hahben inen k-*nokh*en-brookh/iner fair-*shtouwkh*oong

You need a few stitches	***Sie brauchen ein paar Stiche**	Zee *brouwkh*en ine pahr *shtikh*er
You must stay in bed	***Sie müssen im Bett bleiben**	Zee muissen im bett *bly*ben
Come and see me again in two days' time	***Kommen Sie in zwei Tagen wieder**	*Komm*en zee in tsvy *tah*gun *veed*er
Will you call again?	**Kommen Sie wieder?**	*Komm*en zee *veed*er
Is it serious/ contagious?	**Ist es schlimm/ ansteckend?**	Ist es shlim/*an*-shteckent
Nothing to worry about	***Es besteht kein Grund zur Unruhe**	Es bu*shtayt* kine groont tsoor *oon*roo-wer
I feel better now	**Mir geht es jetzt wieder besser**	Meer gait es yetst *veed*er besser
When can I travel again?	**Wann kann ich wieder reisen?**	Van kan ikh *veed*er *ry*zen
You should not travel until . . .	***Sie sollten bis . . . nicht reisen**	Zee zollten bis . . . nikht *ry*zen
How much do I owe you?	**Wie viel schulde ich Ihnen?**	Vee feel *shool*der ikh eenen
I'd like a receipt for the health insurance	**Ich hätte gern einen Beleg für die Krankenkasse**	Ikh hetter gairn inen bu*laig* fuir dee *kran*ken-kasser
ambulance	**der Rettungswagen**	*rett*oongs-*vah*gun
anaesthetic	**das Betäubungsmittel**	be*toy*boongs-mittel
bandage	**der Verband**	fair*bant*
chiropodist	**der Fußpfleger**	*foos-pflayg*ur
first aid station/A&E	**Erste Hilfe-Station/ Notaufnahme**	airster hilfer-shtats-*yon*/*noht*-owf-*nah*mer

hospital	**das Krankenhaus**	*kran*ken-hows
injection	**die Spritze**	*shprits*er
laxative	**das Abführmittel**	*ap*-fuir-mittel
nurse	**der (Kranken-) Pfleger/** **die (Kranken-) Pflegerin**	(*kranken*-) *pflay*gur/ *pflay*gurin
operation	**die Operation**	operats-*yon*
osteopath	**der Osteopath**	osteo*paht*
(adhesive) plaster	**das Pflaster**	*pflas*ter
prescription	**das Rezept**	rayt*sept*
X-ray	**die Röntgenaufnahme**	*rernt*gun-owf-*nah*mer

Optician

Key Phrases

I have broken my glasses; can you repair them?	**Meine Brille ist kaputt; können Sie sie reparieren?**	Miner *bril*ler ist kah*poot*; kernen zee zee repah*ree*ren
Can you give me a new pair of glasses to the same prescription?	**Können Sie mir eine neue Brille mit der gleichen Stärke verschreiben?**	Kernen zee meer iner *noy*er *bril*ler mit dair *glyk*hen *shter*ker fair*shry*ben
Please test my eyes	**Testen Sie bitte meine Augen**	Testen zee bitter miner *ow*gun
I am short-sighted/ long-sighted	**Ich bin kurzsichtig/ weitsichtig**	Ikh bin *koorts*-zikhtig/*vite*-zikhtig

I have broken the frame/arm	**Der Rahmen/Bügel ist kaputt**	Dair *rahmen*/*bui*gul ist kah*poot*
When will they be ready?	**Wann wird sie fertig sein?**	Van veert zee *fair*tihk zine
I have difficulty with reading/with long distance vision	**Ich habe Schwierigkeiten beim Lesen/beim weit sehen**	Ikh hahber *shveer*ikh-kiten bime *lay*zen/bime vite *zay*en
I have lost one of my contact lenses	**Ich habe eine Kontaktlinse verloren**	Ikh hahber miner kon*takt*-linzer fair*lohr*en
I should like to have contact lenses	**Ich hätte gern Kontaktlinsen**	Ikh *het*ter gairn kon*takt*-linzen
My vision is blurred	**Meine Sicht ist verschwommen**	Miner zikht ist fair*shwom*men
I can't see clearly	**Ich sehe nicht klar**	Ikh *zay*er nikht klar

Parts of the Body

ankle	**der Fußknöchel**	*foos*-k-*nerkh*el
arm	**der Arm**	arm
artery	**die Arterie**	ahr*tair*ee-yer
back	**der Rücken**	*ruick*en
bladder	**die Blase**	*blah*ser
blood	**das Blut**	bloot
body	**der Körper**	*kerp*er

bone	der Knochen	k-*nokh*en
bowels	der Darm	darm
brain	das Gehirn	gu*heern*
breast/chest	die Brust	broost
cheek	die Wange	vang-er
chin	das Kinn	kin
collar-bone	das Schlüsselbein	*shluis*sel-bine
ear	das Ohr	ohr
elbow	der Ellbogen	*el*bohgun
eye	das Auge	*owg*ur
eyelid	das Augenlid	*owg*un-lit
face	das Gesicht	gu*zikht*
finger	der Finger	fing-er
foot	der Fuß	foos
forehead	die Stirn	shteern
gums	das Zahnfleisch	*zahn*-flysh
hand	die Hand	hant
head	der Kopf	kopf
heart	das Herz	hairts
heel	die Ferse	*fair*zer
hip	die Hüfte	*huif*ter
jaw	der Kiefer	*kee*fer
joint	das Gelenk	gu*lenk*

kidney	**die Niere**	neerer
knee	**das Knie**	k-nee
knee-cap	**die Kniescheibe**	k-*nee-shy*ber
leg	**das Bein**	bine
lip	**die Lippe**	*lip*per
liver	**die Leber**	*lay*ber
lung	**die Lunge**	loong-er
mouth	**der Mund**	moont
muscle	**der Muskel**	*moos*kell
nail	**der Nagel**	*nah*gul
neck	**der Hals**	hals
nerve	**der Nerv**	nairf
nose	**die Nase**	*nah*zer
pelvis	**das Becken**	*becken*
pulse	**der Puls**	pools
rib	**die Rippe**	ripper
shoulder	**die Schulter**	*shool*ter
skin	**die Haut**	howt
stomach	**der Magen**	*mah*gun
temple	**die Schläfe**	*shlay*fer
thigh	**der Schenkel**	*shen*kel
throat	**der Hals**	hals
thumb	**der Daumen**	*dow*men

toe	**der Zeh**	tsay
tongue	**die Zunge**	tsoong-er
tonsils	**die Mandeln**	*man*deln
tooth	**der Zahn**	tsahn
vein	**die Ader**	*ah*der
wrist	**das Handgelenk**	*hant*-gulenk

MEETING PEOPLE

Key Phrases

Glad to meet you/ Delighted	**Es freut mich, Sie kennenzulernen/ Angenehm**	Es froyt mikh zee *kennen*-tsoo-*lair*nen/ *An*-gunaym
How are you?	**Wie geht es Ihnen?**	Vee gait es eenen
My name is . . .	**Mein Name ist . . .**	Mine *nah*mer ist . . .
I'm on holiday/a business trip	**Ich bin auf Urlaub/ geschäftlich hier**	Ikh bin owf *oor*lowp/ gu-*sheft*likh here
What is your telephone number?	**Wie ist Ihre Telefonnummer?**	Vee ist eerer tele*fohn*-noommer
Thanks for the invitation	**Vielen Dank für die Einladung**	Feelen dank fuir dee *ine*-lahdoong
Yes, I'd like to come	**Ja, sehr gern**	Ya, zair gairn
I'm sorry, I can't come	**Tut mir leid, ich kann nicht kommen**	Toot meer lite, ikh *kan* nikht *kommen*

Introductions

May I introduce . . .?	**Darf ich . . . vorstellen?**	Darf ikh . . . *for-shtel*len
Have you met . . .?	**Kennen Sie . . .?**	Kennen zee . . .
How are things?	**Wie steht's?**	Vee shtaits

Fine, thanks, and you?	**Gut, danke, und Ihnen?**	Goot danker, oont eenen
What is your name?	**Wie heißen Sie?**	Vee *hy*sen zee
This is ...	**Dies ist ...**	Dees ist ...
Am I disturbing you?	**Störe ich Sie?**	*Shter*-rer ikh zee
Sorry to have troubled you	**Entschuldigen Sie die Störung**	Ents*hool*digun zee dee *shter*-roong
Leave me alone	**Lassen Sie mich in Ruhe**	Lassen zee mikh in roo-wer

Getting Acquainted

Are you on holiday?	**Sind Sie auf Urlaub?**	Zint zee owf *oor*lowp
Do you live/are you staying here?	**Wohnen Sie hier?**	*Voh*nen zee heer
We've been here for a week	**Wir sind seit einer Woche hier**	Veer zint zite iner *wokh*er heer
Is this your first time here?	**Sind Sie zum ersten Mal hier?**	Zint zee tsoom airsten mahl heer
Do you like it here?	**Gefällt es Ihnen hier?**	*Gu*felt es eenen heer
Are you on your own?	**Sind Sie allein(e)?**	Zint zee a*line*(-er)
Where do you come from?	**Woher sind Sie?**	Voh-hair zint zee
I come from ...	**Ich komme aus ...**	Ikh *kom*mer ows ...

Have you been to England/America?	**Waren Sie schon in England/Amerika?**	*Vah*ren zee shohn in *aing*-lant/*amair*eekah
It's been nice talking to you	**Es war nett, mit Ihnen zu plaudern**	Es vahr nett mit eenen tsoo *plow*dern
Can I see you again?	**Können wir uns wiedersehen?**	Kernen veer oons *veeder*-*zay*en

Personal Information

I am with	**Ich bin mit**	Ikh bin mit
a colleague	**einem Kollegen**	inem kol*lay*gun
a friend	**einem Freund/ einer Freundin**	inem froynd/iner *froyn*din
my family	**meiner Familie**	miner fa*meel*-yer
my husband	**meinem Mann**	minem man
my parents	**meinen Eltern**	minen *el*tern
my wife	**meiner Frau**	miner frow
I have a boyfriend/ girlfriend	**Ich habe einen Freund/eine Freundin**	Ikh hahber inen froynt/*froyn*din
I live with my partner	**Ich wohne mit meinem Partner/ meiner Partnerin zusammen**	Ikh *voh*ner mit minem partner/miner partnerin tsoo-*zammen*
I am separated/ divorced	**Ich lebe getrennt/Ich bin geschieden**	Ikh *lay*ber gu*trennt*/ Ikh bin gu-*shee*den

I am a widow(er)	**Ich bin Witwe(r)**	Ikh bin *veet*ver
Are you married/ single?	**Sind Sie verheiratet/ single?**	Zint zee fair-*hy*-rahtet/ single
Do you have children/ grandchildren?	**Haben Sie Kinder/ Enkel?**	Hahben zee kin-der/*en*kel
What do you do?	**Was machen Sie beruflich?**	Vas makhen zee bu*roof*-likh
I work for . . .	**Ich arbeite bei . . .**	Ikh *arb*yter by . . .
I work freelance	**Ich arbeite freiberuflich**	Ikh *arb*yter *fry*-bu*roof*-likh
I'm a consultant	**Ich bin Berater**	Ikh bin bu*rah*ter
We're retired	**Wir sind Rentner**	Veer zint rentner
What are you studying?	**Was studieren Sie?**	Vas shtoo*deer*en zee
What do you do in your spare time?	**Was machen Sie in Ihrer Freizeit?**	Vas makhen zee in eerer *fry*-tsite
I like sailing/ swimming/walking	**Ich segle/ schwimme/ wandere gern**	Ikh *zayg*ler/*shvim*mer/ *vand*erer gairn
I don't like cycling	**Ich fahre nicht gern Rad**	Ikh *fahr*er nikht gairn raht
I don't like (playing) tennis	**Ich spiele nicht gern Tennis**	Ikh *shpee*ler nikht gairn *tennis*
I'm interested in art/ music	**Ich interessiere mich für Kunst/ Musik**	Ikh interes*seer*er mikh fuir koonst/ moo*zeek*

Going Out[1]

Could we have coffee/a drink somewhere?	Können wir irgendwo einen Kaffee trinken/ etwas trinken?	Kernen veer eergunt-voh inen kaffay trinken/ etvas trinken
I'd like ... please	Ich hätte gern ...	Ikh hetter ... gairn
No thanks, I'm all right	Nein danke, ich möchte nichts	Nine danker, ikh merkhte nikhts
Cheers!	Prost!	Prohst
Would you like to have lunch with us tomorrow?	Möchten Sie morgen mit uns zu Mittag essen?	Merkhten zee morgun mit oons tsoo mit-tahg essen
Can you come to dinner/for a drink?	Können Sie zum Abendessen/auf ein Gläschen zu uns kommen?	Kernen zee tsoom ahbent-essen/owf ine glays-khen tsoo oons kommen
We're giving/There is a party. Would you like to come?	Wir geben/Es gibt eine Party. Möchten Sie auch kommen?	Veer gayben/Es geebt iner party. Merkhten zee owkh kommen
May I bring a (girl) friend?	Kann ich einen Freund (eine Freundin) mitbringen?	Kan ikh inen froynt (iner froyndin) mit-bring-en
Shall we go to the cinema/theatre?	Sollen wir ins Kino/ Theater gehen?	Zollen veer ins keenoh/ ins tayahter gayen
Shall we go for a walk?	Sollen wir einen Spaziergang machen?	Zollen veer inen spatseergang makhen

1. See also Entertainment (pp. 135–38).

Would you like to go dancing/for a drive?	**Möchten Sie tanzen gehen/eine Spritztour mit dem Auto machen?**	*Merkh*ten zee *tantsen gay*en/iner *shprits*-toor mit dem *ow*toh makhen
Do you know a good disco/restaurant?	**Kennen Sie eine gute Diskothek/ein gutes Restaurant?**	Kennen zee iner gooter diskoh-*taik*/ine gootes restor-*rant*
Are you doing anything tonight/ tomorrow afternoon?	**Haben Sie heute Abend/morgen Nachmittag etwas vor?**	Hahben zee *hoy*ter *ah*bent/*morg*un *nahkh*-mit-tahg etvas for
Let's go to a gay bar	**Gehen wir in eine Schwulenbar**	*Gay*en veer in iner *shwoo*len-bar

Arrangements

Where shall we meet?	**Wo sollen wir uns treffen?**	Voh zollen veer oons *treffen*
What time shall I/ we come?	**Wann soll ich/sollen wir kommen?**	Van zoll ikh/zollen veer *kommen*
I could pick you up at ...	**Ich könnte Sie von ... abholen**	Ikh *kern*ter zee oom ... fon ... *ap*-hohlen
Could you meet me at ... *(time)*?	**Könnten wir uns um ... treffen?**	Kernten veer oons oom ... *treffen*
May I see you home?	**Darf ich Sie nach Hause begleiten?**	Darf ikh zee nahkh *how*zer bug*ly*ten
Can we give you a lift home/to your hotel?	**Können wir Sie nach Hause/zu Ihrem Hotel fahren?**	Kernen veer zee nahkh *how*zer/tsoo eerem hoh*tel* fahren
Where do you live?	**Wo wohnen Sie?**	Voh vohnen zee

What is your telephone number?	**Wie ist Ihre Telefonnummer?**	Vee ist eerer tele*fohn*-noommer
Hope to see you again soon	**Hoffentlich sehen wir uns bald wieder**	*Hoff*entlikh *zay*en veer oons balt *vee*der
See you soon/later/tomorrow	**Bis bald/später/morgen**	Bis balt/*shpay*ter/*morg*un
Are you free at the weekend?	**Sind Sie am Wochenende frei?**	Zint zee am *wokh*en-ender fry

Accepting, thanking and declining

Yes, I'd like to come	**Ja, sehr gern**	Ya, zair gairn
Thanks for the invitation	**Vielen Dank für die Einladung**	Feelen dank fuir dee *ine*-lahdoong
Thanks for the evening/nice time	**Vielen Dank für den netten Abend/die netten Stunden**	Feelen dank fuir dain netten *ah*bent/dee netten *shtoon*den
Did you enjoy it?	**Hat es Ihnen gefallen?**	Hat es eenen gu*fal*-len
It was lovely	**Es war sehr nett**	Es vahr zair nett
I've enjoyed myself very much	**Ich habe viel Spaß gehabt**	Ikh hahber feel shpahs guhabt
It was interesting/funny/fantastic	**Es war sehr interessant/witzig/fantastisch**	Es var zehr interes*sant*/*veet*sik/fan*tas*tish
Thanks for the drink/ride	**Vielen Dank für den Drink/das Mitnehmen**	Feelen dank fuir dain drink/das *mit-nay*men
I'm sorry, I can't come	**Tut mir leid, ich kann nicht kommen**	Toot meer lite, ikh *kan* nikht *kom*men

Maybe another time	**Vielleicht ein andermal**	Feel-*lyhkht* ine *and*er-mahl
No thanks, I'd rather not	**Nein danke, lieber nicht**	Nine danker, *leeb*er nikht
Go away	**Gehen Sie weg**	*Gay*en zee vek
Leave me alone	**Lassen Sie mich in Ruhe**	Lassen zee mikh in roo-wer

MONEY

Key Phrases

Where is the nearest ATM?	**Wo ist der nächste Geldautomat?**	Voh ist der *naikh*ster *gelt*-owtoh-*maht*
Do you take credit cards?	**Nehmen Sie Kreditkarten?**	*Nay*men zee kray*deet*-karten
Is there a bank/ exchange bureau near here?	**Gibt es eine Bank/ Wechselstube hier in der Nähe?**	Geebt es iner bank/*veck*sel-*shtoo*ber heer in der *nay*er
Can you give me some small change?	**Können Sie mir etwas Kleingeld geben?**	Kernen zee meer etvas *kline*-gelt *gay*ben
I want to open a bank account	**Ich möchte ein Bankkonto eröffnen**	Ikh *merkh*ter ine bank-*kon*toh air-*erf*nen

Credit and Debit Cards

I'd like to get some cash with my credit/ cash (debit) card	**Ich würde gern etwas Bargeld mit meiner Kredit-/ Debitkarte abheben**	Ikh *vuir*der gairn etwas *bar*-gelt mit miner kray*deet*-/*day*bit-karter *ap*-*hay*ben
Please enter your PIN number	**Geben Sie bitte Ihre PIN-Nummer ein**	*Gay*ben zee bitter eerer PIN-noommer ine
The ATM has swallowed my card	**Der Geldautomat hat meine Karte verschluckt**	Der *gelt*-owtoh-*maht* hat miner karter fair*shlookt*

Exchange

Do you cash traveller's cheques?	**Lösen Sie Reiseschecks ein?**	*Lerzen* zee *ryzer*-sheks ine
Where can I cash traveller's cheques?	**Wo kann ich Reiseschecks einlösen?**	Voh kan ikh *ryzer*-sheks *ine-lerzen*
I want to change some English/ American money	**Ich möchte englisches/ amerikanisches Geld einwechseln**	Ikh *merkh*ter *aing*-lishes/ amaireekahnishes gelt *ine-veck*zeln
Your passport, please	*****Ihren Pass bitte**	Eeren pass bitter
Where do I sign?	**Wo soll ich unterschreiben?**	Voh zoll ikh *oonter-shry*ben
Sign here, please	*****Unterschreiben Sie hier bitte**	*Oonter-shry*ben zee heer bitter
Go to the cashier	*****Gehen Sie zur Kasse**	*Gay*en zee tsoor kasser
What is the rate of exchange?	**Wie ist der Wechselkurs?**	Vee ist dair *veck*sel-koors
How much is your commission?	**Wie viel Kommission nehmen Sie?**	Vee feel kommiss-*yon naymen* zee
Can you give me some small change?	**Können Sie mir etwas Kleingeld geben?**	Kernen zee meer etvas *kline*-gelt *gay*ben
I'd like small notes, please	**Geben Sie mir bitte kleine Scheine**	*Gay*ben zee meer bitter kliner shiner

General Banking

I arranged for money to be transferred from the UK. Has it arrived yet?	**Ich habe Geld von Großbritannien überweisen lassen. Ist es schon angekommen?**	Ikh hahber gelt fon grohs-brit-*tan*-yen *uiber*-vizen lassen. Ist es shohn *an*-gu*kommen*
I want to open a bank account	**Ich möchte ein Bankkonto eröffnen**	Ikh *merkh*ter ine bank-*kont*oh air-*erf*nen
Please credit this to my account	**Schreiben Sie das bitte auf mein Konto gut**	*Shry*ben zee das bitter owf mine *kont*oh goot
I'd like to withdraw some cash with my debit card	**Ich möchte mit meiner Debitkarte Bargeld abheben**	Ikh *merkh*ter mit miner day*bit*-karter *bar*gelt *ap*-hayben
I want to make a transfer	**Ich möchte Geld überweisen**	Ikh *merkh*ter gelt *uiber*-vizen
balance	**der Kontostand**	*kont*oh-shtant
bank card	**die Bankkarte**	bank-karter
cheque book	**das Scheckbuch**	*sheck*-bookh
current account	**das Girokonto**	*jeero*-*kont*oh
deposit account	**das Sparkonto**	*shpar*-*kont*oh
foreign currency	**die Devisen**	de*veez*en
statement	**der Kontoauszug**	*kont*oh-ows-tsoog

SHOPS¹ AND SERVICES

Where to Go

antique shop	**der Antiquitätenladen**	anteek-veetayten-lahden
audio-equipment shop	**der Hifi-Laden**	hifi-lahden
bakery	**der Bäcker, die Bäckerei**	becker, becker-rye
barber (see p. 187)	**der Friseur**	freezeur
beauty and spa treatments (see p. 176)	**die Schönheitspflege**	shernhites-pflaygur
bicycle-repair shop (see p. 47)	**der Fahrradladen**	fahr-raht-lahden
bookshop (see p. 177)	**die Buchhandlung**	bookh-hantloong
building supplies (see p. 189)	**der Baumarkt**	bow-markt
butcher (see p. 114)	**die Metzgerei, Schlachterei**	metsgur-rye, shlakhter-rye
cake shop (see p. 121)	**die Konditorei**	kondeetor-rye
camping equipment (see p. 189)	**die Campingausstattung**	camping-ows-shtattoong
carpenter	**der Schreiner**	shriner

1. See tables (p. 184) for continental sizes in clothing.

chemist (see pp. 180 and 196)	die Apotheke (*for medicines*), Drogerie (*for cosmetics, etc.*)	apoh*tayker*, droh-gair-*ee*
confectioner (see p. 121)	die Konditorei	kon*deetor-rye*
consulate (see p. 128)	das Konsulat	konsoo*laht*
craft shop	das Kunsthandwerk	*koonst-hant*-verk
decorator, painter	der Anstreicher, Maler	*an-stryk*her, *mahler*
delicatessen	Feinkost	fine-kost
dentist (see p. 139)	der Zahnarzt	*tsahn*-artst
department store	das Kaufhaus	*kowf*-hows
DIY store (see p. 189)	der Heimwerkermarkt	*hyme*-verker-markt
doctor (see p. 141)	der Arzt	artst
dry cleaner (see p. 191)	die (chemische) Reinigung	(*kay*misher) *ryni*goong
electrical appliances	Elektrogeräte	e*lek*troh-gu*rayter*
electrician	der Elektriker	e*lek*tricker
embassy (see p. 128)	die Botschaft	*boht*-shaft
fishmonger (see p. 112)	die Fischhandlung	*fish-hant*loong
florist	das Blumengeschäft	*bloomen*-gu-*sheft*
furniture shop (see p. 75)	das Möbelgeschäft	*merbel*-gu-*sheft*
garden centre	das Gartenzentrum	garten-*tsentrum*

gift shop	die Geschenkboutique	gu-*shenk*-boutique
greengrocer (see pp. 117 and 123)	die Gemüsehandlung	gu*muiser*-*hant*loong
grocery (see p. 185)	das Lebensmittelgeschäft	*lay*bens-mittel-gu-*sheft*
haberdashery	die Kurzwaren	*koorts*-*vahr*en
hairdresser (see p. 187)	der Friseur	free*zeur*
handyman	Handlanger	*hant*-lang-er
hardware store (see p. 189)	die Eisenwarenhandlung	izen-*vahren*-*hant*loong
health-food shop	der Bioladen	*bee*-oh-*lahden*
home-entertainment shop	das Geschäft für Unterhaltungs- elektronik	gu-*sheft* fuir *oonter*-*halt*oongs-elek*tronik*
interior design shop	der Designladen	design-*lahden*
jeweller (see p. 194)	der Juwelier	yoo-vel-*eer*
kitchen shop (see p. 78)	der Küchenshop	*kuikh*en-shop
launderette	die Schnellwäscherei	*shnell*-vesher-*rye*
laundry (see p. 191)	die Wäscherei	vesher-*rye*
lighting shop	das Beleuchtungsgeschäft	bu*loykh*toongs-gu-*sheft*
liquor/wine store (see p. 125)	die Spirituosen-/ Weinhandlung	spee-ree-too-*ohzen*-/*vine*-*hant*loong

market (see p. 192)	**der Markt**	markt
mobile/cell phone shop (see p. 86)	**der Handy-Shop**	handy-shop
newsagent (see p. 177)	**das Zeitungsgeschäft**	*tsite*-oongs-gu-*sheft*
optician (see p. 150)	**der Optiker**	opt*eeker*
outdoor equipment shop (see p. 189)	**das Outdoor-Geschäft**	outdoor-gu-*sheft*
pastry shop (see p. 121)	**die Konditorei**	kond*eetor-rye*
photographer	**der Fotograf**	fohtoh-*grahf*
photographic equipment (see p. 193)	**der Fotoladen**	fohtoh-*lah*den
plasterer	**der Verputzer**	fair*pootser*
plumber (for plumbing problems, see p. 71)	**der Klempner**	*klemp*ner
police (see p. 128)	**die Polizei**	pohli*tsy*
post office (see p. 85)	**das Postamt**	*post*-amt
shoe repairs (see p. 194)	**die Schuhreparatur**	*shoo*-reparah*toor*
shoe shop (for shoe sizes, see p. 184)	**das Schuhgeschäft**	*shoo*-gu-*sheft*
shopping centre	**das Einkaufszentrum**	*ine*-kowf-*tsen*trum
souvenir shop	**der Souvenirladen**	souvenir-*lah*den
sports shop	**das Sportgeschäft**	*shport*-gu-*sheft*

stationer (see p. 177)	**das Schreibwarengeschäft**	*shryp*-vahren-gu-*sheft*
supermarket (see p. 185)	**der Supermarkt**	*zooper*-markt
tobacconist	**der Tabakladen**	tabak-*lahden*
tourist information office	**das Verkehrsamt**	fair*kairs*-amt
toy shop	**das Spielwarengeschäft**	*shpeel*-vahren-gu-*sheft*
travel agency	**das Reisebüro**	*ryzer*-buiroh
travel goods shop	**das Reiseartikelgeschäft**	*ryzer*-arteekel-gu-*sheft*

Which is the best …?	**Welches ist der/die/das beste …?**	*Velkhes* ist dair/dee/das bester …
Where is the nearest …?	**Wo ist der/die/das nächste …?**	Voh ist dair/dee/das *naikh*ster …
Can you recommend a …?	**Können Sie einen/eine/ein … empfehlen?**	Kernen zee inen/iner/ine … emp*fay*len
Where is the market?	**Wo ist der Markt?**	Voh ist dair markt
Is there a market every day?	**Ist jeden Tag Markt?**	Ist *yay*den tahg markt
Where can I buy …	**Wo kann ich … kaufen?**	Voh kan ikh … *kow*fen
When are the shops open?	**Wann sind die Geschäfte geöffnet?**	Van zint dee gu-*sheft*er gu-*erf*net

In the Shop

Checkout/cash desk	*Kasse	Kasser
Manager	der Geschäftsführer	Gu-*shefts-fuirer*
Self-service	*Selbstbedienung	Zelbst-bu*deen*oong
Sale (clearance)	*Schlussverkauf/Ausverkauf	*Shlooss*-fairk*owf*/*ows*-fairk*owf*
Shop assistant	der Verkäufer/die Verkäuferin	Fair*koy*fer/fair*koy*ferin
Where can I get a trolley?	Wo bekomme ich einen Einkaufswagen?	Voh bu*kommer* ikh inen *ine*-kowfs *vahg*un
Can I help you?	*Was darf es sein?	Vas darf es zine
I want to buy . . .	Ich möchte . . . kaufen	Ikh *merkh*ter . . . *kow*fen
Do you sell . . .?	Verkaufen Sie . . .?	Fair*kow*fen zee
I'm just looking round	Ich möchte mich nur umsehen	Ikh *merkh*ter mikh noor *oom-zay*en
I don't want to buy anything now	Ich möchte im Augenblick nichts kaufen	Ikh *merkh*ter im *owgun*-blick nikhts *kow*fen
Could you show me . . .?	Könnten Sie mir bitte . . . zeigen?	Kernten zee meer bitter *tsy*gun
We do not have that	*Das haben wir leider nicht	Das hahben veer *lyder* nikht
You'll find them at that counter	*Sie sind dort auf dem Verkaufstisch	Zee zint dort owf daim fair*kowfs*-tish

We've sold out but we'll have more tomorrow	*Wir sind im Augenblick ausverkauft, aber morgen haben wir mehr	Veer zint im *owgun*-blick *ows*-fair*kowft* ahber *morg*un hahben veer mair
Anything else?	*Sonst noch etwas?	Zonst nokh etvas
That will be all	Das ist alles	Das ist alles
Will you take it with you?	*Möchten Sie es mitnehmen?	*Merkh*ten zee es *mit-nay*men
I will take it with me	Ich nehme es gleich mit	Ikh *nay*mer es glykh mit
Will you gift wrap it please?	Könnten Sie es bitte als Geschenk verpacken?	Kernten zee es bitter als gu-*shenk* fair*pack*en

Choosing

I like the one in the window	Das im Fenster gefällt mir	Das im *fenster* gu*felt* meer
Could I see that one, please?	Darf ich das mal sehen, bitte?	Darf ikh das mahl *zay*en bitter
Is it handmade?	Ist es handgemacht?	Ist es *hant*-gu*makht*
What's it made of?	Woraus ist es gemacht?	Voh-*rows* ist es gu*makht*
I like the colour but not the style	Mir gefällt die Farbe, aber nicht der Schnitt	Meer gu*felt* dee farber ahber nikht dair shnit
I want a darker/ lighter shade	Ich möchte einen dunkleren/helleren Farbton	Ikh *merkh*ter inen *doon*kleren/*hell*eren *farb*-tohn

Do you have one in another colour/size?	**Haben Sie es in einer anderen Farbe/Größe?**	Hahben zee es in iner *an*deren farber/*grer*ser
It's for a three-year-old	**Es ist für ein dreijähriges Kind**	Es ist fuir ine *dry-yair*iges kint
Have you anything better/cheaper?	**Haben Sie etwas Besseres/ Billigeres?**	Hahben zee etvas besseres/*bill*igures
How much is this?	**Was kostet das?**	Vas kostet das
That is too much for me	**Das ist mir zu teuer**	Das ist meer tsoo *toy*er

Colours

beige	**beige**	beige
black	**schwarz**	shvarts
blue	**blau**	blouw
brown	**braun**	brown
gold	**golden**	gohlden
green	**grün**	gruin
grey	**grau**	grouw
mauve	**lila**	leelah
orange	**orangenfarbig**	o*ran*jen-farbikh
pink	**rosa**	rozah
purple	**purpur**	poorpoor
red	**rot**	roht
silver	**silbern**	zilbern
white	**weiß**	vice
yellow	**gelb**	gelp

Materials

canvas	**das Segeltuch**	*zay*gul-tookh
cotton	**die Baumwolle**	*bowm-voll*er
glass	**das Glas**	glahs
lace	**die Spitze**	*shpit*ser
leather	**das Leder**	*lay*der
linen	**das Leinen**	*lyn*en
muslin	**der Musselin**	moo-selin
plastic	**der Plastik**	*plas*tik
silk	**die Seide**	*zy*der
suede	**das Wildleder**	vild-*lay*der
synthetic	**das Synthetik**	zuin-*tay*-tik
velvet	**der Samt**	zamt
wood	**das Holz**	holts
wool	**die Wolle**	*voll*er

Paying

How much is this?	**Wie teuer ist das?**	Vee *toy*er ist das
That's . . . euros, please	***Das macht . . . Euros bitte**	Das makht . . . *oy*rohs bitter
They are . . . euros each	***Sie kosten . . . Euros pro Stück**	Zee kosten . . . *oy*rohs pro shtuick
It's too expensive	**Das ist zu teuer**	Das ist tsoo *toy*er
Is that your best price?	**Ist das Ihr bester Preis?**	Ist das eer bester price

Can you give me a discount?	**Können Sie mir einen Rabatt geben?**	Kernen zee meer inen ra*bat gay*ben
How much does that come to?	**Was macht das?**	Vas makht das
That will be …	***Das macht …**	Das makht …
How would you like to pay?	***Wie möchten Sie zahlen?**	Vee *merkh*ten zee *tsah*len
Cash only please	***Nur mit Bargeld bitte**	Noor mit *bar*-gelt bitter
Do you take credit cards?	**Nehmen Sie Kreditkarten?**	*Naymen zee kraydeet*-karten
Do I have to pay VAT?	**Muss ich Mehrwertsteuer zahlen?**	Mooss ikh *mair*-vairt-*shtoyer tsah*len
Please pay at the cash desk/check out	***Bitte, zahlen Sie an der Kasse**	Bitter *tsah*len zee an dair kasser
May I have a receipt, please	**Kann ich bitte eine Quittung haben?**	Kan ikh bitter iner *k-vitoong* hahben
You've given me too little/too much change	**Sie haben mir zu wenig/zu viel Geld herausgegeben**	Zee hahben meer tsoo *vaynikh*/tsoo feel gelt hair*ows-gugayben*

Complaints

| I want to see the manager | **Ich möchte den Geschäftsführer sprechen** | Ikh *merkh*ter dain gu-*shefts-fuirer shprekh*en |
| I bought this yesterday | **Ich habe dies gestern gekauft** | Ikh hahber dees *gestern* gu*kowft* |

It doesn't work/fit	Es funktioniert/ passt nicht	Es foonkts-yoneert/passt nikht
This is	Es ist	Es ist
bad	schlecht	shlekht
broken	kaputt	kahpoot
dirty	schmutzig	shmootsikh
torn	zerrissen	tsair-rissen
This is stained/ cracked	Es hat Flecken/einen Sprung	Es hat flecken/inen shproong
I'd like to return this	Ich möchte das zurückgeben	Ikh merkhter das tsoo-ruick-gayben
Will you change it please?	Können Sie es bitte umtauschen?	Kernen zee es bitter oom-towshen
Will you refund my money?	Können Sie mir bitte mein Geld zurückgeben?	Kernen zee meer bitter mine gelt tsoo-ruick-gayben
Here is the receipt	Hier ist die Quittung	Heer ist dee k-vitoong

Beauty and Spa Treatments

I'd like a manicure/ pedicure	Ich hätte gern eine Maniküre/Pediküre	Ikh hetter gairn iner maneekuirer/pedeekuirer
I'd like a facial/ massage	Ich hätte gern eine kosmetische Gesichtsbehandlung/ eine Massage	Ikh hetter gairn iner kosmetisher guzikhts-buhantloong/iner massahjer

Do you do waxing?	**Machen Sie Wachsbehandlung?**	Makhen zee *vaks-*buhant*loong
I'd like my eyebrows shaped	**Ich hätte gern meine Augenbrauen geformt**	Ikh hetter gairn miner *owgun-browen* guformt
Do you do aromatherapy?	**Machen Sie Aromatherapie?**	Makhen zee arohmah-terapee
Is there a sauna/ steam room?	**Gibt es eine Sauna/ Dampfsauna?**	Geebt es iner zownah/dampf-zownah
What spa packages are available?	**Welche Thermalbehandlungen haben Sie?**	*Velkh*er termahl-buhandloong-en hahben zee
How much does it cost?	**Wie viel kostet das?**	Vee feel kostet das

Books, Newspapers and Stationery

Do you sell English/American newspapers/ magazines?	**Verkaufen Sie englische/ amerikanische Zeitungen/ Zeitschriften?**	Fairkowfen zee *aing*-lisher/amaireekahnisher *tsite*-oong-en/*tsite*-shriften
Can you get ... magazine for me?	**Können Sie die Zeitschrift ... für mich besorgen?**	Kernen zee dee *tsite*-shrift ... fuir mikh buzorgun
Where can I get the ...?	**Wo kann ich ... bekommen?**	Voh kan ikh ... bukommen
I'd like a map of the city/road map of ...	**Ich möchte einen Stadtplan/ Straßenplan von ...**	Ikh *merkh*ter inen shtat-plahn/*shtrahs*sen-plahn fon ...

I'd like an entertainment guide	Ich möchte ein Veranstaltungsprogramm	Ikh *merkh*ter ine fair*anshtaltoongs*-prohgram
Do you have any books in English?	Haben Sie englische Bücher?	Hahben zee *aing*-lisher buikher
Have you any books by…?	Haben Sie irgendwelche Bücher von…?	Hahben zee *eergunt-velkh*er buikher fon
I want some postcards	Ich möchte einige Ansichtskarten	Ikh *merkh*ter ine-igur *anzikhts-karten*
Do you sell souvenirs/toys?	Verkaufen Sie Reiseandenken/ Spielwaren?	Fairkowfen zee *ryzer-andenken/shpeel-vah*ren
ballpoint pen	der Kugelschreiber	*koogul-shry*ber
calculator	der Taschenrechner	*tashen-rekh*ner
card	die Karte	karter
dictionary	das Wörterbuch	*verter*-bookh
drawing paper	das Zeichenpapier	*tsykhen-pa*peer
drawing pin	die Reißzwecke	rice-*tsveck*er
elastic band	das Gummiband	*goommee-bant*
envelope	der Umschlag, das Kuvert	*oom*shlag, kouvair
felt-tip pen	der Filzstift	*filts*-shtift
glue/paste	der Leim/Klebstoff	lime/*klayb*-shtoff
guide book	der Reiseführer	*ryzer-fui*rer
ink	die Tinte	tinter

notebook	**das Notizbuch**	noh*tits*-bookh
paperclip	**die Heftklammer**	*heft*-klammer
pen	**der Stift**	shtift
pen cartridge	**die Füllerpatrone**	*fü*ler-pat*rohn*er
(coloured) pencil	**der Bleistift (Farbstift)**	*bly*-shtift (farb-shtift)
pencil sharpener	**Der Spitzer**	*shpit*ser
postcard	**die Postkarte**	*post*-karter
rubber/eraser	**der Radiergummi**	ra*deer-goom*mee
sellotape	**das Tesafilm**	*tay*zah-film
string	**das Band**	bant
sketch pad	**der Skizzenblock**	*skit*sen-block
(writing) paper	**das (Schreib-) Papier**	(*shryb*-) pa*peer*
wrapping paper	**das Packpapier**	*pack*-pa*peer*

CDs/DVDs

Can you recommend any CDs of local music?	**Können Sie CDs mit hiesiger Musik empfehlen?**	*Kern*en zee tsay-days mit *hee*zigur moo*zeek* emp*fay*len
Are there any new CDs by . . .?	**Gibt es neue CDs von . . .?**	Geebt es *noy*er tsay-days fon . . .
Have you any CDs by . . .?	**Haben Sie CDs von . . .?**	*Hah*ben zee tsay-days fon . . .
I'm looking for DVDs of . . .	**Ich suche DVDs von . . .**	Ikh *zook*her day-fow-days fon . . .

Chemist[1]

Can you prepare this prescription for me, please?	**Können Sie bitte dieses Rezept für mich zubereiten?**	Kernen zee bitter deezes ray*tsept* fuir mikh tsoo-bu-*ryten*
Have you a small first-aid kit?	**Haben Sie einen kleinen Verbandkasten?**	Hahben zee inen klinen *fair*bant-*kast*en
I'd like	**Ich möchte**	Ikh *merkh*ter
a pack of adhesive plasters	**eine Schachtel Hansaplast/ Heftpflaster**	iner *shakh*tel *hanzah*-plast/*heft*-pflaster
some aspirin	**Aspirin**	aspi*reen*
sun cream (for children)	**Sonnencreme (für Kinder)**	zonnen-*kray*mer (fuir kin-der)
Can you suggest something for	**Können Sie etwas gegen ... empfehlen?**	Kernen zee etvas *gay*gun ... emp*fay*len
constipation?	**Verstopfung**	fair*shtop*foong
diarrhoea?	**Durchfall**	*doorkh*fall
indigestion?	**Verdauungsstörung**	fair*dowoongs-shter*-roong
an upset stomach	**Magenverstimmung**	*mah*gun-fairsht*immung*
I'd like something for insect bites	**Ich möchte etwas gegen Insektenstiche**	Ikh *merkh*ter etvas *gay*gun inzekten-*shtikh*er

1. You go to an *Apotheke* for prescriptions, medicines, etc., and to a *Drogerie* for toiletries (see p. 196). See also Doctor (p. 141).

Can you give me something for sunburn?	**Können Sie mir etwas gegen Sonnenbrand geben?**	Kernen zee meer etvas *gay*gun zonnen-*brant gay*ben
I need some	**Ich brauche**	Ikh *browkher*
antiseptic cream	**antiseptische Creme**	antee-*zep*tisher *kray*mer
disinfectant	**Desinfektionsmittel**	des-infekts-*yons*-mittel
mouthwash	**Mundwasser**	*moont-vas*ser
nose drops	**Nasentropfen**	*nahsen-tropf*en
throat lozenges	**Halspastillen**	*hals*-pastillen
Do you have sanitary towels/tampons?	**Haben Sie Binden/ Tampons?**	Hahben zee binden/*tampons*
Do you sell contraceptives?	**Verkaufen Sie Verhütungsmittel?**	Fair*kow*fen zee fair*hui*toongs-mittel
I need something for a hangover/travel sickness	**Ich brauche etwas für einen Kater/ gegen Reiseübelkeit**	Ikh *browkh*er etvas fuir inen *kahter/gay*gen ryzer-*uib*el-kite

Clothes, Shoes and Accessories[1]

| I'd like a hat/sunhat | **Ich möchte einen Hut/Sonnenhut** | Ikh *merkh*ter inen hoot/*zonnen*-hoot |
| Where are beach clothes? | **Wo finde ich Strandkleidung?** | Voh fin-der ikh *shtrant-kly*doong |

1. For sizes see p. 184.

I'd like a short-/long-sleeved shirt, collar size ...	**Ich möchte ein Hemd mit kurzen/langen Ärmeln, Kragenweite ...**	Ikh *merkh*ter ine hemt mit *koorts*en/*lang*-en ermeln, *krah*gun-viter ...
Where is the underwear/haberdashery/coats department?	**Wo ist die Unterwäsche-/Kurzwaren-/Mantelabteilung?**	Voh ist dee *oonter*-vesher-/*koorts-vahren*-/*mantel*-*ap*-tyloong
Where can I find socks/tights?	**Wo finde ich Socken/Strumpfhosen?**	Voh fin-der ikh *zocken*/shroompf-*hoh*zen
I am looking for	**Ich suche**	Ikh zooker
a blouse	**eine Bluse**	iner *bloozer*
a bra	**einen BH**	inen bay-hah
a jumper	**einen Pullover**	inen pool-*ohv*er
I need	**Ich brauche**	Ikh *browkh*er
a coat	**einen Mantel**	inen *mantel*
a jacket	**eine Jacke**	iner *yacke*r
a raincoat	**einen Regenmantel**	inen *raygun-man*tel
a pair of trousers	**eine Hose**	iner *hohz*er
Do you have other colours?	**Haben Sie andere Farben?**	Hahben zee *anderer* farben
What size is this?	**Welche Größe ist das?**	Velkher *grers*er ist das
I take size ...	**Ich brauche Größe ...**	Ikh *brouwkh*er *grers*er ...

May I try it on?	**Kann ich es anprobieren?**	Kan ikh es *anprohbeer*en
Is there a mirror?	**Gibt es einen Spiegel?**	Geebt es inen *shpee*gul
It's too	**Es ist zu**	Es ist tsoo
long	**lang**	lang
loose	**weit**	vite
short	**kurz**	koorts
tight	**eng**	aing
Have you a larger/ smaller one?	**Haben Sie ein größeres/kleineres**	Hahben zee ine *grer*seres/klineres
I need something warmer/thinner	**Ich brauche etwas Wärmeres/ Dünneres**	Ikh *browkh*er etvas *vair*meres/*duin*neres
Is it colour fast?	**Ist es farbecht?**	Ist es farb-ekht
Is it machine washable?	**Ist es waschmaschinenfest?**	Ist es *vash*-ma*sheen*en-fest
Will it shrink?	**Läuft es ein?**	Loyft es ine
I'd like a pair of	**Ich möchte ein Paar**	Ikh *merkh*ter ine pahr
black shoes	**schwarze Schuhe**	*shvarts*er shoo-wer
boots	**Stiefel**	*shtee*fel
sandals	**Sandalen**	san*dah*len
trainers	**Turnschuhe**	*toorn*-shoo-wer
walking shoes	**Wanderschuhe**	*vander*-shoo-wer

Clothing sizes
WOMEN'S CLOTHING
coats, dresses, skirts, tops, trousers

UK/Australia	8	10	12	14	16	18
USA/Canada	6	8	10	12	14	16
Europe	38	40	42	44	46	48

shoes

UK	4	5	6	7	8	9	10
USA/Canada	5$\frac{1}{2}$	6$\frac{1}{2}$	7$\frac{1}{2}$	8$\frac{1}{2}$	9$\frac{1}{2}$	10$\frac{1}{2}$	11$\frac{1}{2}$
Europe	37	38	39/40	41	42	43	44

MEN'S CLOTHING
suits and coats

UK/USA/Canada	36	38	40	42	44	46
Europe	46	48	50	52	54	56

shirts

UK/USA/Canada	14	14$\frac{1}{2}$	15	15$\frac{1}{2}$	16	16$\frac{1}{2}$	17
Europe	36	37	38	39	40	41	42

shoes

UK	9$\frac{1}{2}$	10	10$\frac{1}{2}$	11	11$\frac{1}{2}$
USA/Canada	10	10$\frac{1}{2}$	11	11$\frac{1}{2}$	12
Europe	43	44	44	44	45

Food[1]

Give me a kilo/half a kilo (pound) of ... please	**Geben Sie mir bitte ein Kilo/ein halbes Kilo (ein Pfund) ...**	*Gay*ben zee meer ine keeloh/ine halbes keeloh (ine pfoont) ...
100 grams of sweets, please	**Ich möchte bitte hundert Gramm Bonbons**	Ikh *merkh*ter bitter *hoon*dert gramm bonbons
A bottle of wine/beer, please	**Eine Flasche Wein/ Bier bitte**	Iner *flash*er vine/beer bitter
A litre of semi-skimmed/full milk please	**Ein Liter halbfette Milch/Vollmilch**	Ine liter halb-fetter milkh/*foll*-milkh
A carton of plain yoghurt	**Eine Packung Naturjoghurt**	Iner packoong natoor-*yogh*urt
A dozen eggs	**Ein Dutzend Eier**	Ine *doot*sent eyer
A bottle of mineral water	**Eine Flasche Mineralwasser**	Iner *flash*er mine*rahl-vass*er
I'd like	**Ich möchte**	Ikh *merkh*ter
a jar of ...	**ein Glas ...**	ine glahs ...
a packet of ...	**ein Paket ...**	ine pa*kayt* ...
... slices of ham	**... Scheiben Schinken**	... *shyben shinken*
300 grams of cheese	**dreihundert Gramm Käse**	dry-*hoon*dert gramm *kayzer*
a tin (can) of ...	**eine Dose ...**	iner *dohz*er ...

1. See also the various menu sections (p. 111 onwards) and Weights and Measures (pp. 237–41).

Do you sell frozen foods?	**Verkaufen Sie Tiefkühlkost?**	Fair*kow*fen zee *teef*-kuil-kost
These pears are too hard/soft	**Diese Birnen sind zu hart/weich**	Deezer birnen zint tsoo hart/vykh
Is it fresh?	**Ist es frisch?**	Ist es frish
Are they ripe?	**Sind sie reif?**	Zind zee rife
This is bad/stale	**Dies ist schlecht/alt**	Deez ist shlekht/alt
A loaf of bread, please	**Ein Brot bitte**	Ine broht bitter
Wholemeal/Dark ryebread	**das Vollkornbrot/ Schwarzbrot**	Foll-korn-broht/ shvarts-broht
Ryebread	**das Graubrot**	Grouw-broht
White bread	**das Weißbrot**	Vice-broht
How much a kilo/ bottle?	**Wie teuer ist ein Kilo/eine Flasche?**	Vee *toyer* ist ine keeloh/ iner *flash*er
A kilo of sausages	**Ein Kilo Wurst**	Ine keeloh voorst
Four pork chops	**Vier Schweinekoteletts**	Feer *shvine*-er-koteletts
Will you mince the meat?	**Können Sie das Fleisch hacken?**	Kernen zee das flysh hacken
Please can you clean the fish?	**Können Sie bitte den Fisch ausnehmen?**	Kernen zee bitter den fish *ows-naymen*
Is there any shellfish?	**Haben Sie Schalentiere?**	Hahben zee *shahlen- teerer*
Shall I help myself?	**Darf ich mich bedienen?**	Darf ikh mikh bu*dee*enen

Hairdresser and Barber

May I make an appointment for this morning/tomorrow afternoon?	**Kann ich mich für heute Morgen/morgen Nachmittag anmelden?**	Kan ikh mikh fuir *hoyter morgun/morgun* nahkh-mit-tahg *an*-melden
What time?	**Zu welcher Zeit?**	Tsoo *velkher* tsite
I'd like my hair cut	**Ich möchte mir die Haare schneiden lassen**	Ikh *merkh*ter meer dee hahrer *shnyd*en lassen
I'd like my hair trimmed, please	**Schneiden Sie mein Haar bitte nur ein bisschen kürzer**	*Shnyd*en zee mine hahr bitter noor ine *bissk*hen *kuirt*ser
Not too short at the sides	**Nicht zu kurz an den Seiten**	Nikht tsoo koorts an dain ziten
I'll have it shorter at the back, please	**Hinten möchte ich es bitte kürzer haben**	Hinten *merkh*ter ikh es bitter *kuirt*ser hahben
That's fine, thank you	**So ist es gut, danke**	Zoh ist es goot danker
Could you give me a shave, please?	**Könnten Sie mich rasieren?**	Kernten zee mikh rah*zee*ren
Could you trim my beard/moustache?	**Könnten Sie meinen Bart/Schnurrbart beschneiden?**	Kernten zee meer minen bart/shnoor-bart bu-*shnyd*en
My hair is oily/dry	**Mein Haar ist fettig/trocken**	Mine hahr ist *fett*ikh/trocken
I'd like a shampoo	**Waschen bitte**	Vashen bitter

Please use conditioner	Benutzen Sie bitte Haarspülung	Bunootsen zee bitter *hahr-shpui*loong
I'd like my hair washed, styled and blow-dried	Ich möchte mir die Haare waschen, stylen und fönen lassen	Ikh *merkh*ter meer dee hahrer vashen, *stylen* oont *fern*en lassen
Please do not use hairspray	Bitte benutzen Sie kein Haarspray	Bitter bunootsen zee kine hahr-shpray
I want a colour rinse	Ich möchte einen Farbfestiger	Ikh *merkh*ter inen *farb*-festigur
May I see a colour chart, please	Kann ich bitte eine Farbskala sehen?	Kan ikh bitter iner *farbs*-kahlah *zay*en
I'd like a darker/ lighter shade	Ich möchte einen dunkleren/helleren Farbton	Ikh *merkh*ter inen *doon*kleren/*hell*eren *farb*-tohn
I'd like a tint/ highlights	Ich hätte gern eine Farbtönung/ Strähnchen	Ikh hetter gairn iner *farb*-ternoong/ *shtren*-khen
The water is too cold	Das Wasser ist zu kalt	Das *vasser* ist tsoo kalt
The dryer is too hot	Die Trockenhaube ist zu heiß	Dee trocken-*how*ber ist tsoo hice
Thank you, I like it very much	Danke, so gefällt es mir gut	Danker, zoh ge*felt* es meer goot
I'd like a manicure	Ich möchte mich maniküren lassen	Ikh *merkh*ter mikh manee*kui*ren lassen

Hardware and Outdoors[1]

Where is the camping equipment?	Wo ist die Camping-/Zeltausrüstung?	Voh ist dee *kamping-/*tselt-*ows*-ruistoong
Do you have a battery for this?	Haben Sie hierfür eine Batterie?	Hahben zee heer-fuir iner batt*ree*
Where can I get butane gas?	Wo kann ich Butangas bekommen?	Voh kan ikh boo*tahn*-gahs bu*kom*men
I need a	Ich brauche einen	Ikh *browkh*er inen
bottle opener	Flaschenöffner	*flashen-erf*ner
corkscrew	Korkenzieher	*korken*-tsee-yer
tin opener	Dosenöffner	*dohzen-erf*ner
A small/large screwdriver	Ein kleiner/großer Schraubenzieher	Ine kliner/grosser *shrowben*-tsee-yer
I'd like	Ich möchte	Ikh *merkh*ter
a (pen) knife	ein (Taschen-) Messer	ine (tashen-) *messer*
a pair of scissors	eine Schere	iner *shay*rer
some candles/matches	Kerzen/Streichhölzer	*strykh-herl*tser
a torch	Taschenlampe	*tashen-lam*per
Do you sell string/rope?	Verkaufen Sie Schnur/Tau?	Fair*kow*fen zee shnoor/tow
Where can I find	Wo finde ich	Voh fin-der ikh
cleaning cream?	Scheuercreme?	*shoyer-kray*mer
a dishcloth?	ein Geschirrtuch?	ine gu-*sheer*-tookh
a scrubbing sponge?	einen Scheuerschwamm?	*shoyer*-shvam
washing-up liquid?	Spülmittel?	*spuil*-mittel

1. See also Camping plot and Apartments and Villas p. 74

I need	**Ich brauche**	Ikh *browkh*er
a bucket	**einen Eimer**	inen *eye*mer
a brush	**eine Bürste**	iner *buir*ster
a frying pan	**eine Bratpfanne**	iner *braht*-pfanner
a groundsheet	**eine Zeltbahn**	iner tselt-bahn
I want to buy a barbecue	**Ich möchte einen Grill kaufen**	Ikh *merkh*ter inen grill *kow*fen
Do you sell charcoal?	**Verkaufen Sie Holzkohle?**	Fair*kow*fen zee *holts*-kohler
adaptor	**der Adapter**	adapter
basket	**der Korb**	korb
duster	**das Staubtuch**	*shtowp*-tuikh
electrical flex	**die Leitungsschnur**	*lite*-oongs-shnoor
extension lead	**die Verlängerungsschnur**	fair*leng*-eroongs-shnoor
fuse	**die Sicherung**	*zikh*eroong
fuse wire	**der Sicherungsdraht**	*zikh*eroongs-draht
insulating tape	**das Isolierband**	iso*leer*-band
light bulb	**die Glühbirne**	*glui-beer*ner
plug (*bath*)	**der Badewannenstopfen**	*bah*der-vannen-shtopfen
plug (*electric*)	**der Stecker**	*shtec*ker

Laundry and Dry Cleaning

Where is the nearest launderette/dry cleaner?	**Wo ist die nächste Schnellwäscherei/ Reinigung?**	Voh ist dee *naikh*ster *shnell*-vesher-*eye*/rynigoong
I'd like to have these things washed/ cleaned	**Ich möchte diese Sachen waschen lassen/reinigen lassen**	Ikh *merkh*ter deezer zackhen *vash*en lassen/rynigun lassen
Can you get this stain out?	**Können Sie diesen Flecken rausmachen?**	Kernen zee deezen flecken *rows*-makhen
It is coffee/wine/ grease	**Es ist Kaffee/Wein/ Fett**	Es ist kaf*fay*/vine/fett
These stains won't come out	***Diese Flecken gehen nicht raus**	Deezer flecken *gay*en nikht rows
It only needs to be pressed	**Es muss nur geplättet (gebügelt) werden**	Es mooss noor gu*plet*et (gu*buig*elt) *vair*den
This is torn. Can you mend it?	**Dies ist zerrissen. Können Sie es ausbessern?**	Dees ist tsair-*rissen*. Kernen zee es *ows*-bessern
There's a button missing	**Hier fehlt ein Knopf**	Heer failt ine k-nopf
Will you sew on another one, please?	**Würden Sie bitte einen anderen annähen?**	*Vuir*den zee bitter inen *an*deren *an*-na*yen*
When will they be ready?	**Wann sind sie fertig?**	Van zint zee *fair*tikh
I need them by this evening/tomorrow	**Ich brauche sie bis heute Abend/Morgen**	Ikh *browkh*er zee bis *hoyter* ahbent/*morgun*

Call back at five o'clock	*Kommen Sie um fünf Uhr wieder	Kommen zee oom fuinf oor veeder
We can't do it until Tuesday	*Wir können es nicht vor Dienstag machen	Veer kernen es nikt for deens-tahg makhen
It will take three days	*Es dauert drei Tage	Es dowert dry tahgur
This isn't mine	Das ist nicht von mir	Das ist nikht fon mir
I've lost my ticket	Ich habe mein Ticket verloren	Ikh hahber mine ticket fairlohren

Household laundry

bath towel	das Badehandtuch	bahder-hant-tookh
(woollen) blanket	die (Woll-) Decke	(voll-) decker
napkin	die Serviette	servee-yetter
pillowcase	der Kissenbezug	kissen-bu-tsoog
sheet	das Laken	lahken
tablecloth	die Tischdecke	tish-decker
tea towel	das Geschirrtuch	gu-sheer-tookh

Markets

Which day is market day?	An welchem Tag ist Markt?	An velkhem tahg ist markt
Where is the market held?	Wo ist der Markt?	Voh ist dair markt
Is it a permanent/ covered market?	Ist es eine Markthalle/ein überdachter Markt?	Ist es iner markt-haller/ ine uiber-dakhter markt

What time does it start?	**Wann fängt der Markt an?**	Van fengt dair markt an
When does it finish?	**Wann schließt er?**	Van shleest er
Is there a market today in a nearby town?	**Gibt es heute in der Umgebung einen Markt?**	Geebt es *hoy*ter in der oom*gay*boong inen markt

Photography

I'd like to buy	**Ich möchte ... kaufen**	Ikh *merkh*ter ... *kow*fen
a camcorder	**einen Camcorder**	inen camcorder
a digital camera	**eine Digitalkamera**	iner dig-ee-*tahl*-kamairah
a disposable camera	**eine Wegwerfkamera**	iner *vek*-wairf-kamairah
Do you have a memory card for this camera?	**Haben Sie eine Speicherkarte für diese Kamera?**	Hahben zee iner *shpykh*er-karter fuir deezer kamairah
Can you print photos from this card/disk/USB?	**Können Sie von dieser Karte/Diskette/USB-Stick Fotos drucken?**	Kernen zee fon deezer karter/dis*ket*ter/oo-ess-bay-shtick fohtohs *drook*en
I'd like ... prints of this image	**Ich möchte ... Fotoabzüge von diesem Bild**	Ikh *merkh*ter ... fohtoh-*ap*-tsuigur fon deezem bilt
I'd like to enlarge this image	**Ich möchte dieses Bild vergrößern lassen**	Ikh *merkh*ter deezez bilt fair*grer*sern lassen
I'd like the express service please	**Ich hätte gern den Schnelldienst**	Ikh hetter gairn den *shnell*-deenst

When will it be ready?	**Wann ist es fertig?**	Van ist es *fair*tikh
Will it be done tomorrow?	**Ist es morgen fertig?**	Ist es *morgun fair*tikh
My camera's not working. Can you mend it?	**Meine Kamera funktioniert nicht. Können Sie sie reparieren?**	Miner kamair*ah* foonkts-yon*eert* nikht. Kernen zee zee repah*reeren*
You will have to leave it for a few days	***Sie müssen sie ein paar Tage hier lassen**	Zee muissen zee ine pahr *tah*gur heer lassen

battery	**die Batterie**	battair*ee*
filter	**der Filter**	*fil*tair
lens	**die Linse**	*lin*zer
lens cap	**die Linsenkappe**	*lin*zenkapper
light meter	**der Lichtmesser**	*likht*messair

Repairs

This is broken; could you mend it?	**Dies ist kaputt; können Sie es reparieren?**	Dees ist kah*poot*; kernen zee es repah*reeren*
Could you do it while I wait?	**Können Sie es machen, während ich warte?**	Kernen zee es makhen *vair*ent ikh *var*ter
When should I come back for it?	**Wann kann ich es abholen?**	Van kan ikh es *ap*-hohlen

I'd like these shoes soled (with leather)	**Ich möchte an diesen Schuhen (Leder-) Sohlen haben**	Ikh *merkh*ter an deezen shoo-wen (*layder-*) zohlen hahben
I'd like them heeled (with rubber)	**Ich möchte (Gummi-) Absätze haben**	Ikh *merkh*ter (*goommee-*) *ap*-zetser hahben
Do you sell shoelaces?	**Verkaufen Sie Schnürsenkel?**	Fair*kow*fen zee shnuir-zenkel
My watch is broken	**Meine Uhr ist kaputt**	Miner oor ist kah*poot*
I have broken the glass/strap	**Das Glas/Der Riemen ist kaputt**	Das glahs/Dair *ree*men ist kah*poot*
Could you mend this bag for me, please?	**Könnten Sie bitte diese Tasche reparieren?**	Kernten zee bitter deezer tasher repah*ree*ren
Could you put in a new zip?	**Könnten Sie den Reißverschluss erneuern?**	Kernten zee den *rice*-fair*shlooss* ernoyern
The stone/charm/ screw has come loose	**Der Stein/Der Anhänger/Die Schraube ist lose**	Dair shtine/Dair *an*-heng-er/Die *shrow*ber ist *loh*zer
The fastener/clip/ chain is broken	**Der Verschluss/ Die Spange/ Die Kette is kaputt**	Dair fair*shlooss*/ Dee *shpang*-er/ Dee ketter is kah*poot*
It can't be repaired	***Es kann nicht repariert werden**	Es kan nikht raypah*reert* vairden
You need a new one	***Sie brauchen etwas Neues**	Zee *brouwkh*en etvas *noy*es
How much would a new one cost?	**Wie viel kostet ein neuer/eine neue/ein neues?**	Vee feel kostet ine *noy*er/ iner *noy*er/ine *noy*es

Toiletries[1]

A packet of razor blades, please	**Eine Schachtel Rasierklingen bitte**	Iner *shakh*tel rah*zeer*-kling-en bitter
How much is this aftershave lotion?	**Wie teuer ist dieses Rasierwasser?**	Vee toyer ist deezes rah*zeer*-vasser
A tube of toothpaste, please	**Eine Tube Zahnpasta bitte**	Iner toober *tsahn*-pasta bitter
A box of paper handkerchiefs, please	**Eine Packung Papiertaschentücher bitte**	Iner *packoong* pa*peer* tashen-*tuikh*er bitter
A roll of toilet paper, please	**Eine Rolle Toilettenpapier bitte**	Iner *rol*-ler twah*letten*-pa*peer* bitter
I'd like some eau-de-cologne/perfume	**Ich möchte Kölnisch Wasser/Parfüm**	ikh *merkh*ter *kern*lish vasser/parfoom
May I try it?	**Kann ich es ausprobieren?**	Kan ikh es *ows*-prohbeeren
A bottle/tube of shampoo, please, for dry/greasy hair	**Eine Flasche/Tube Schampoo bitte für trockenes/fettiges Haar**	Iner *flasher*/toober *shampoh* fuir trockenes/*fett*iges hahr
Do you have any sun cream?	**Haben Sie Sonnencreme?**	Hahben zee *zonnen*-*kray*mer
I'd like	**Ich möchte**	Ikh *merkh*ter
a bar of soap	**ein Stück Seife**	ine shtuick *zyfer*
cleansing cream/lotion	**Reinigungslotion**	*rynigoongs*-lots-*yon*

1. You go to an *Apotheke* for prescriptions, medicines, etc. (see Chemist, p. 180), and to a *Drogerie* for toiletries.

hair conditioner	**Haarspülung**	hahr-*shpui*loong
hand cream	**Handcreme**	hant-*kray*mer
lip salve	**Labello**	labello
moisturizer	**Feuchtigkeitscreme**	*fuikh*tik-kites-*kray*mer

SIGHTSEEING[1]

1. See also Getting Around (pp. 18–54).

What should we see here?	**Was ist hier sehenswert?**	Vas ist here *zayens*-vert
Can you suggest an interesting half-day excursion?	**Können Sie einen interessanten Halbtagsausflug empfehlen?**	Kernen zee inen interess*anten* halp-tahgs-*ows*-floog emp*faylen*
Can we take a boat cruise/balloon flight?	**Können wir eine Bootsfahrt/einen Ballonflug machen?**	Kernen veer iner *bohts*-fahrt/inen ballon-floog makhen
We want to go hiking.	**Wir möchten wandern gehen**	Veer *merkh*ten *vand*ern *gay*en
Do we need a guide?	**Brauchen wir einen Führer?**	*Browkh*en veer inen *fuirer*
It's	**Das ist**	Das ist
beautiful	**wunderschön**	*voond*er-shern
funny	**komisch**	*kohm*ish
impressive	**beeindruckend**	bu-*ine*-drookent
romantic	**romantisch**	rom*antish*
stunning	**herrlich**	*hair*likh
unusual	**ungewöhnlich**	*oon*-guvern*likh*

Exploring

| I'd like to walk around the old town | **Ich möchte durch die Altstadt bummeln** | Ikh *merkh*ter doorkh dee *alt*-shtat boomeln |
| Is there a good street plan showing the monuments? | **Gibt es einen guten Stadtplan mit den Sehenswürdigkeiten?** | Geebt es inen gooten shtat-plahn mit den *zayens*-*vuir*dikh-kiten |

Which bus goes to the castle?	**Welcher Bus fährt zum Schloss?**	*Velkh*er boos fairt tsoom shloss
We want to visit	**Wir möchten ... besichtigen**	Veer *merkh*ten ... buz*ikh*tigun
the cathedral	**die Kathedrale**	dee katay-*drah*ler
the cloister	**das Kloster**	das *klohs*ter
the fortress	**die Burg**	dee boorg
the library	**die Bibliothek**	dee beeblee-yoh-*taik*
the monastery	**das Stift**	das shteeft
the palace	**den Palast**	dain pa*last*
May we walk around the walls?	**Können wir an den Mauern entlang gehen?**	Kernen veer un den *mou*wern ent*lang gay*en
May we go up the tower?	**Können wir auf den Turm steigen?**	Kernen veer owf dain toorm *shty*gun
Where do we find antique shops/the flea market?	**Wo finden wir Antikläden/ Flohmärkte?**	Voh fin-den veer an*teek*-*lay*den/ floh-*mairk*ter
What's this building?	**Was für ein Gebäude is das?**	Vas fuir ine gu*boy*der ist das
Which is the oldest building in the city?	**Welches ist das älteste Gebäude in der Stadt?**	*Velkh*es ist das *el*tester gu*boy*der in dair shtat
What's the name of this church?	**Wie heißt diese Kirche?**	Vee hyst deezer *kirkh*er

Gardens, Parks and Zoos

Where is the botanic garden/zoo?	**Wo ist der botanische Garten/ der Zoo?**	Voh ist der bo*tah*nisher garten/der tsoh
How do I get to the park?	**Wie komme ich zum Park?**	Vee *komm*er ikh tsoom park
Can we walk there?	**Können wir zu Fuß gehen?**	Kernen veer tsoo foos *gay*en
Can we drive through the park?	**Können wir durch den Park fahren?**	Kernen veer doorkh den park fahren
Are the gardens open to the public?	**Sind die Gärten für Publikum geöffnet?**	Zint dee gerten fuir *poo*blikoom gu-*erf*net
What time do the gardens close?	**Wann schließen die Gärten?**	Van *shlees*sen dee gerten
Is there a plan of the gardens?	**Gibt es eine Karte von den Gärten?**	Geebt es iner karter fon den gerten
Who designed the gardens?	**Wer hat die Gärten entworfen?**	Vair hat dee gerten ent-*vor*fen
Where is the tropical plant house/lake?	**Wo ist das Gewächshaus/der See?**	Voh ist das guvekhshows/der zay

Historic Sites

We want to visit ... Can we get there by car?	**Wir möchten nach ... mit dem Auto hinfahren. Geht das?**	Veer *merkh*ten nahkh ... mit dem *ow*toh *hin*fahren. Gayt das

Is it far to walk?	**Ist es weit zu Fuß?**	Ist es vite tsoo foos
Is it an easy walk?	**Ist es leicht zu Fuß?**	Ist es lykht tsoo foos
Is there access for wheelchairs?	**Gibt es Zugang für Rollstühle?**	Geebt es *tsoo*gang fuir *rol-shtui*ler
Is it far to	**Ist es weit bis**	Ist es vite bis
the acqueduct?	**zum Aquädukt?**	tsoom ak-vay-*dookt*
the castle?	**zum Schloss?**	tsoom shloss
the fort?	**zur Burg?**	tsoor boorg
the fortifications?	**zur Befestigungsanlage?**	tsoor bu*fes*tigoongs-*an*-lahgur
the fountain?	**zum Brunnen?**	tsoom broonen
the gate?	**zum Tor?**	tsoom tohr
the ruins?	**zu den Ruinen?**	tsoo dain roo-*wee*nen
the walls?	**zu den Mauern?**	tsoo dain *mou*wern
When was it built?	**Wann wurde es gebaut?**	Van voorder es gu*bowt*
Who built it?	**Wer hat es gebaut?**	Vair hat es gu*bowt*

Museums and Galleries

When is the museum open?	**Wann ist das Museum geöffnet?**	Van ist das moo*zay*oom gu-*erf*net
Is it open every day?	**Ist es jeden Tag geöffnet?**	Ist es *yay*den tahg gu-*erf*net

The gallery is closed on Mondays	*Die Galerie ist montags geschlossen	Dee galai*ree* ist *mohn*-tahgs gu-*shlossen*
Is there wheelchair access?	Gibt es Zugang für Rollstühle?	Geebt es *tsoo*gang fuir *rol-shtui*ler
How much does it cost?	Wie viel Eintritt kostet es?	Vee feel *ine*-tritt kostet es
Are there reductions for	Gibt es Ermäßigungen für	Geebt es air*messi*goong-un fuir
children?	Kinder?	kin-der
seniors?	Senioren?	zenee-*yohren*
students?	Studenten?	shtoo*denten*
Is there a family ticket?	Gibt es ein Familienticket?	Geebt es ine fa*meel*-yen-ticket
Are admission fees reduced on any particular day?	Gibt es an bestimmten Tagen eine Eintrittsermäßigung?	Geebt es an bu-*shtimm*ten *tahg*un iner *ine*-trits-air*messi*goong
Admission free	*Eintritt frei	*Ine*-tritt fry
Have you a ticket?	*Haben Sie eine Eintrittskarte?	Hahben zee iner *ine*-trits-karter
Where do I get tickets?	Wo bekomme ich Eintrittskarten?	Voh bu*komme* ikh *ine*-trits-karten
Are there guided tours of the museum?	Gibt es Führungen durch das Museum?	Geebt es *fuir*oong-en durkh das moo*za*yoom
Does the guide speak English?	Spricht der Führer Englisch?	Shprikht dair *fui*rer *aing*-lish

Is there an audio guide in English?	**Gibt es einen Audioführer auf Englisch?**	Geebt es inen owdee-yoh-*fuirer* owf *aing*-lish
We don't need a guide	**Wir brauchen keinen Führer**	Veer *browkh*en kinen *fuirer*
Where is the ... collection/exhibition?	**Wo ist die Sammlung/ Ausstellung ...?**	Voh ist dee ... *zam*loong/ *ows-shtel*loong
Please leave your bag in the cloakroom	***Bitte lassen Sie Ihre Tasche in der Garderobe**	Bitter lassen zee eerer tasher in dair garder-*rohb*er
It's over there	***Es ist dort drüben**	Es ist dort druiben
Can I take photographs?	**Kann ich fotografieren?**	Kan ikh fohtoh-grah*feer*en
Photographs are prohibited	***Fotografieren ist verboten**	Fohtoh-grah*feer*en ist fair*boht*en
Where can I get a catalogue?	**Wo kann ich einen Katalog bekommen?**	Voh kann ikh inen kata*lohg* bu*komm*en

Places of Worship

Where is	**Wo ist**	Voh ist dee
the Catholic church?	**die katholische Kirche?**	dee ka*tohl*isher *kirkh*er
the Protestant church?	**die evangelische Kirche?**	dee evan-*gay*-lisher *kirkh*er
the cathedral?	**die Kathedrale?**	dee katay-*drah*ler

the mosque?	**die Moschee?**	dee mo*shay*
the shrine?	**der Schrein?**	dair shrine
the synagogue?	**die Synagoge?**	dee zuinah-*gohg*ur
When is the mass/ service?	**Wann ist der Gottesdienst/ die Messe?**	Van ist dair *gottes-*deenst/dee messer

Tours

We'd like to take a coach tour round the sights	**Wir möchten eine Stadtrundfahrt machen**	Veer *merkh*ten iner *shtat-*roont-fahrt makhen
Is there boat ride?	**Gibt es eine Bootsfahrt?**	Geebt es iner *bohts*-fahrt
Is there an excursion to . . . tomorrow?	**Gibt es morgen einen Ausflug nach . . .?**	Geebt es *mor*gun inen *ows*-floog nahkh . . .
Is there a walking tour of the town?	**Gibt es einen geführten Rundgang durch die Stadt?**	Geebt es inen gufuirten roont-gang doorkh dee shtat
How long does the tour take?	**Wie lange dauert der Rundgang?**	Vee lang-er *dow*ert dair roont-gang
When does it leave?	**Wann geht es los?**	Van gait es los
When does it return?	**Wann ist er zu Ende?**	Van ist es tsoo ender
Does the coach stop at our hotel?	**Hält der Bus am Hotel?**	Helt dair boos am hoh*tel*
How much does the tour cost?	**Wie viel kostet die Tour?**	Vee feel kostet dee toor

Are all admission fees included?	**Sind die Eintrittspreise einbegriffen?**	Zint dee *ine*-trits-pryzer *ine*-bugriffen
Does it include lunch?	**Ist das Mittagessen einbegriffen?**	Ist das *mit*-tahg-essen *ine*-bugriffen
Could we stop here	**Können wir anhalten**	Kernen veer *an*-halten
to buy souvenirs?	**um Souvenirs zu kaufen?**	oom souvenirs tsoo *kow*fen
to get a bottle of water?	**um eine Flasche Wasser zu kaufen?**	oom iner *flasher vasser* tsoo *kow*fen
to take photographs?	**um Fotos zu machen?**	oom fohtohs tsoo makhen
to use the toilet?	**um zur Toilette zu gehen?**	oom tsoor twah*letter* tsoo *gay*en
How long do we stay here?	**Wie lange bleiben wir hier?**	Vee lang-er *bly*ben veer heer

SPORTS AND LEISURE[1]

Where is the nearest tennis court/golf course?	**Wo ist der nächste Tennisplatz/ Golfplatz?**	Vo ist dair *naikh*ster *tennis*-plats/*golf*-plats
Is there a gym/ running track?	**Gibt es ein Fitnesszentrum/ eine Laufbahn?**	Geebt es ine fitness-*tsen*trum/iner *lowf*-bahn
What is the charge per	**Wieviel kostet es pro**	Vas kostet es pro
day?	**Tag?**	tahg
game?	**Spiel?**	shpeel
hour?	**Stunde?**	*stoon*der
Is it a club?	**Ist es ein Verein?**	Ist es ine fair-*ine*
Do I need temporary membership?	**Muss ich Mitglied sein?**	Mooss ikh *mit*-gleet zine
Where can we go fishing?	**Wo können wir angeln?**	Voh kernen veer *ang*-eln
Can I hire	**Kann ich . . . mieten?**	Kan ikh . . . *mee*ten
clubs?	**Golfschläger**	golf-*shlay*gur
fishing tackle?	**ein Angelgerät**	ine *ang*-el-gurait
a racket?	**einen Tennisschläger?**	inen *tennis*-shlay*gur

---

1. See also By Bike or Moped (p. 47).

I want to go fishing. Do I need a permit?	**Ich möchte angeln gehen. Brauche ich einen Angelschein?**	Ikh *merkh*ter *ang*-eln *gay*en. *Browkh*er ikh inen *ang*-el-*shine*
Where do I get a permit?	**Wo bekomme ich einen (Angel-) Schein?**	Voh bu*kommer* ikh inen (*ang*-el-) shine
Is there a skating rink?	**Gibt es eine Eisbahn?**	Geebt es inerice-bahn
Can I hire skates?	**Kann ich Rollschuhe mieten?**	Kan ikh *rol*-shoo-wer *meeten*
I'd like to ride	**Ich würde gern reiten**	Ikh *vuird*er gairn *ry*ten
Is there a stable nearby?	**Gibt es in der Nähe einen Reitstall?**	Geebt es in dair *nay*er inen rite-shtal
Do you give riding lessons?	**Geben Sie Reitunterricht?**	*Gay*ben zee *rite*-oonterikht
I am an inexperienced/ a good rider	**Ich bin nie geritten/ Ich kann gut reiten**	Ikh bin nee gu-ritten/Ikh kan goot *ry*ten

Winter Sports

Can I hire skiing equipment?	**Kann ich eine Skiausrüstung leihen?**	Kan ikh iner *shee-ows*-ruistoong *ly*-en
Can I take lessons here?	**Kann ich hier Unterricht nehmen?**	Kan ikh here *oonter*-rikht *nay*men
I've never skied before	**Ich bin noch nie Ski gelaufen**	Ikh bin nokh nee *shee*-gu*low*fen

Are there runs for beginners/average skiers?	**Gibt es Pisten für Anfänger/ mittelmäßige Skiläufer?**	Geebt es pisten fuir *an*-feng-er/mittel-*messi*gur *shee-loy*fer
I'd like to go cross-country skiing	**Ich würde gern Skilanglauf machen**	Ikh vuirder gairn *shee*-lang-lowf makhen
Are there ski lifts?	**Gibt es Skilifts?**	Geebt es *shee*-lifts
Is there a cable car?	**Gibt es eine Seilbahn?**	Geebt es iner zile-bahn
Can I buy a lift pass?	**Kann ich einen Liftpass kaufen?**	Kan ikh inen lift-pass *kow*fen
Can we go snow-boarding?	**Können wir Snowboard fahren?**	Kernen veer snow-board fahren

At the Beach

Which is the best beach?	**Welches ist der beste Strand?**	*Velkhe*s ist dair bester shtrant
Is there a quiet beach near here?	**Gibt es einen ruhigen Strand in der Nähe?**	Geebt es inen roo-igun shtrant in dair *nay*er
Is it far to walk?	**Ist es weit zu gehen?**	Ist es vite tsoo *gay*en
Is there a bus to the beach?	**Fährt ein Bus zum Strand?**	Fairt ine boos tsoom shtrant
Is it a sandy/pebbly/ rocky beach?	**Ist es ein Sand-/ Kies-/Felsstrand?**	Ist es ine zant-/kees-/ fels-shtrant
Is swimming safe from this beach/bay?	**Ist das Baden an diesem Strand/ in dieser Bucht ungefährlich?**	Ist das *bah*den an deezem shtrant/ in deezer bookht *oon*-gu*fair*likh

Is it safe for small children?	**Können kleine Kinder hier ohne Gefahr baden?**	Kernen kliner kin-der heer ohner g*ufahr* *bah*den
Is there a lifeguard?	**Gibt es einen Rettungsschwimmer?**	Geebt es inen rettoongs-*shvim*mer
Bathing prohibited	***Baden verboten**	*Bah*den fair*boht*en
It's dangerous	***Es ist gefährlich**	Es ist g*ufair*likh
Is the tide rising/ falling?	**Ist Flut oder Ebbe?**	Ist floot ohder ebber
I'd like to hire a cabin for the day/morning	**Ich möchte eine Kabine für den Tag/ Morgen mieten**	Ikh *merkh*ter iner *kabee*ner fuir dain tahg/*morgun mee*ten
I'd like to hire a deckchair/sunshade	**Ich möchte einen Liegestuhl/ Sonnenschirm mieten**	Ikh *merkh*ter inen *leegur*-shtool/ *zonnen*-sheerm *mee*ten
Where can I buy	**Wo kann ich . . . kaufen?**	Vo kan ikh . . . *kow*fen
flippers?	**Schwimmflossen?**	*shvim*-flossen
a bucket and spade?	**einen Eimer und eine Schaufel?**	inen *eye*mer oont iner *show*fel
a snorkel?	**einen Schnorchel?**	inen *shnor*khel
ball	**der Ball**	bal
beach bag	**die Strandtasche**	shtrant-tasher
boat	**das Boot**	boht
crab	**der Krebs**	krebs

first aid	**der Verbandskasten**	fair*bants*-kasten
jellyfish	**die Qualle**	*k-vah*ler
lifevest	**die Rettungsweste**	*ret*toongs-vester
lighthouse	**der Leuchtturm**	loykht-toorm
outboard motor	**der Außenmotor**	*owssen*-moh*tor*
rockpool	**der Gezeitentümpel**	gu-*tsite*-en-tuimpel
sandbank	**die Sandbank**	zant-bank
sandcastle	**die Sandburg**	zant-boorg
shell	**die Muschel**	*moo*shel
sunglasses	**die Sonnenbrille**	*zonnen-brill*er
wave	**die Welle**	veller

Swimming

Is there an indoor/ outdoor swimming pool?	**Gibt es ein Hallenbad/Freibad?**	Geebt es ine *hal*-len-bat/*fry*-bat
Is it heated?	**Ist es beheizt?**	Ist es bu-*hyts*t
Is the water cold?	**Ist das Wasser kalt?**	Ist das *vass*er kalt
It's warm	**Es ist warm**	Es ist varm
Is it salt or fresh water?	**Ist es Salz- oder Süßwasser?**	Ist es zalts- ohder *zuis-vass*er
Can one swim in the lake/river?	**Kann man im See/ im Fluss baden?**	Kan man im zay/ im flooss *bah*den
There's a strong current here	***Die Strömung ist hier sehr stark**	Dee *shtrer*moong ist heer zair shtark

Are you a strong swimmer?	***Sind Sie ein tüchtiger Schwimmer?**	Zint zee ine *tuikh*tigur *shvim*mer
Is it deep?	**Ist es tief?**	Ist es teef
Are there showers?	**Gibt es Duschen?**	Geebt es *doo*shen
No lifeguard on duty	***Keine Rettungsschwimmer**	Kiner *ret*toongs-*shvim*mer
armbands	**die Armbinde**	*arm*-bin-der
goggles	**die Schwimmbrille**	*shvim*-bril*ler
rubber ring	**der Gummischlauch**	*goom*mee-shlowkh
swimsuit	**der Badeanzug**	*bah*der-an-tsoog
towel	**das Handtuch**	hant-tookh
trunks	**die Badehose**	*bah*der-*hoh*zer

Watersports

Can we water ski here?	**Können wir hier Wasserski laufen?**	Kernen veer here *vas*ser-shee *low*fen
I've never waterskied before	**Ich bin noch nie Wasserski gelaufen**	Ikh bin nokh nee *vas*ser-shee gu*low*fen
Can we hire the equipment?	**Können wir die Ausrüstung mieten?**	Kernen veer dee *ows*-ruistoong *mee*ten
Should I wear a life jacket?	**Soll ich eine Schwimweste tragen?**	Zoll ikh iner *shvim*-vester *trah*gun

Can I hire	**Kann ich ... mieten?**	Kan ikh ... *meet*en
diving equipment?	**Tauchausrüstung?**	*towkh*-ows-ruistoong
a jet ski?	**einen Jetski?**	inen jet-shee
a motor boat?	**ein Motorboot?**	ine moh*tor*-boht
a rowing boat?	**ein Ruderboot?**	ine *rooder*-boht
a sailing boat?	**ein Segelboot?**	ine *zay*gul-boht
waterskis?	**Wasserskis?**	*vasser*-shees
Do you have a course on windsurfing for beginners?	**Haben Sie einen Anfängerkurs für Windsurfing?**	Hahben zee inen *an*-feng-er-koors fuir windsurfing
Is there a map/chart of the river?	**Gibt es eine Karte/ Skizze des Flusses?**	Geebt es iner karter/*skitser* des floosses
Are there many locks to pass?	**Müssen wir durch viele Schleusen?**	Muissen veer durkh feeler *shlui*zen
Can we get fuel here?	**Können wir hier Treibstoff bekommen?**	Kernen veer here *tribe*-shtof bu*kommen*
Where's the harbour?	**Wo ist der Hafen?**	Voh ist dair hahfen
Can we go out in a fishing boat?	**Können wir in einem Fischkutter hinausfahren?**	Kernen veer in inem *fish*-kootter hinows-fahren
What does a boat cost by the hour?	**Wie viel kostet ein Boot pro Stunde?**	Vee feel kostet ine boht proh *shtoon*der

Walking[1]

I'd like a map of the area showing walking trails	**Ich hätte gern eine Landkarte mit Wanderwegen**	Ikh hetter gairn iner *lant*-karter mit *vander*-*vayg*un
Can we walk?	**Können wir zu Fuß gehen?**	Kernen veer tsoo foos *gayen*
How long is the walk to …?	**Wie lange ist es zu Fuß bis …?**	Vee lang-er ist es tsoo foos bis …
It's an hour's walk to …	***Man geht eine Stunde nach …**	Man gait iner *shtoon*der nahkh …
How far is the next village?	**Wie weit ist es bis zum nächsten Dorf?**	Vee vite ist es bis tsoom *naihkh*sten dorf
Which way is	**Wo liegt**	Voh leegt
the lake?	**der See?**	zay
the nature reserve?	**das Naturschutzgebiet?**	das na*toor*-shoots-gu*beet*
the waterfall?	**der Wasserfall?**	dair *vasser*-fal
Is there a scenic walk to …?	**Gibt es einen malerischen Weg nach …?**	Geebt es inen *mahl*erishen vayg nahkh …
Is it steep/far/difficult?	**Ist es steil/weit/schwer?**	Ist es shtile/vite/shvair
Is there a footpath to …?	**Gibt es einen Wanderweg nach …?**	Fuirt ine *vander*-vayg nahkh …
Is there a short cut?	**Gibt es einen kürzeren Weg?**	Geebt es inen *kuirt*seren vayg

1. See also Directions (p. 52).

| Is there a bridge across the stream? | **Gibt es eine Brücke über den Bach?** | Geebt es iner *bruicker uiber* den bakh |
| Can you give me a lift to …? | **Können Sie mich bis … mitnehmen?** | Kernen zee mikh bis… *mit-nay*men |

Spectator Sports and Indoor Games

We want to go to a football match/the tennis tournament	**Wir möchten uns ein Fußballspiel/ das Tennisturnier ansehen**	Veer *merkh*ten oons ine *foos*-bal-shpeel / das *tennis-toorneer an-zay*en
Where is the stadium?	**Wo ist das Stadion?**	Voh ist das shtad-*yon*
Are there any seats left in the grandstand?	**Gibt es noch Plätze auf der Haupttribüne?**	Geebt es nokh *plet*ser owf der *howpt*-tribuiner
Can you get us tickets?	**Können Sie uns Karten besorgen?**	Kernen zee oons karten bu*zorg*un
How much are the cheapest seats?	**Wie viel kosten die billigsten Plätze?**	Vee feel kosten dee *bil*likh-sten *plet*ser
Who's playing?	**Wer spielt?**	Vair shpeelt
When does it start?	**Wann fängt es an?**	Van fengt es an
What is the score?	**Wie steht's?**	Vee shtayts
Who's winning?	**Wer gewinnt?**	Vair gu*vinnt*
Where's the race course?	**Wo ist die Rennbahn?**	Voh ist dee *renn*-bahn
When's the next meeting?	**Wann ist das nächste Rennen?**	Vann ist das *naikh*ster rennen

Which is the favourite?	**Wer ist der Favorit?**	Vair ist dair favoh*reet*
What are the odds?	**Wie ist der Wettkurs?**	Vee ist dair *vett*-koors
Where can I place a bet?	**Wo kann ich eine Wette einreichen?**	Voh kan ikh iner *vetter ine-rykh*en
Do you play cards?	**Spielen Sie Karten?**	*Shpee*len zee karten
Would you like a game of chess?	**Möchten Sie Schach spielen?**	*Merkh*ten zee shakh *shpee*len

TRAVELLING WITH CHILDREN

Key Phrases

Are there any organized activities for children?	**Gibt es organisierte Aktivitäten für Kinder?**	Geebt es organzeerter aktiv*i*tayten fuir kin-der
Are children allowed?	**Sind Kinder zugelassen?**	Zint kin-der *tsoo*-gulassen
Is there a lower price for children?	**Gibt es eine Ermäßigung für Kinder?**	Geebt es air*mess*igoong fuir kin-der
Where can I feed/change my baby?	**Wo kann ich mein Baby füttern/frisch machen?**	Voh kan ikh mine baby fuittern/frish makhen
Can you put a child's bed/cot in our room?	**Können Sie ein Kinderbett in unser Zimmer stellen?**	Kernen zee ine kin-der-bet in oonzer tsimmer *shtel*len
My son/daughter is missing	**Mein Sohn/Meine Tochter wird vermisst**	Mine zohn/Miner *tokh*ter veert fair*mist*

Out and About[1]

Is there a park/ amusement park nearby?	**Gibt es in der Nähe einen Park/ Vergnügungspark?**	Geebt es in der *nayer* inen park/fair-*gnui*goongs park
Is there a toyshop here?	**Gibt es einen Spielzeugladen?**	Geebt es inen *shpeel*-tsoyg-*lahden*
Where is the aquarium/zoo?	**Wo ist das Aquarium/der Zoo?**	Voh ist das ak-*vahree*-oom/der tsoh
Is there	**Gibt es**	Geebt es
a children's swimming pool?	**ein Kinderschwimmbad?**	ine kin-der-*shvim*-baht
a games room?	**ein Spielzimmer?**	ine *shpeel*-tsimmer
a paddling pool?	**ein Planschbecken?**	ine plansch-becken
a playground?	**einen Spielplatz?**	inen *shpeel*-plats
Is the beach safe for children?	**Ist der Strand ungefährlich für Kinder?**	Ist der shtrant *oon*-gu*fair*likh fuir kin-der
Can we hire a canoe/ paddle boat?	**Können wir ein Kanu/Paddelboot mieten?**	kernen veer ine kah*noo*/paddel-boht *mee*ten
Are there snorkeling/ riding/skiiing lessons for children?	**Gibt es Schnorchel-/ Reit-/Skiunterricht für Kinder?**	Geebt es shn*or*khel-/*rite*-/*shee*-*oon*terikht fuir kin-der

1. See also At the Beach (p. 209).

I'd like	**Ich hätte gern**	Ikh hetter gairn
a doll	**eine Puppe**	iner poopper
roller skates	**Rollschuhe**	*rol*-shoo-wer
some playing cards	**Spielkarten**	*shpeel*-karten
He has lost his toy	**Er hat sein Spielzeug verloren**	Er hat zine *shpeel*-tsoyg fair*lohr*en
I'm sorry if they have bothered you	**Tut mir leid, dass sie sie gestört haben**	Toot meer lite dass zee zee gu-*shtert* hahben

Everyday Needs

Can you put a child's bed/cot in our room?	**Können Sie ein Kinderbett in unser Zimmer stellen?**	Kernen zee ine kin-der-bet in oonzer tsimmer *shtel*len
Can you give us adjoining rooms?	**Können Sie uns Nebenzimmer geben?**	Kernen zee oons *nay*ben-tsimmer *gay*ben
Does the hotel have a babysitting service?	**Hat das Hotel einen Babysitter-Service?**	Hat das hoh*tel* inen babysitter-service
Can you find me a babysitter?	**Können Sie mir einen Babysitter besorgen?**	Kernen zee meer inen babysitter buz*or*gun
We shall be out for a couple of hours	**Wir gehen für ein paar Stunden weg**	Veer *gay*en fuir ine pahr *shtoon*den vek
We shall be back at …	**Wir sind um … zurück**	Veer zint oom … tsoo-*ruick*

You can reach me at this number	**Sie können mich unter dieser Nummer erreichen**	Zee kernen mikh *oon*ter deezer noommer er-*rykh*en
This is my mobile (cell) number	**Das ist meine Handynummer**	Das ist miner handy-noommer
Is there a children's menu?	**Gibt es ein Kindermenü?**	Geebt es ine kin-der-menui
Do you have half portions for children?	**Haben Sie Kinderportionen?**	Hahben zee kin-der-portsee-*yon*en
Have you got a high chair?	**Haben Sie einen Kinderstuhl?**	Hahben zee inen kin-der-shtool
Where can I feed/change my baby?	**Wo kann ich mein Baby füttern/frisch machen?**	Voh kan ikh mine baby fuittern/frish makhen
Can you heat this bottle for me?	**Können Sie diese Flasche wärmen?**	Kernen zee deezer *flasher vair*men
I need	**Ich brauche**	Ikh *browkh*er
baby wipes	**Babyfeuchttücher**	baby-*foykht*-tuikher
a bib	**einen Schnuller**	inen *shnoo*ller
a feeding bottle	**eine Saugflasche**	iner *zowg-flasher*
some baby food	**Babynahrung**	baby-*nah*roong
some disposable nappies	**Wegwerfwindeln**	*vek*-vairf-*vind*eln

Health and Emergencies[1]

My daughter suffers from travel sickness	**Meiner Tochter ist von der Reise übel**	Miner *tokh*ter ist fon der *ryz*er uibel
She has hurt herself	**Sie hat sich verletzt**	Zee hat zikh fair*letst*
My son is ill	**Mein Sohn ist krank**	Mine zohn ist krank
He is allergic to...	**Er ist allergisch gegen...**	Er ist al*lairg*ish *gay*gun...
My son/daughter is missing	**Mein Sohn/Meine Tochter wird vermisst**	Mine zohn/Miner *tokh*ter veert fair*mist*
He/She is...years old	**Er/Sie ist...Jahre alt**	Er/Zee ist...*yahr*er alt
He/She is wearing...	**Er/Sie trägt...**	Er/Zee traigt...

1. See also Doctor (p. 141).

WORK[1]

I'm here on business	**Ich bin geschäftlich hier**	Ikh bin gu-*sheft*likh heer
Where is the conference centre?	**Wo ist das Konferenzzentrum?**	Voh ist das konfe*rence*-*tsen*trum
I'm here for the ... trade fair	**Ich bin hier für die ... Messe**	Ikh bin here fuir dee ... messer
I'm here for a conference/seminar	**Ich bin hier auf einer Konferenz/ einem Seminar**	Ikh bin here owf iner konfe*rence*/inem zemi*nar*
This is my colleague	**Das ist mein Kollege/meine Kollegin**	Das ist mine kol*layg*ur/ miner kol*layg*in
I have an appointment with ...	**Ich habe einen Termin mit ...**	Ikh hahber inen ter*meen* mit ...
Here is my card	**Hier ist meine Karte**	Here ist miner karter
Can you provide an interpreter?	**Können Sie mir einen Dolmetscher besorgen?**	Kernen zee meer inen *dol*metsher buzo*rg*un

1. See also Telephones, Mobiles and SMS (p. 86).

TIME AND DATES[1]

Telling the Time

What time is it?	Wie spät ist es?	Vee shpayt ist es
It's	Es ist	Es ist
one o'clock	ein Uhr	ine oor
two o'clock	zwei Uhr	tsvy oor
five past eight[2]	fünf (Minuten) nach acht	fuinf (minooten) nahkh akht
quarter past five	viertel nach fünf	feertel nahkh fuinf
twenty-five past eight	fünf vor halb neun	fuinf for halb noyn
half past nine	halb zehn	halb tsayn
twenty-five to seven	fünf nach halb sieben	fuinf nahkh halb zeeben
twenty to three	zwanzig vor drei	tsvan-tsikh for dry
quarter to ten	viertel vor zehn	feertel vor tsayn
7 a.m./7 p.m.	Sieben Uhr morgens/Sieben Uhr abends	Zeeben oor morguns/Zeeben oor ahbents
Second	die Sekunde	Zekoonder

1. Germany uses the 24-hour clock in formal contexts.
2. The basic sequence is: five, ten, quarter *past*; ten, five *to half*; half *to next hour*; five, ten *past half*; quarter, ten, five *to next hour*.

Minute	**die Minute**	Mee*noo*ter
Hour	**die Stunde**	*Shtoon*der
It's early/late	**Es ist früh/spät**	Es ist fruih/shpayt
My watch is slow/fast	**Meine Uhr geht nach/vor**	Miner oor gait nahkh/for
The clock has stopped	**Die Uhr ist stehengeblieben**	Dee oor ist *shtayen*gu*bleeben*
Sorry I'm late	**Entschuldigen Sie die Verspätung**	Ent*shool*digun zee dee fair*shpay*toong

Days of the Week

Monday	**Montag**	*Mohn*-tahg
Tuesday	**Dienstag**	*Deens*-tahg
Wednesday	**Mittwoch**	*Mit*-vokh
Thursday	**Donnerstag**	*Donners*-tahg
Friday	**Freitag**	*Fry*-tahg
Saturday	**Samstag, Sonnabend**	*Zams*-tahg, *Zon-ah*bent
Sunday	**Sonntag**	*Zon*-tahg

Months of the Year

January	**Januar**	*Yan*ooar
February	**Februar**	*Feb*rooar
March	**März**	Mairts

April	**April**	*April*
May	**Mai**	*My*
June	**Juni**	*Yoonee*
July	**Juli**	*Yoolee*
August	**August**	*Owgoost*
September	**September**	*Zeptember*
October	**Oktober**	*Octohber*
November	**November**	*Nohvember*
December	**Dezember**	*Daytsember*

Seasons

Spring	**der Frühling, das Frühjahr**	*Fruiling, frui-yahr*
Summer	**der Sommer**	*Zommer*
Autumn	**der Herbst**	*Hairbst*
Winter	**der Winter**	*Vinter*

Periods of Time

morning	**der Morgen**	*morgun*
this morning	**heute Morgen**	*hoyter morgun*
in the morning	**am Morgen/ Morgens**	am *morgun/morguns*

midday, noon	**der Mittag**	*mit*-tahg
at noon	**zu Mittag**	tsoo *mit*-tahg
afternoon	**der Nachmittag**	*nahkh-mit*-tahg
tomorrow afternoon	**morgen Nachmittag**	*morgun nahkh-mit*-tahg
evening	**der Abend**	*ahbent
night	**die Nacht**	nahkht
midnight	**Mitternacht**	*mit*ter-nahkht
tonight	**heute Abend**	*hoyter ahbent
last night	**gestern Abend**	*gestern ahbent
day	**der Tag**	tahg
today	**heute**	*hoyter
by day	**am Tag**	am tahg
yesterday	**gestern**	*gestern
day before yesterday	**vorgestern**	*for-gestern
two days ago	**vor zwei Tagen**	for tsvy *tahgun
tomorrow	**morgen**	*morgun
day after tomorrow	**übermorgen**	*uiber-morgun
in three days	**in drei Tagen**	in dry *tahgun
on Tuesday	**(am) Dienstag**	(am) *deens*-tahg
on Sundays	**sonntags**	*zon*-tahgs

week	**die Woche**	*vokh*er
weekend	**das Wochenende**	*vokh*en-ender
on weekdays	**an Wochentagen**	an *vokh*en-tahgun
every week	**jede Woche**	*yay*der *vokh*er
once a week	**einmal pro Woche**	ine-mahl pro *vokh*er
fortnight	**zwei Wochen/ vierzehn Tage**	tsvy *vokh*en/*feer*-tsayn *tah*ger
month	**der Monat**	moh*nat*
in March	**im März**	im mairts
since June	**seit Juni**	zite *yoo*nee
year	**das Jahr**	yahr
this year	**dieses Jahr**	*dee*zes yahr
last year	**voriges/ vergangenes Jahr**	*for*iges/fair*gang*-enes yahr
next year	**nächstes Jahr**	*naykh*stes yahr
in spring	**im Frühjahr**	im *frui*-yahr
during the summer	**während des Sommers**	*vair*ent des *zom*mers
sunrise	**der Sonnenaufgang**	*zonnen-owf*-gang
dawn	**das Morgengrauen, der Tagesanbruch**	*morgun-grouw*en/*tahges*-anbrookh
sunset	**der Sonnenuntergang**	*zonnen-oon*ter-gang
dusk, twilight	**das Zwielicht**	*tsvee*-likht

Dates

What's the date?	**Welches Datum ist heute?**	*Velkh*es *dah*toom ist *hoy*ter
It's December 9th	**Es ist der neunte Dezember**	Es ist dair *noyn*ter day*tsember*
We're leaving on January 5th	**Wir fahren am fünften Januar ab**	Veer fahren am *fuinf*ten *yan*ooar ap
We got here on July 27th	**Wir sind am siebenundzwanzigsten Juli angekommen**	Veer zint am *zeeben*-oont-*tsvan*-tsigsten *yoo*lee *an*-gu*kommen*

Public Holidays

1 January	**der Neujahrstag**	New Year's Day
6 February	**das Dreikönigsfest**	Epiphany (Austria only)
	der Karfreitag	Good Friday
	der Ostermontag	Easter Monday
1 May	**der Tag der Arbeit**	Mayday (not Switzerland)
	der Himmelfahrtstag	Ascension Day
	der Pfingstmontag	Whit Monday
	der Fronleichnam	Corpus Christi (Austria only)
15 August	**Mariä Himmelfahrt**	Ascension of the Virgin (Austria only)

3 October	**Tag der Deutschen Einheit**	Day of German Unity
1 November	**Allerheiligen**	All Saints (Austria only)
16 November	**Buß- und Bettag**	Day of Repentance and Prayer (Germany only)
8 December	**Mariä Empfängnis**	Conception Day (Austria only)
25 December	**der (erste) Weihnachtstag**	Christmas Day
26 December	**der zweite Weihnachtstag**	Boxing Day
31 December	**Silvester**	New Year's Eve

WEATHER

What is the weather forecast?	**Wie ist die Wettervorhersage?**	Vee ist dee *vetter*-for-hair-*zah*gur
What is the temperature?	**Wie ist die Temperatur?**	Vee ist dee tempera*toor*
It's going to be hot/cold today	**Heute wird es heiß/kalt**	*Hoy*ter veert es hice/kalt
It's	**Es ist**	Es ist
cloudy	**wolkig**	*vol*kikh
misty/foggy	**neblig**	*nay*blikh
sunny	**sonnig**	*zon*nikh
windy	**windig**	*vin*dikh
The mist will clear later	**Der Nebel wird sich später lichten**	Der *nay*bul veert zikh *shpay*ter *likh*ten
Will it be fine tomorrow?	**Ist morgen schönes Wetter?**	Ist *mor*gun *sher*nes *vet*ter
What lovely/awful weather	**Was für ein tolles/schreckliches Wetter**	Vas fuir ine *tol*les/*shreck*likhes *vet*ter
Do you think it will rain/snow?	**Glauben Sie, es wird regnen/schneien?**	*Glow*ben zee es veert *rayg*nen/*shny*-en
frost	**der Frost**	frost
hail	**der Hagel**	*hah*gul
humid	**feucht**	foykht
ice	**das Eis**	ice
storm	**das Gewitter**	gu*vit*ter

OPPOSITES

before/after	**vor/nach**	for/nahkh
early/late	**früh/spät**	frui/shpayt
first/last	**erste/letzte**	airster/letster
now/later, then	**jetzt/dann**	yetst/dan
far/near	**weit/nah**	vite/nah
here/there	**hier/dort**	heer/dort
in/out	**in/aus**	in/ows
inside/outside	**drinnen/draußen**	drinnen/*drowssen*
under/over	**unter/über**	*oonter/ui*ber
big, large/small	**groß/klein**	grohs/kline
deep/shallow	**tief/seicht**	teef/zykht
empty/full	**leer/voll**	layer/fol
fat/lean	**fett, dick/mager**	fet, dick/*mahg*ur
heavy/light	**schwer/leicht**	shvair/lykht
high/low	**hoch/niedrig**	hohkh/*need*rikh
long, tall/short	**lang/kurz**	lang/koorts
narrow/wide	**schmal/breit**	shmahl/brite
thick/thin	**dick/dünn**	dick/duin

least/most	**mindest/meist**	mindest/myst
many/few	**viel(e)/wenig(e)**	feel(er)/*vay*nikh (*vay*nigur)
more/less	**mehr/weniger**	mair/*vay*nigur
much/little	**viel/wenig**	feel/*vay*nikh
beautiful/ugly	**schön/hässlich**	shern/*hess*likh
better/worse	**besser/schlechter**	*besser/shlekh*ter
cheap/dear	**billig/teuer**	*bil*likh/*toy*er
clean/dirty	**sauber/schmutzig**	*zow*ber/*shmoot*sikh
cold/hot, warm	**kalt/heiß, warm**	kalt/hice, varm
easy/difficult	**leicht/schwierig**	lykht/*shvee*rikh
free/taken	**frei/besetzt**	fry/buze*tst*
fresh/stale	**frisch/schal, alt**	frish/shahl, alt
good/bad	**gut/schlecht**	goot/shlekht
new, young/old	**neu, jung/alt**	noy, yoong/alt
nice/nasty	**nett/eklig**	net/*ayk*-likh
open/closed, shut	**offen/geschlossen**	*off*en/gu-*shlos*sen
quick/slow	**schnell/langsam**	shnell/*lang*zam
quiet/noisy	**ruhig/laut**	roo-ikh/lowt
right/wrong	**richtig/falsch**	*rikh*-tikh/falsh
sharp/blunt	**scharf/stumpf**	sharf/*shtoompf*

NUMBERS

Cardinal

0	null	nool
1	eins	ines
2	zwei	tsvy
3	drei	dry
4	vier	feer
5	fünf	fuinf
6	sechs	zekhs
7	sieben	*zee*ben
8	acht	akht
9	neun	noyn
10	zehn	tsayn
11	elf	elf
12	zwölf	tsverlf
13	dreizehn	*dry*-tsayn
14	vierzehn	*feer*-tsayn
15	fünfzehn	*fuinf*-tsayn
16	sechzehn	*zekh*-tsayn
17	siebzehn	*zeeb*-tsayn

18	**achtzehn**	*akht*-tsayn
19	**neunzehn**	*noyn*-tsayn
20	**zwanzig**	*tsvan*-tsikh
21	**einundzwanzig**	ine-oont-*tsvan*-tsikh
22	**zweiundzwanzig**	tsvy-oont-*tsvan*-tsikh
30	**dreißig**	*dry*-sikh
31	**einunddreißig**	ine-oont-*dry*-sikh
32	**zweiunddreißig**	tsvy-oont-*dry*-sikh
40	**vierzig**	*feer*-tsikh
41	**einundvierzig**	ine-oont-*feer*-tsikh
50	**fünfzig**	*fuinf*-tsikh
51	**einundfünfzig**	ine-oont-*fuinf*-tsikh
60	**sechzig**	*zekh*-tsikh
61	**einundsechzig**	ine-oont-*zekh*-tsikh
70	**siebzig**	*zeeb*-tsikh
71	**einundsiebzig**	ine-oont-*zeeb*-tsikh
80	**achtzig**	*akht*-tsikh
81	**einundachtzig**	ine-oont-*akh*-tsikh
90	**neunzig**	*noyn*-tsikh
91	**einundneunzig**	ine-oont-*noyn*-tsikh
100	**hundert**	*hoon*dert
101	**hunderteins**	*hoon*dert-*ines*
200	**zweihundert**	*tsvy-hoon*dert

1,000	**tausend**	*towzent*
2,000	**zweitausend**	*tsvy-towzent*
1,000,000	**eine Million**	iner meel-*yon*

Ordinal

1st	**der erste**	airster
2nd	**zweite**	tsviter
3rd	**dritte**	*dritter*
4th	**vierte**	*feerter*
5th	**fünfte**	*fuinfter*
6th	**sechste**	*zekhster*
7th	**siebte**	*zeebter*
8th	**achte**	*akhter*
9th	**neunte**	*noynter*
10th	**zehnte**	*tsaynter*
11th	**elfte**	*elfter*
12th	**zwölfte**	*tsverlfter*
13th	**dreizehnte**	*dry-tsaynter*
14th	**vierzehnte**	*feer-tsaynter*
15th	**fünfzehnte**	*fuinf-tsaynter*
16th	**sechzehnte**	*zekh-tsaynter*
17th	**siebzehnte**	*zeeb-tsaynter*
18th	**achtzehnte**	*akh-tsaynter*

19th	**neunzehnte**	*noyn-tsayn*ter
20th	**zwanzigste**	*tsvan*-tsikhster
21st	**einundzwanzigste**	*ine*-oont-*tsvan*-tsikhster
30th	**dreißigste**	*dry*-sikhster
40th	**vierzigste**	*feer*-tsikhster
50th	**fünfzigste**	*fuinf*-tsikhster
60th	**sechzigste**	*zekh*-tsikhster
70th	**siebzigste**	*zeeb*-tsikhster
80th	**achtzigste**	*akht*-tsikhster
90th	**neunzigste**	*noyn*-tsikhster
100th	**hundertste**	*hoon*dertster
1,000th	**tausendste**	*tow*zentster

half	**(ein) halb**	halp
quarter	**(ein) Viertel**	*feer*tel
three-quarters	**dreiviertel**	*dry-feer*tel
a third	**ein Drittel**	*drit*tel
two-thirds	**zwei Drittel**	*tsvy drit*tel

WEIGHTS AND MEASURES

Distance

kilometres – miles

km	miles or km	miles		km	miles or km	miles
1.6	1	0.6		14.5	9	5.6
3.2	2	1.2		16.1	10	6.2
4.8	3	1.9		32.2	20	12.4
6.4	4	2.5		40.2	25	15.3
8	5	3.1		80.5	50	31.1
9.7	6	3.7		160.9	100	62.1
11.3	7	4.4		402.3	250	155.3
12.9	8	5		804.7	500	310.7

A rough way to convert from miles to kilometres: divide by 5 and multiply by 8; from kilometres to miles: divide by 8 and multiply by 5.

Length and Height

centimetres – inches

cm	inches or cm	inches	cm	inches or cm	inches
2.5	1	0.4	17.8	7	2.7
5.1	2	0.8	20.0	8	3.2
7.6	3	1.2	22.9	9	3.5
10.2	4	1.6	25.4	10	3.9
12.7	5	2.0	50.8	20	7.9
15.2	6	2.4	127.0	50	19.7

A rough way to convert from inches to centimetres: divide by 2 and multiply by 5; from centimetres to inches: divide by 5 and multiply by 2.

metres – feet

m	ft or m	ft	m	ft or m	ft
0.3	1	3.3	2.4	8	26.3
0.6	2	6.6	2.7	9	29.5
0.9	3	9.8	3.0	10	32.8
1.2	4	13.1	6.1	20	65.6
1.5	5	16.4	15.2	50	164.0
1.8	6	19.7	30.5	100	328.1
2.1	7	23.0	304.8	1,000	3,280

A rough way to convert from feet to metres: divide by 10 and multiply by 3; from metres to feet: divide by 3 and multiply by 10.

metres – yards

m	yds or m	yds	m	yds or m	yds
0.9	1	1.1	7.3	8	8.8
1.8	2	2.2	8.2	9	9.8
2.7	3	3.3	9.1	10	10.9
3.7	4	4.4	18.3	20	21.9
4.6	5	5.5	45.7	50	54.7
5.5	6	6.6	91.4	100	109.4
6.4	7	7.7	457.2	500	546.8

A rough way to convert from yards to metres: subtract 10% from the number of yards; from metres to yards: add 10% to the number of metres.

Liquid Measures

litres – gallons

litres	galls or litres	galls	litres	galls or litres	galls
4.6	1	0.2	36.4	8	1.8
9.1	2	0.4	40.9	9	2.0
13.6	3	0.7	45.5	10	2.2
18.2	4	0.9	90.9	20	4.4
22.7	5	1.1	136.4	30	6.6
27.3	6	1.3	181.8	40	8.8
31.8	7	1.5	227.3	50	11.0

1 pint = 0.6 litre; 1 litre = 1.8 pints

A rough way to convert from gallons to litres: divide by 2 and multiply by 9; from litres to gallons: divide by 9 and multiply by 2.

Weight

kilograms – pounds

kg	lb or kg	lb	kg	lb or kg	lb
0.5	1	2.2	3.2	7	15.4
0.9	2	4.4	3.6	8	17.6
1.4	3	6.6	4.1	9	19.8
1.8	4	8.8	4.5	10	22.1
2.3	5	11.0	9.1	20	44.1
2.7	6	13.2	22.7	50	110.2

A rough way to convert from pounds to kilograms: divide by 11 and multiply by 5; from kilograms to pounds: divide by 5 and multiply by 11.

grams – ounces

grams	oz	oz	grams
100	3.5	2	57.1
250	8.8	4	114.3
500	17.6	8	228.6
1,000 (1kg)	35.0	16 (1lb)	457.2

Temperature

Centigrade (°C)	Fahrenheit (°F)
°C	°F
−10	14
−5	23
0	32
5	41
10	50
15	59
20	68
25	77
30	86
35	95
37	98.4
38	100.5
39	102
40	104
100	180

To convert °F to °C: deduct 32, divide by 9, multiply by 5; to convert °C to °F: divide by 5, multiply by 9 and add 32.

BASIC GRAMMAR

There are four cases in German: *nominative* (used for the subject or initiator of an action or speech), *accusative* (used for the person or thing directly affected by the action), *dative* (used for the recipient), *genitive* (used for the possessor). These cases are used for articles, nouns, pronouns and adjectives according to their position.

German also has three genders: *masculine*, *feminine* and *neuter*. They apply not only to living beings but also to inanimate objects: e.g. *der Tisch* (the table), *die Tür* (the door), *das Bett* (the bed). There are no clear rules for the use of the different genders. Similarly there are no precise easy rules on how to decline German nouns and these declensions have therefore been omitted.

Definite Article – the
The definite article is declined as follows:

	Masculine	Feminine	Neuter	Plural for all genders	
Nom.	der	die	das	die	the
Acc.	den	die	das	die	the
Dat.	dem	der	dem	den	to the
Gen.	des	der	des	der	of the

The following words are declined in the same way as *der*, *die*, *das*:

Masculine	Feminine	Neuter	Plural for all genders	
dieser	diese	dieses	diese	this
jener	jene	jenes	jene	that
jeder	jede	jedes	jede	every, each
mancher	manche	manches	manche	many (a)
solcher	solche	solches	solche	such (a)
welcher?	welche?	welches?	welche?	which (one)?

Indefinite Article – a, an

The indefinite article is declined as follows:

	Masculine	Feminine	Neuter	
Nom.	ein	eine	ein	a
Acc.	einen	eine	ein	a
Dat.	einem	einer	einem	to a
Gen.	eines	einer	eines	of a

The following words are declined in the same way as *ein*, *eine*, *ein* and, in addition, have a plural – given just for *keine* but applicable to all:

Masculine	Feminine	Neuter	Plural for all genders	
mein	meine	mein	meine	my
dein	deine	dein	deine	your
sein	seine	sein	seine	his, its
ihr	ihre	ihr	ihre	her, their
unser	uns(e)re	unser	uns(e)re	our
euer	eu(e)re	euer	eu(e)re	your
Ihr	Ihre	Ihr	Ihre	your
kein	keine	kein	keine	no, not a

Plural	
Nom.	keine
Acc.	keine
Dat.	keinen
Gen.	keiner

Adjectives

The declension of adjectives is complex, but falls into a rigid pattern:

With the definite article:

masculine

	Singular		*Plural*
Nom.	der alte Mann	the old man	die alten Männer
Acc.	den alten Mann	the old man	die alten Männer
Dat.	dem alten Mann	to the old man	den alten Männern
Gen.	des alten Mannes	of the old man, the old man's	der alten Männer

feminine

	Singular		*Plural*
Nom.	die junge Frau	the young woman	die jungen Frauen
Acc.	die junge Frau	the young woman	die jungen Frauen
Dat.	der jungen Frau	to the young woman	den jungen Frauen
Gen.	der jungen Frau	of the young woman, the young woman's	der jungen Frauen

neuter

	Singular		Plural
Nom.	das kleine Kind	the small child	die kleinen Kinder
Acc.	das kleine Kind	the small child	die kleinen Kinder
Dat.	dem kleinen Kind	to the small child	den kleinen Kindern
Gen.	des kleinen Kindes	of the small child, the small child's	der kleinen Kinder

With the indefinite article:

masculine

Nom.	ein alter Mann	an old man
Acc.	einen alten Mann	an old man
Dat.	einem alten Mann	to an old man
Gen.	eines alten Mannes	of an old man, an old man's

feminine

Nom.	eine junge Frau	a young woman
Acc.	eine junge Frau	a young woman
Dat.	einer jungen Frau	to a young woman
Gen.	einer jungen Frau	of a young woman, a young woman's

neuter

Nom.	ein kleines Kind	a small child
Acc.	ein kleines Kind	a small child
Dat.	einem kleinen Kind	to a small child
Gen.	eines kleinen Kindes	of a small child, a small child's

Personal Pronouns

Nom.		*Acc.*		*Dat.*		*Gen.*	
ich	I	mich	me	mir	to me	meiner	mine
du	you	dich	you	dir	to you	deiner	yours
er	he	ihn	him	ihm	to him	seiner	his
sie	she	sie	her	ihr	to her	ihrer	hers
es	it	es	it	ihm	to it	seiner	its
wir	we	uns	us	uns	to us	unser	ours
ihr	you	euch	you	euch	to you	euer	yours
sie	they	sie	them	ihnen	to them	ihrer	theirs
Sie	you	Sie	you	Ihnen	to you	Ihrer	yours

The pronouns *du* (singular) and *ihr* (plural) are the familiar address used towards friends, relatives and children. *Sie* (singular and plural) is the formal address used towards all other people. It is written with a capital 'S' when it means 'you' and small 's' when it means 'she' or 'they'.

Prepositions

The English meanings given in the list below are often only approximations, as prepositions in German are used to indicate a number of different meanings, e.g.

> *Ich wohne* bei *meinen Eltern* – I am living *with* my parents.
> *Biegen Sie rechts* bei *den Verkehrsampeln ab* = Turn right
> *at* the traffic lights.

With the *accusative* (i.e. they always govern the noun or pronoun in the accusative case):

durch	through
für	for
gegen	against
wider	against
ohne	without
um	round, at (of time)

With the *dative*:

mit	with
zu	to
nach	to (a place), after, according to
von	of, from, by
aus	out of

bei	with, near, by
seit	since
gegenüber	opposite
ausser	except, besides

With the *accusative* or *dative*:

in	in, into, inside
auf	on, onto
unter	under
über	over, above
an	at, on, against
vor	before, in front of
hinter	behind
zwischen	between
neben	near, beside

These prepositions are used with the *dative* when they indicate position or rest (e.g. *Ich bin in dem Haus* = I am in the house) or motion within a confined area (e.g. *Ich gehe in dem Garten auf und ab* = I am walking up and down in the garden). They are used with the *accusative* if they indicate motion towards something or a change from one place to another (e.g. *Ich gehe in das Haus* = I go into the house). Most German prepositions take either the dative or the accusative or both.

Interrogatives

Nom.	wer?	who?	was?	what?
Acc.	wen?	whom?	was?	what?
Dat.	wem?	to whom?	wem?	to what?
Gen.	wessen?	whose?	wessen?	of what?

For 'welcher?' and 'which?' see Definite Article (p. 242).

Negatives

nicht	not
nie, niemals	never

The position of these words in a sentence depends very much on the stress the speaker wants to put on them. Generally, however, they stand in front of the word or idea to be negated.

Basic Verbs

In German, as in English, there are two basic verbs that one uses over and over again:

sein = to be

Present		*Future*	
ich bin	I am	ich werde sein	I will be
du bist	you are	du wirst sein	you will be

er ⎫	he ⎫	er ⎫	he ⎫
sie ⎬ ist	she ⎬ is	sie ⎬ wird sein	she ⎬ will be
es ⎭	it ⎭	es ⎭	it ⎭
wir sind	we are	wir werden sein	we will be
ihr seid	you are	ihr werdet sein	you will be
sie sind	they are	sie werden sein	they will be
Sie sind	you are	Sie werden sein	you will be

Perfect		*Imperfect*	
ich bin gewesen	I have been	ich war	I was
du bist gewesen	you have been	du warst	you were
er ⎫	he ⎫	er ⎫	he ⎫
sie ⎬ ist gewesen	she ⎬ has been	sie ⎬ war	she ⎬ was
es ⎭	it ⎭	es ⎭	it ⎭
wir sind gewesen	we have been	wir waren	we were
ihr seid gewesen	you have been	ihr wart	you were
sie sind gewesen	they have been	sie waren	they were
Sie sind gewesen	you have been	Sie waren	you were

haben = to have

Present		Future	
ich habe	I have	ich werde haben	I will have
du hast	you have	du wirst haben	you will have
er sie } hat es	he she } has it	er sie } wird haben es	he she } will have it
wir haben	we have	wir werden haben	we will have
ihr habt	you have	ihr werdet haben	you will have
sie haben	they have	sie werden haben	they will have
Sie haben	you have	Sie werden haben	you will have

Perfect		Imperfect	
ich habe gehabt	I have had	ich hatte	I had
du hast gehabt	you have had	du hattest	you had
er sie } hat gehabt es	he she } has had it	er sie } hatte es	he she } had it
wir haben gehabt	we have had	wir hatten	we had
ihr habt gehabt	you have had	ihr hattet	you had
sie haben gehabt	they have had	sie hatten	they had
Sie haben gehabt	you have had	Sie hatten	you had

Most German verbs are conjugated with *haben* (e.g. *Ich habe gesehen* – I have seen). The exceptions are the verb *sein* – to be, and all verbs of motion, which are conjugated with *sein* (e.g. *Ich bin gelaufen* – I have run; *Ich bin gefahren* – I have travelled).

Auxiliary Verbs

These verbs are mostly used with the infinitive of another verb, and the latter always goes to the end of the sentence:

dürfen = to be permitted (may)

Present	Imperfect
ich darf	ich durfte
du darfst	du durftest
er ⎱	er ⎱
sie ⎬ darf	sie ⎬ durfte
es ⎰	es ⎰
wir dürfen	wir durften
ihr dürft	ihr durftet
sie dürfen	sie durften
Sie dürfen	Sie durften

e.g. *Darf ich rauchen?* = May I smoke?

können = to be able to (can)

Present	Imperfect
ich kann	ich konnte
du kannst	du konntest
er	er
sie } kann	sie } konnte
es	es
wir können	wir konnten
ihr könnt	ihr konntet
sie können	sie konnten
Sie können	Sie konnten

e.g. *Ich kann Sie nicht verstehen* = I cannot understand you.

mögen = to like, to enjoy

Present	Imperfect
ich mag	ich mochte
du magst	du mochtest
er	er
sie } mag	sie } mochte
es	es
wir mögen	wir mochten
ihr mögt	ihr mochtet
sie mögen	sie mochten
Sie mögen	Sie mochten

e.g. *Es mag richtig sein* = It may well be right.

Ich mag diesen Tee nicht = I don't like this tea.

sollen = to have to, ought to

Present	Imperfect
ich soll	ich sollte
du sollst	du solltest
er ⎫	er ⎫
sie ⎬ soll	sie ⎬ sollte
es ⎭	es ⎭
wir sollen	wir sollten
ihr sollt	ihr solltet
sie sollen	sie sollten
Sie sollen	Sie sollten

e.g. *Er soll zu mir kommen* = He has to come to me.

müssen = to have to (must)

Present	Imperfect
ich muss	ich musste
du musst	du musstest
er ⎫	er ⎫
sie ⎬ muss	sie ⎬ musste
es ⎭	es ⎭
wir müssen	wir mussten
ihr müsst	ihr musstet
sie müssen	sie mussten
Sie müssen	Sie mussten

e.g. *Sie müssen um zehn Uhr hier sein* = You have to be here at ten o'clock.

wollen = to want to, wish to (will)

Present	Imperfect
ich will	ich wollte
du willst	du wolltest
er ⎫	er ⎫
sie ⎬ will	sie ⎬ wollte
es ⎭	es ⎭
wir wollen	wir wollten
ihr wollt	ihr wolltet
sie wollen	sie wollten
Sie wollen	Sie wollten

e.g. *Ich will mit dem Zug fahren* = I want to go by train.

Regular Verbs

A large group of German verbs – known as 'weak verbs' – are conjugated by changing their endings:

machen = to make, do

Present		Future	
ich mache	I make	Ich werde machen	I will make
du machst	you make	du wirst machen	you will make

er ⎫	he ⎫	er ⎫	he ⎫
sie ⎬ macht	she ⎬ makes	sie ⎬ wird machen	she ⎬ will make
es ⎭	it ⎭	es ⎭	it ⎭
wir machen	we make	wir werden machen	we will make
ihr macht	you make	ihr werden machen	you will make
sie machen	they make	sie werden machen	they will make
Sie machen	you make	Sie werden machen	you will make

Imperfect		*Perfect*	
ich machte	I made	ich habe gemacht	I have made
du machtest	you made	du hast gemacht	you have made
er ⎫	he ⎫	er ⎫	he ⎫
sie ⎬ machte	she ⎬ made	sie ⎬ hat gemacht	she ⎬ has made
es ⎭	it ⎭	es ⎭	it ⎭
wir machten	we made	wir haben gemacht	we have made
ihr machtet	you made	ihr habt gemacht	you have made
sie machten	they made	sie haben gemacht	they have made
Sie machten	you made	Sie haben gemacht	you have made

Irregular Verbs

Many of the verbs in this phrase book can be grouped together as 'strong verbs', which means their form changes more radically in different tenses than do regular verbs (see above):

sprechen = to talk, speak

Present		Future	
ich spreche	I speak	ich werde sprechen	I will speak
du sprichst	you speak	du wirst sprechen	you will speak
er sie } spricht es	he she } speaks it	er sie }wird sprechen es	he she } will speak it
wir sprechen	we speak	wir werden sprechen	we will speak
ihr sprecht	you speak	ihr werdet sprechen	you will speak
sie sprechen	they speak	sie werden sprechen	they will speak
Sie sprechen	you speak	Sie werden sprechen	you will speak

Imperfect		*Perfect*	
ich sprach	I spoke	ich habe gesprochen	I have spoken
du sprachst	you spoke	du hast gesprochen	you have spoken
er ⎫ sie ⎬ sprach es ⎭	he ⎫ she ⎬ spoke it ⎭	er ⎫ sie ⎬ hat gesprochen es ⎭	he ⎫ she ⎬ has spoken it ⎭
wir sprachen	we spoke	wir haben gesprochen	we have spoken
ihr spracht	you spoke	ihr habt gesprochen	you have spoken
sie sprachen	they spoke	sie haben gesprochen	they have spoken
Sie sprachen	you spoke	Sie haben gesprochen	you have spoken

A list of the most common 'strong' verbs is given below:

Infinitive	*3rd person sing. present*	*Imperfect*	*Past participle*	
beginnen	beginnt	begann	begonnen	to begin
biegen	biegt	bog	gebogen	to bend, turn

bitten	bittet	bat	gebeten	to entreat, beg (. . . *um* = ask for)
bleiben	bleibt	blieb	geblieben	to remain, stay
bringen	bringt	brachte	gebracht	to bring
denken	denkt	dachte	gedacht	to think
empfehlen	empfiehlt	empfahl	empfohlen	to recommend
essen	isst	aß	gegessen	to eat
fahren	fährt	fuhr	gefahren	to drive, travel
fangen	fängt	fing	gefangen	to catch
finden	findet	fand	gefunden	to find
fliegen	fliegt	flog	geflogen	to fly
geben	gibt	gab	gegeben	to give
gefallen	es gefällt (mir)	gefiel	gefallen	to like
gehen	geht	ging	gegangen	to go
geschehen	es geschieht	geschah	geschehen	to happen
halten	hält	hielt	gehalten	to hold
heissen	heißt	hieß	geheissen	to be called
helfen	hilft	half	geholfen	to help
kennen	kennt	kannte	gekannt	to know
kommen	kommt	kam	gekommen	to come
lassen	lässt	ließ	gelassen	to leave, let

laufen	läuft	lief	gelaufen	to run
liegen	liegt	lag	gelegen	to lie
nehmen	nimmt	nahm	genommen	to take
rufen	ruft	rief	gerufen	to call
schließen	schließt	schloss	geschlossen	to close, shut
schreiben	schreibt	schrieb	geschrieben	to write
sehen	sieht	sah	gesehen	to see
sitzen	sitzt	saß	gesessen	to sit
sprechen	spricht	sprach	gesprochen	to speak, talk
stehen	steht	stand	gestanden	to stand
tragen	trägt	trug	getragen	to carry, wear
treffen	trifft	traf	getroffen	to meet
treten	tritt	trat	getreten	to step
trinken	trinkt	trank	getrunken	to drink
tun	tut	tat	getan	to do, make
vergessen	vergisst	vergaß	vergessen	to forget
verlieren	verliert	verlor	verloren	to lose
verstehen	versteht	verstand	verstanden	to understand
werden	wird	wurde	geworden	to become
wissen	weiß	wusste	gewusst	to know

Separable Verbs

There are some verbs in German which, by having a prefix added, modify their meaning, as in the following, for example:

kommen	to come
ankommen	to arrive
fangen	to catch
anfangen	to start
fahren	to travel, drive
abfahren	to depart

When conjugated the prefix is separated from the verb in the present and imperfect and put at the end of the sentence. Take *abfahren*, for instance:

Der Zug fährt *bald* ab = The train leaves soon.

VOCABULARY

For additional words, please see the specific vocabulary lists elsewhere in the book:

A

a, an	**ein, eine, ein**	ine, iner, ine
able (to be)	**können**	kernen
about	**ungefähr**	*oon*-gufair
above	**über**	*ui*ber
abroad	**im Ausland**	im *ows*-lant
accept (to)	**annehmen**	*an-nay*men
accident	**der Unfall**	*oon*fal
ache (to)	**schmerzen**	*shmairt*sen
acquaintance	**der Bekannte**	bu*kann*ter
across	**über, jenseits**	*ui*ber, *yayn*zites

act (to)	**handeln**	*handeln*
on the stage	**spielen**	*shpee*len
add (to)	**hinzufügen**	hin-*tsoo*-fuigun
address	**die Adresse**	ad*res*ser
admire (to)	**bewundern**	bu*voon*dern
admission	**der Eintritt**	*ine*-tritt
advice	**der Rat**	raht
aeroplane	**das Flugzeug**	*floog*-tsoyg
afford (to)	**sich leisten**	zikh *lys*ten
afraid	**ängstlich**	*aingst*likh
after	**nach**	nahkh
again	**wieder**	*vee*der
against	**gegen, wider**	*gay*gun, vider
age	**das Alter**	alter
agree (to)	**zustimmen**	*tsoo*-shtimmen
ahead	**vorn**	forn
air	**die Luft**	looft
air conditioning	**die Klimaanlage**	*klee*ma-*an*-lahgur
alarm clock	**der Wecker**	vecker
alike	**ähnlich**	*ayn*likh
all	**alles**	alles
allow (to)	**erlauben**	air*low*ben
all right	**in Ordnung/OK**	in *ord*noong/OK

almost	**fast**	fast
alone	**allein**	a*line*
along	**entlang**	ent*lang*
already	**schon**	shohn
also	**auch**	owkh
alter (to)	**ändern**	*end*ern
alternative	**die Alternative**	altairnah*teever*
although	**obgleich**	op*glykh*
always	**immer**	immer
ambulance	**der Krankenwagen**	*kran*ken-*vahg*un
America	**Amerika**	a*mair*eekah
American *adj.*	**amerikanisch**	amairee*kahn*ish
noun	**der Amerikaner, die Amerikanerin**	amairee*kahn*er, amairee*kahn*erin
among	**zwischen, bei**	*ts-vish*en, by
amuse (to)	**amüsieren**	amui*zeer*en
amusing	**amüsant**	amui*zant*
ancient	**sehr alt**	zair alt
and	**und**	oont
angry	**zornig**	tsornikh
animal	**das Tier**	teer
anniversary	**die Jahresfeier**	*yahres-fyer*
annoyed	**geärgert, verärgert**	gu-*air*gert, fair-*air*gert

another	**ein anderer**	ine *anderer*
answer	**die Antwort**	*ant*vort
answer (to)	**antworten**	*ant*vorten
antique	**die Antike**	an*teek*er
any	**irgendein**	*eer*gunt-ine
anyone	**irgendeiner**	*eer*gunt-iner
anything	**irgend etwas**	*eer*gunt etvas
anyway	**jedenfalls**	*yay*den-fals
anywhere	**irgendwo**	*eer*gunt-voh
apartment	**die Wohnung**	*voh*noong
apologize (to)	**sich entschuldigen**	zikh ents*hool*digun
appetite	**der Appetit**	appe*teet*
appointment	**die Verabredung, der Termin**	fair-*ap*-raydoong, ter*meen*
architect	**der Architekt**	arkhee*tekt*
architecture	**die Architektur**	arkheetek*toor*
area	**das Gebiet**	gu*beet*
arm	**der Arm**	arm
armchair	**der Lehnstuhl**	*layn*-shtool
army	**das Heer, die Armee**	hayer, ar*may*
around	**rings herum**	rings hai*room*
arrange (to)	**festsetzen**	*fest*-zetsen
arrival	**die Ankunft**	*an*-koonft

arrive (to)	**ankommen**	*an-kommen*
art	**die Kunst**	koonst
art gallery	**die Kunstgalerie**	*koonst*-galair*ee*
artist	**der Künstler**	*kuinst*ler
as	**wie**	vee
as much as	**soviel wie**	zoh*feel* vee
as soon as	**sobald**	zoh*balt*
as well/also	**auch**	owkh
ashtray	**der Aschenbecher**	*ashe*n-bekher
ask (to)	**fragen**	*frah*gun
asleep	**eingeschlafen**	*ine*-gu-*shlah*fen
at	**an, zu, bei, um**	an, tsoo, by, oom
at last	**endlich**	*ent*likh
at once	**sofort**	zoh*fort*
atmosphere	**die Atmosphäre**	atmohs*fair*er
attention	**die Aufmerksamkeit**	*owf*-mairk-zamkite
attractive	**reizend**	*ry*-tsent
auction	**die Auktion**	owkts-*yon*
audience	**die Zuhörer**	*tsoo*-her-rer
aunt	**die Tante**	tanter
Australia	**Australien**	ow*strah*lee-yen
Australian *adj.*	**australisch**	ow*strah*lish
noun	**der Australier, die Australierin**	ow*strah*lee-yer, ow*strah*lee-yerin

Austria	**Österreich**	*erstair-rykh*
Austrian *adj.*	**österreichisch**	*erstair-rykh*ish
noun	**der Österreicher, die Österreicherin**	*erstair-rykh*er, *erstair-rykh*erin
author	**der Schriftsteller, Autor**	*shrift-shtel*ler, *owtor*
available	**vorhanden**	for-*handen*
avenue	**die Allee**	al*lay*
average	**durchschnittlich**	*doorkh-shnit*likh
awake	**wach**	vakh
away	**weg**	vek
awful	**schrecklich**	*shreck*likh

B

baby	**das Baby**	baby
baby food	**die Babynahrung**	baby-*nah*roong
baby sitter	**der Babysitter**	babysitter
back	**zurück**	tsoo*ruick*
bad	**schlecht**	shlekht
bag	**die Tasche**	tasher
baggage	**das Gepäck**	gu*peck*
bait	**der Köder**	kerder
balcony	**der Balkon**	bal*kohn*

ball *sport*	**der Ball**	bal
ballet	**das Ballet**	ba*let*
band *music*	**die Band**	bant
bank	**die Bank**	bank
bare	**nackt**	nackt
basket	**der Korb**	korp
bath	**das Bad**	baht
bathe (to)	**baden**	*bah*den
bathing cap	**die Bademütze**	*bah*der-muitser
bathing suit	**der Badeanzug**	*bah*der-an-tsoog
bathing trunks	**die Badehose**	*bah*der-*hoh*zer
bathroom	**das Badezimmer**	*bah*der-tsimmer
battery	**die Batterie**	batter*ee*
bay	**die Bucht**	bookht
be (to)	**sein**	zine
beach	**der Strand**	shtrant
beard	**der Bart**	bart
beautiful	**schön**	shern
because	**weil**	vile
become (to)	**werden**	*vair*den
bed	**das Bett**	bet
bed and breakfast	**Zimmer mit Frühstück**	tsimmer mit *frui*-shtuick

bedroom	**das Schlafzimmer**	*shlahf*-tsimmer
before	**vor, bevor**	for, bu-*for*
begin (to)	**beginnen**	bu*ginn*en
beginning	**der Anfang**	*an*-fang
behind	**hinter**	*hin*ter
believe (to)	**glauben**	*glow*ben
bell	**die Glocke**	glocker
belong (to)	**gehören**	gu*her*-ren
below	**unter**	*oon*ter
belt	**der Gürtel**	*guir*tel
bench	**die Bank**	bank
bend (to)	**biegen**	*bee*gun
beneath	**unter**	*oon*ter
berth	**das Bett**	bet
beside	**neben**	*nay*ben
besides	**außerdem**	owsair*daim*
best	**das Beste**	bester
bet	**die Wette**	*vet*ter
better	**besser**	besser
between	**zwischen**	ts-*vish*en
bicycle	**das Fahrrad**	*fahr*-raht
big	**groß**	grohs
bill	**die Rechnung**	*rekh*noong

binoculars	**das Fernglas**	fern-glahs
bird	**der Vogel**	*foh*gel
birthday	**der Geburtstag**	gu*boorts*-tahg
bite (to)	**beißen**	*by*sen
bitter	**herb**	herp
(woollen) blanket	**die (Woll-) Decke**	(*voll*-) decker
bleed (to)	**bluten**	*bloo*ten
blind	**blind**	blint
blond	**blond**	blont
blood	**das Blut**	bloot
blouse	**die Bluse**	*bloo*zer
blow (to)	**blasen**	*blah*zen
(on) board	**an Bord**	an bort
boarding house	**die Pension**	pens-*yon*
boat	**das Boot, Schiff**	boht, shif
body	**der Körper**	*ker*per
bolt	**der Türriegel**	*tuir-ree*gul
bone	**der Knochen**	k-*nokh*en
book	**das Buch**	bookh
book (to)	**buchen**	*bookh*en
boot	**der Stiefel**	*shtee*fel
border	**die Grenze**	grentser
borrow (to)	**borgen**	borgun

both	**beide**	*byder*
bottle	**die Flasche**	*flasher*
bottle opener	**der Flaschenöffner**	*flashen-erfner*
bottom	**der Boden**	*bohden*
bowl	**die Schüssel**	*shuissel*
box *container*	**die Schachtel**	*shakhtel*
theatre	**die Loge**	*lohjer*
box office	**die Kasse**	*kasser*
boy	**der Junge**	*yoong-er*
bracelet	**das Armband**	*arm*-bant
braces	**der Hosenträger**	*hohzen-tray*gur
brain	**das Gehirn**	*guheern*
branch	**der Zweig**	ts-vyg
brand	**die Marke**	marker
brassière	**der Büstenhalter**	*buis*ten-halter
break (to)	**brechen**	brekhen
breakfast	**das Frühstück**	*frui*-shtuick
breathe (to)	**atmen**	*aht*men
bridge	**die Brücke**	*bruic*ker
briefs	**der Schlüpfer**	*shluip*fer
bright	**leuchtend, hell**	*loykh*tent, hell
bring (to)	**bringen**	bring-en
British	**britisch**	*bri*tish

broadband	**Breitband**	brite-bant
broken	**gebrochen, zerbrochen**	gu*brokh*en, tsair-*brokh*en
brooch	**die Brosche**	brosher
brother	**der Bruder**	brooder
bruise (to)	**quetschen**	*k-vets*hen
brush	**die Bürste**	*buir*ster
brush (to)	**bürsten**	*buir*sten
bucket	**der Eimer**	*eye*mer
buckle	**die Schnalle**	shnaller
build (to)	**bauen**	*bow*en
building	**das Gebäude**	gu*boy*der
bundle	**das Bündel**	*buin*del
burn (to)	**brennen**	brennen
burst (to)	**bersten**	bairsten
bus	**der Bus**	boos
bus stop	**die Bushaltestelle**	*boos*-halter-*shtel*ler
business	**das Geschäft**	gu-*sheft*
busy	**beschäftigt**	bu-*sheft*ikht
but	**aber**	ahber
button	**der Knopf**	k-nopf
buy (to)	**kaufen**	*kow*fen
by	**von, bei**	fon, by

C

cabin	**die Kabine**	ka*bee*ner
call *telephone*	**der Anruf**	*an*-roof
visit	**der Besuch**	bu*zookh*
call (to) *summon*	**rufen**	roofen
name	**nennen**	nennen
telephone	**anrufen**	*an*-roofen
visit	**besuchen**	bu*zookh*en
calm	**ruhig**	roo-ikh
camera	**die Kamera, der Fotoapparat**	kamai*rah, foh*toh-appa*raht*
camp (to)	**zelten**	tselten
campsite	**der Campingplatz**	camping-plats
can (to be able)	**können**	kernen
can *tin*	**die Dose**	*doh*zer
Canada	**Kanada**	*kan*ahdah
Canadian	**kanadisch**	ka*nah*dish
cancel (to)	**abbestellen**	*ap*-bu-*shtel*len
candle	**die Kerze**	*kairt*ser
canoe	**das Kanu**	kah*noo*
cap	**die Mütze**	muitser
capable	**fähig**	fay-ikh

capital city	**die Hauptstadt**	*howpt*-shtaht
car	**das Auto**	*ow*toh
car park	**der Parkplatz**	*park*-plats
caravan	**der Wohnwagen**	*vohn-vah*gun
card	**die Karte**	karter
care (to)	**sorgen**	*zorg*un
careful	**sorgsam**	*zorg*zahm
careless	**unachtsam**	*oon-akht*zahm
carry (to)	**tragen**	*trah*gun
cash	**das Bargeld**	*bar*-gelt
cash (to)	**einlösen**	*ine*-lerzen
cashier	**der Kassierer**	kaseerer
casino	**das Kasino**	kazeenoh
castle	**das Schloss, die Burg**	shloss, boorg
cat	**die Katze**	katser
catalogue	**der Katalog**	kata*lohg*
catch (to)	**fangen**	fang-en
cathedral	**der Dom, die Kathedrale**	dohm, katay-*drah*ler
catholic	**katholisch**	ka*toh*lish
cause	**der Grund**	groont
cave	**die Höhle**	*her*ler
central	**zentral**	tsen*trahl*
centre	**das Zentrum**	*tsen*troom

century	**das Jahrhundert**	yahr-*hoon*dert
ceremony	**die Zeremonie**	tsay-raymoh-*nee*
certain	**sicher**	*zikh*er
certainly	**gewiss**	gu*viss*
chair	**der Stuhl**	shtool
chambermaid	**das Zimmermädchen**	tsimmer-*mayt*-khen
chance	**die Möglichkeit**	*merk*likh-kite
(by) chance	**(durch) Zufall**	*tsoo*fal
(small) change	**das Kleingeld**	*kline*-gelt
change (to)	**einwechseln**	*ine-veck*zeln
charge	**der Preis**	price
charge (to)	**berechnen**	bu*rekh*nen
cheap	**billig**	*bil*likh
check (to)	**nachrechnen**	*nahkh*-rekhnen
checkout/till	**die Kasse**	kasser
cheque	**der Scheck**	sheck
child	**das Kind**	kint
china	**das Porzellan**	portsel-*lahn*
choice	**die Wahl**	vahl
choose (to)	**(aus)wählen**	(*ows*)*vay*len
church	**die Kirche**	*kirkh*er
cigar	**die Zigarre**	tsi*garr*er
cigarettes	**die Zigaretten**	tsiga*retten*
cinema	**das Kino**	*kee*noh

circus	**der Zirkus**	*tseer*koos
city	**die (Groß-) Stadt**	(grohs-) shtat
class	**die Klasse**	klasser
clean	**rein**	rine
clean (to)	**reinigen**	*ry*nigun
clear	**klar**	klar
clerk	**der Beamte**	bu-*am*ter
cliff	**die Klippe**	klipper
climb (to)	**besteigen**	bu-*shty*gun
cloakroom	**die Toilette**	twah*let*ter
clock	**die Uhr**	oor
close (to)	**schließen**	*shlee*ssen
closed	**geschlossen**	gu-*shlo*ssen
cloth	**der Stoff**	shtof
clothes	**die Kleider**	*kly*der
cloud	**die Wolke**	volker
coach	**der (Auto-) Bus**	(*ow*toh-) boos
coast	**die Küste**	kuister
coat	**der Mantel**	*man*tel
coathanger	**der (Kleider-) Bügel**	(*kly*der-) *bui*gul
coin	**die Münze**	muintser
cold	**kalt**	kalt
collar	**der Kragen**	*krah*gun

collect (to)	**sammeln**	*zammeln*
colour	**die Farbe**	farber
comb	**der Kamm**	kam
come (to)	**kommen**	*kom*men
come in (to)	**hereinkommen**	hair-*ine*-kommen
comfortable	**bequem**	bu-*k-vaym*
common	**allgemein**	algu*mine*
company	**die Gesellschaft**	guze*l*shaft
complain (to)	**sich beschweren**	zikh bu-*shvairen*
complaint	**die Beschwerde**	bu-*shvair*der
complete	**komplett**	kom*plet*
completely	**ganz**	gants
concert	**das Konzert**	kon*tsairt*
condition	**der Zustand**	*tsoo*-shtant
condom	**das Kondom**	kon*dohm*
conductor *bus*	**der Schaffner**	*shaf*ner
orchestra	**der Dirigent**	deeree*ghent*
congratulations	**herzlichen Glückwunsch**	*hairts*-likhen *gluick*-woonsh
connect (to)	**verbinden**	fair*bin*-den
connection *train, etc.*	**der Anschluss**	*an*-shlooss
consul	**der Konsul**	*kon*zool
consulate	**das Konsulat**	*kon*zoolaht

contain (to)	**enthalten**	ent*hal*ten
convenient	**günstig**	*guin*stikh
conversation	**die Unterhaltung**	*oon*ter-*hal*toong
cook	**der Koch, die Köchin**	kokh, kerkhin
cook (to)	**kochen**	kokhen
cool	**kühl**	kuil
copy	**das Exemplar, die Kopie**	eksem*plar*, koh*pee*
copy (to)	**kopieren**	koh*pee*ren
cork	**der Korken**	korken
corkscrew	**der Korkenzieher**	korken-tsee-yer
corner	**die Ecke**	ecker
correct	**richtig**	*rikh*-tikh
corridor	**der Korridor**	*korreedor*
cosmetics	**die Kosmetikartikel**	kos*meteek*-artikel
cost	**der Preis**	price
cost (to)	**kosten**	kosten
cotton	**die Baumwolle**	*bowm*-voller
cotton wool	**die Watte**	vatter
couchette	**der Liegeplatz**	*lee*gur-plats
count (to)	**zählen**	*tsay*len
country	**das Land**	lant
couple	**das Paar**	pahr
course *dish*	**das Gericht**	gu*rikht*

courtyard	**der Hof**	hohf
cousin	**der Vetter, die Kusine**	*fetter*, koo-zeener
cover	**die Decke**	decker
cover (to)	**bedecken**	bu*decken*
cow	**die Kuh**	koo
crash *collision*	**der Zusammenstoß, Unfall**	tsoo-*zammen*-shtohs, *oon*fal
credit	**das Guthaben, der Kredit**	goot-hahben, kray*deet*
credit card	**die Kreditkarte**	kray*deet*-karter
crew	**die Besatzung**	bu*zat*soong
cross	**das Kreuz**	kroyts
cross (to)	**hinübergehen**	hin-*uiber*-*gay*en
crossroads	**die Kreuzung**	*kroyts*oong
crowd	**die Menge**	meng-er
crowded	**voll**	fol
cry (to)	**schreien**	*shry*en
cup	**die Tasse**	tasser
cupboard	**der Schrank**	shrank
cure (to)	**heilen**	*hy*len
curious	**neugierig**	*noy*geerig
curl	**die Locke**	locker
current	**die Strömung**	*shtrer*moong

curtain	**der Vorhang**	*for*-hang
curve	**die Kurve**	koorver
cushion	**das Kissen**	kissen
customs	**der Zoll**	tsoll
customs officer	**der Zollbeamte**	*tsoll*-bu-*am*ter
cut	**der Schnitt**	shnit
cut (to)	**schneiden**	*shny*den
cycling	**Fahrrad fahren**	*fahr*-raht fahren
cyclist	**Fahrradfahrer**	*fahr*-raht-fahrer

D

daily	**täglich**	*tayg*likh
damaged	**beschädigt**	bu-*shay*dikht
damp	**feucht**	foykht
dance	**der Tanz**	tants
danger	**die Gefahr**	gu*fahr*
dangerous	**gefährlich**	gu*fair*likh
dark	**dunkel**	*doon*kel
date *day/year*	**das Datum**	*dah*toom
appointment	**die Verabredung**	fair-*ap*-raydoong
daughter	**die Tochter**	*tokh*ter
day	**der Tag**	tahg

dead	**tot**	toht
deaf	**taub**	towb
dear *expensive*	**teuer**	*toyer*
decide (to)	**entscheiden**	ent*shyden*
deck	**das Deck**	deck
deckchair	**der Liegestuhl**	*leeg*ur-shtool
declare (to)	**erklären**	air*klairen*
customs	**verzollen**	fair-*tsoll*en
deep	**tief**	teef
delay	**die Verzögerung**	fair-*tserg*uroong
deliver (to)	**austragen**	*ows*-trahgun
delivery	**die Austragung**	*ows*-trahgoong
dentist	**der Zahnarzt**	*tsahn*-artst
deodorant	**das Deodorant**	day-odor*ant*
depart (to)	**abfahren**	*ap*-fahren
department	**die Abteilung**	*ap*-ty loong
department store	**das Warenhaus**	*vahren*-hows
departure	**die Abfahrt**	*ap*-fahrt
dessert	**der Nachtisch**	*nahkh*-tish
detour	**der Umweg**	*oom*-vayg
dial (to)	**wählen**	*vay*len
diamond	**der Diamant**	dee-ah*mant*
dice	**der Würfel**	*vuir*fel

dictionary	**das Wörterbuch**	*verter*-bookh
diet	**die Diät**	dee-*yet*
diet (to)	**Diät halten**	dee-*yet* halten
different	**verschieden**	fair*sheed*en
difficult	**schwierig**	*shveer*ikh
dine (to)	**speisen, essen**	*shpy*zen, essen
dining room	**der Speisesaal**	*shpy*zer-zahl
dinner	**das Abendessen**	*ahb*ent-essen
direct	**direkt**	dee*rekt*
direction	**die Richtung**	*rikh*toong
dirty	**schmutzig**	*shmoot*sikh
disappointed	**enttäuscht**	ent-*toysht*
discount	**der Preisnachlass, die Ermäßigung**	*price*-nahkh-lass, air*messi*goong
dish	**die Schüssel**	*shuiss*el
disinfectant	**das Desinfektionsmittel**	des-infekts-*yons*-mittel
distance	**die Entfernung**	ent*fair*noong
disturb (to)	**stören**	*shter*-ren
ditch	**der Graben**	*grahb*en
dive (to)	**tauchen**	*towkh*en
diving board	**das Sprungbrett**	*sproong*-bret
divorced	**geschieden**	gu-*sheed*en
do (to)	**tun**	toon

dock (to)	**anlegen**	an-*lay*gun
doctor	**der Arzt**	artst
dog	**der Hund**	hoont
doll	**die Puppe**	pooper
door	**die Tür**	tuir
double	**doppelt**	doppelt
double bed	**das Doppelbett**	doppel-bet
double room	**das Doppelzimmer**	doppel-tsimmer
down	**hinunter**	hin*oon*ter
downstairs	**unten**	oonten
dozen	**das Dutzend**	*doot*sent
drawer	**die Schublade**	shoob-*lah*der
dream	**der Traum**	trowm
dress	**das Kleid**	klite
dressing-gown	**der Morgenrock**	*mor*gun-rock
drink (to)	**trinken**	trinken
drinking water	**das Trinkwasser**	*trink-vas*ser
drive (to)	**fahren**	fahren
driver	**der Fahrer**	fahrer
drop (to)	**fallen lassen**	*fal*-len lassen
drunk	**betrunken**	but*roon*ken
dry	**trocken**	trocken
during	**während**	*vair*ent

E

each	**jeder, jede, jedes**	*yay*der, *yay*der, *yay*des
early	**früh**	frui
earrings	**die Ohrringe**	*ohr*-ring-er
east	**der Osten**	osten
easy	**leicht**	lykht
eat (to)	**essen**	essen
edge	**der Rand**	rant
elastic	**das Gummiband**	*goom*mee-bant
electric point	**die Steckdose**	*shteck-doh*zer
electricity	**die Elektrizität, der Strom**	aylek-tritsi*tayt*, shtrohm
elevator	**der Fahrstuhl**	*fahr*-shtool
embarrass (to)	**in Verlegenheit bringen**	in fair*lay*gunhite bring-en
embassy	**die Botschaft**	*boht*shaft
emergency exit	**der Notausgang**	*noht-ows*-gang
empty	**leer**	layer
end	**das Ende**	ender
engaged *marriage*	**verlobt**	fair*lohbt*
telephone	**besetzt**	buze*tst*
engine	**der Motor**	moh*tor*
England	**England**	*aing*-lant

English	**englisch**	*aing*-lish
Englishman/-woman	**der Engländer, die Engländerin**	*aing*-lender, *aing*-lenderin
enjoy (to)	**genießen**	gu*neessen*
enough	**genug**	gunoog
enquiries	**die Auskunft**	*ows*-koonft
enter (to)	**hineintreten**	hin-*ine-trayt*en
entrance	**der Eingang**	*ine*-gang
envelope	**der (Brief-) Umschlag**	(breef-) *oom*shlahg
equipment	**die Ausrüstung**	*ows*-ruistoong
escape (to)	**entkommen**	ent*kommen*
Europe	**Europa**	oy*rohp*ah
EU	**EU**	ay-oo
even *not odd*	**gerade**	gu*rah*der
event	**der Vorfall**	*for*-fal
ever	**immer**	immer
every	**jeder, jede, jedes**	*yay*der, *yay*der, *yay*des
everybody	**jedermann**	*yay*der-man
everything	**alles**	alles
everywhere	**überall**	*ui*beral
example	**das Beispiel**	*by*-shpeel
excellent	**ausgezeichnet**	*ows*-gu-*tsykh*net
except	**außer**	*ows*ser

excess	das Übermaß	*ui*ber-mahss
exchange bureau	die Wechselstube	*veck*sel-*shtoo*ber
exchange rate	der Wechselkurs	*veck*sel-koors
excursion	der Ausflug	*ows*-floog
excuse	die Entschuldigung	ent*shool*digoong
exhausted	erschöpft	air*sherpft*
exhibition	die Ausstellung	*ows*-shtel*loong
exit	der Ausgang	*ows*-gang
expect (to)	erwarten	air*varten*
expensive	teuer	*toyer*
explain (to)	erklären	air*klairen*
express train	der Schnellzug	*shnell*-tsoog
extra	zusätzlich	*tsoo*-zetslikh

F

fabric	der Stoff	shtof
face	das Gesicht	gu*zikht*
face cream	die Gesichtscreme	gu*zikhts*-kraym
fact	die Tatsache	*taht*-zakher
factory	die Fabrik	*fabreek*
fade (to)	verblassen	fair*blassen*
faint (to)	in Ohnmacht fallen	in *ohn*-makht *fal*-len

fair *colouring*	blond	blont
fête	der Jahrmarkt, die Kirmes	*yahr*-markt, *keer*mes
fall (to)	fallen	*fal*-len
family	die Familie	fa*meel*-yer
far	weit	vite
fare	das Fahrgeld	*fahr*-gelt
farm	der Bauernhof	*bowern*-hohf
farmer	der Bauer	*bower*
farther	weiter	*viter*
fashion	die Mode	*mohder*
fast	schnell	shnell
fat	dick	dick
father	der Vater	*fahter*
fault	der Fehler	*failer*
fear	die Angst	angst
feed (to)	ernähren	air*nayren*
feel (to)	fühlen	*fuilen*
female *adj.*	weiblich	*vipe*-likh
ferry	die Fähre	*fairer*
fetch (to)	holen	*hohlen*
few	wenig	*vay*nikh
fiancé(e)	der/die Verlobte	fair*lohbter*

field	**das Feld**	felt
fight (to)	**kämpfen**	kempfen
fill (to)	**füllen**	fuillen
film	**der Film**	film
find (to)	**finden**	fin-den
fine	**die Geldstrafe**	*gelt-shtrah*fer
finish (to)	**vollenden**	fol*len*den
finished	**fertig**	*fair*tikh
fire	**das Feuer**	*foyer*
fire escape	**der Notausgang**	*noht-ows*-gang
first	**erste**	airster
first-aid	**die erste Hilfe**	airster hilfer
fish	**der Fisch**	fish
fish (to)	**angeln**	*ang*-eln
fisherman	**der Fischer**	fisher
fit	**fähig**	fay-ikh
fit (to)	**passen**	passen
flag	**die Fahne**	fahner
flat *adj.*	**flach**	flakh
noun	**die Wohnung**	*voh*noong
flight	**der Flug**	floog
flippers	**Schwimmflossen**	*shvim*-flossen
float (to)	**obenauf schwimmen**	ohben-*owf shvim*men

flood	**die Flut**	floot
floor	**der Fußboden**	*foos-boh*den
storey	**der Stock**	shtock
floor show	**das Kabarett**	kaba*ret*
flower	**die Blume**	*bloo*mer
fly	**die Fliege**	*flee*gur
fly (to)	**fliegen**	*flee*gun
fog	**der Nebel**	*nay*bul
fold (to)	**falten**	falten
follow (to)	**folgen**	folgun
food	**das Essen**	essen
foot	**der Fuß**	foos
football	**der Fußball**	*foos*-bal
footpath	**der Fußweg**	*foos*-vayg
for	**für**	fuir
foreign	**fremd**	fremt
forest	**der Wald**	valt
forget (to)	**vergessen**	fair*gessen*
fork	**die Gabel**	*gah*bul
forward	**vorwärts**	*for*-vairts
forward (to)	**nachschicken**	*nahkh*-shicken
fountain	**der (Spring-) Brunnen**	(shpring-) broonen
fragile	**zerbrechlich**	tsair*brekh*likh

free	**frei**	fry
fresh	**frisch**	frish
fresh water	**das Süßwasser**	*zuis-vas*ser
friend	**der Freund, die Freundin**	froynt, *froyn*din
friendly	**freundlich**	*froynt*likh
from	**von**	fon
front	**die Vorderseite**	*forder*-ziter
frontier	**die Grenze**	grentser
frozen	**gefroren**	gufrohren
fruit	**die Frucht**	frookht
full	**voll**	foll
fun	**der Spaß**	shpahs
funny	**komisch**	*koh*mish
fur	**der Pelz**	pelts
furniture	**die Möbel, der Hausrat**	*mer*bel, *hows*-raht

G

gallery	**die Galerie**	galai*ree*
gamble (to)	**(um Geld) spielen**	(oom gelt) *shpee*len
game	**das Spiel**	shpeel
garage	**die Garage**	ga*rah*jer

garbage	**der Abfall**	*ap*-fal
garden	**der Garten**	garten
gas	**das Gas**	gahs
gate	**das Tor**	tohr
gentlemen	**die Herren, Männer**	hairren, menner
German *adj.*	**deutsch**	doytsh
noun	**der/die Deutsche**	doytsher
Germany	**Deutschland**	*doytsh*-lant
get (to)	**bekommen**	bu*kommen*
get off (to)	**aussteigen**	*ows-shty*gun
get on (to)	**einsteigen**	*ine-shty*gun
gift	**das Geschenk**	gu-*shenk*
girl	**das Mädchen**	*mayt*-khen
give (to)	**geben**	*gay*ben
glad	**froh**	froh
glass	**das Glas**	glahs
glasses	**die Brille**	*briller*
gloomy	**dunkel, schwermütig**	*doon*kel, *shvair*muitikh
glorious	**herrlich**	*hair*likh
glove	**der Handschuh**	*hant*shoo
go (to)	**gehen**	*gay*en
goal	**das Ziel**	tseel

goal (to score a)	**ein Tor schießen**	tohr *sheess*en
god	**Gott**	got
gold	**das Gold**	gohlt
good	**gut**	goot
government	**die Regierung**	re*geer*oong
granddaughter	**die Enkelin**	*enk*ellin
grandfather	**der Großvater**	*grohs*-fahter
grandmother	**die Großmutter**	*grohs*-mootter
grandson	**der Enkel**	*enk*el
grass	**das Gras**	grahs
grateful	**dankbar**	dankbar
gravel	**der Kies**	kees
great	**groß**	grohs
Great Britain	**Großbritannien**	grohs-brit*tan*-yen
groceries	**die Lebensmittel**	*lay*bens-mittel
ground	**der Grund, Boden**	groont, *boh*den
grow (to)	**wachsen**	vakhsen
guarantee	**die Garantie**	garan*tee*
guard	**der Schaffner**	*shaf*ner
guest	**der Gast**	gast
guide	**der Führer**	*fuir*er
guide book	**der Reiseführer**	ryzer-*fuir*er

H

hail	**der Hagel**	*hah*gul
hair	**das Haar**	hahr
hair brush	**die Haarbürste**	*hahr-buir*ster
hairgrip	**die Haarklammer**	*hahr*-klammer
hairpin	**die Haarnadel**	*hahr-nah*del
half	**halb**	halp
half fare	**der halbe Preis**	halber price
hammer	**der Hammer**	hammer
hand	**die Hand**	hant
handbag	**die Handtasche**	*hant*-tasher
handkerchief	**das Taschentuch**	*tash*en-tookh
hang (to)	**hängen**	heng-en
happen (to)	**geschehen**	gu-*shay*en
happy	**glücklich**	gluicklikh
happy birthday	**viel Glück zum Geburtstag**	feel gluick tsoom gu*boorts*-tahg
harbour	**der Hafen**	hahfen
hard *solid*	**hart**	hart
difficult	**schwierig**	*shveer*ikh
hardly	**kaum**	kowm
hat	**der Hut**	hoot
have (to)	**haben**	hahben

he	er	air
health	die Gesundheit	guzoont-hite
hear (to)	hören	her-ren
heart	das Herz	hairts
heat	die Hitze	hitser
heating	die Heizung	hytsoong
heavy	schwer	shvair
height	die Höhe	her-wer
help	die Hilfe	hilfer
help (to)	helfen	helfen
hem	der Saum	zowm
her	sie, ihr, ihre	zee, eer, eerer
here	hier	heer
hers	ihr	eer
high	hoch	hohkh
hike (to)	wandern	vandern
hill	der Hügel, Berg	huigel, bairg
him	ihn, ihm	een, eem
hire (to)	mieten	meeten
his	sein, seine	zine, ziner
hitch hike (to)	per Anhalter fahren	pair an-halter fahren
hold (to)	(fest)halten	(fest)halten
hole	das Loch	lokh
holiday	der Feiertag	fyer-tahg

holidays	**die Ferien**	*fayree-yen*
hollow	**hohl**	hohl
(at) home	**zu Hause**	tsoo *howzer*
honeymoon	**die Hochzeitsreise**	*hohkh*-tsites-*ryzer*
hope	**die Hoffnung**	hofnoong
hope (to)	**hoffen**	hoffen
horse	**das Pferd**	pfairt
horse races	**das Pferderennen**	*pfairder*-rennen
horse riding	**das (Pferde-) Reiten**	(*pfairder-*) *ry*ten
hospital	**das Krankenhaus**	*kranken*-hows
host	**der Gastgeber**	*gast-gay*ber
hostess	**die Gastgeberin**	*gast-gay*berin
hot	**heiß**	hice
hotel	**das Hotel**	hoh*tel*
hotel keeper	**der Hotelier**	hoh*tel-yer*
hot-water bottle	**die Wärmflasche**	*vairm-flasher*
hour	**die Stunde**	*shtoon*der
house	**das Haus**	hows
how?	**wie?**	vee
how much/many?	**wie viel/viele?**	vee feel/feeler
hungry	**hungrig**	hoongrikh
hurry (to)	**eilen**	ilen
hurt (to)	**schmerzen, weh tun**	*shmairt*sen, vay toon
husband	**der Mann, Gatte**	man, gatter

I

I	**ich**	ikh
if	**wenn**	ven
immediately	**sofort**	zoh*fort*
important	**wichtig**	*vikh*tikh
in	**in**	in
include (to)	**einschließen**	*ine-shlees*sen
included	**einbegriffen**	*ine-*bugriffen
inconvenient	**ungelegen**	*oon-*gul*ay*gun
incorrect	**unrichtig, falsch**	*oon-rikh*-tikh, falsh
indeed	**tatsächlich**	taht-*sekh*likh
indoors	**ins Haus**	ins hows
information	**die Auskunft**	*ows*-koonft
information bureau	**die Auskunftstelle**	*ows*-koonft-*shtel*ler
ink	**die Tinte**	tinter
inn	**das Gasthaus**	*gast*-hows
insect	**das Insekt**	in*zekt*
insect sting	**der Insektenstich**	in*zekt*en-shtikh
insect repellant	**das Insektenspray**	in*zekt*en-shpray
inside	**drinnen**	drinnen
instead of	**statt**	shtat
instructor	**der Lehrer**	lairer
insurance	**die Versicherung**	fair-*zikh*eroong
insure (to)	**versichern**	fair-*zikh*ern

interested	**interessiert**	interess*eert*
interesting	**interessant**	interess*ant*
internet	**Internet**	internet
interpreter	**der Dolmetscher**	*dol*metsher
into	**in**	in
introduce (to)	**bekanntmachen**	bu*kannt*-makhen
invitation	**die Einladung**	*ine-lah*doong
invite (to)	**einladen**	*ine-lah*den
Ireland	**Irland**	*eer*-lant
Irish	**irisch**	*eer*ish
iron (to)	**bügeln, plätten**	*bui*geln, pletten
island	**die Insel**	*in*zel
it	**es**	es

J

jacket	**die Jacke**	*yack*er
jar	**der Krug, Topf**	kroog, topf
jelly fish	**die Qualle**	*k-vah*ler
jewellery	**der Schmuck**	shmook
Jewish	**jüdisch**	*yui*dish
job	**die Stellung**	*shtel*loong
journey	**die Reise**	*ry*zer
jump (to)	**springen**	shpring-en
jumper	**der Pullover**	pool*oh*ver

K

keep (to)	**halten, behalten**	halten, buhalten
key	**der Schlüssel**	*shluis*sel
kick (to)	**(mit dem Fuß) stoßen**	(mit daim foos) *shtoh*sen
kind (friendly)	**freundlich**	*froynt*likh
king	**der König**	kernikh
kiss	**der Kuss**	kooss
kiss (to)	**küssen**	kuissen
kitchen	**die Küche**	*kuikh*er
knife	**das Messer**	messer
knock (to)	**klopfen**	klopfen
know (to) *fact*	**wissen**	vissen
person	**kennen**	kennen

L

label	**das Etikett**	etee*kett*
lace	**die Spitze**	shpitser
ladies	**die Damen, Frauen**	*dah*men, *frow*en
lake	**der See**	zay
lamp	**die Lampe**	*lamp*er
land	**das Land**	lant
landlady	**die Hauswirtin**	*hows*-veertin

landlord	**der Hauswirt**	*hows*-veert
lane *town*	**die Gasse**	gasser
country	**der Pfad**	pfaht
language	**die Sprache**	*shprahkh*er
large	**groß**	grohs
last	**letzt**	letst
late	**spät**	shpayt
laugh (to)	**lachen**	lakhen
launderette	**der Waschsalon**	*vash*-zalon
lavatory	**die Toilette**	twah*letter*
lavatory paper	**das Toilettenpapier**	twah*letten*-pa*peer*
law	**das Gesetz**	gu*zets*
lawyer	**der Anwalt**	*an*-valt
lead (to)	**führen**	fuiren
leaf	**das Blatt**	blat
leak (to)	**auslaufen**	*ows-low*fen
learn (to)	**lernen**	lairnen
least	**mindest, wenigst**	mindest/*vay*nikhst
(in the) least	**am wenigsten**	am *vay*nikhsten
leather	**das Leder**	*lay*der
leave (to) *abandon*	**verlassen**	fair*lassen*
go away	**abfahren**	*ap*-fahren
(on the) left	**links**	links
left luggage	**die Gepäckaufbewahrung**	gu*peck*-owf-bu*vah*roong

lend (to)	**leihen**	*ly*-en
length	**die Länge**	leng-er
less	**weniger**	*vay*nigur
lesson	**der Unterricht**	*oon*ter-rikht
let (to) *rent*	**vermieten**	fair*meet*en
allow	**erlauben, lassen**	air*low*ben, lassen
letter	**der Brief**	breef
level crossing	**der Bahnübergang**	bahn-*uiber*-gang
library	**die Bibliothek**	beeblee-yoh-*taik*
licence	**die Erlaubnis**	air*low*bnis
life	**das Leben**	*lay*ben
lift	**der Fahrstuhl**	*fahr*-shtool
light *colour*	**hell**	hell
weight	**leicht**	lykht
noun	**das Licht**	likht
light bulb	**die Glühbirne**	*glui-beer*ner
lighthouse	**der Leuchtturm**	*loykht*-toorm
like (to)	**gern haben**	gairn hahben
line	**die Linie**	*leen*-yer
linen *fibre*	**das Leinen**	*ly*nen
household	**die Bettwäsche**	*bet*-vesher
lingerie	**die Unterwäsche**	*oon*ter-vesher
lipstick	**der Lippenstift**	lippen-shtift

liquid *adj.*	**flüssig**	*fluissikh*
noun	**die Flüssigkeit**	*fluissikh-kite*
listen (to)	**zuhören**	*tsoo-*her-ren
little	**klein**	kline
live (to)	**leben**	*lay*ben
loaf	**das Brot**	broht
local	**lokal, hiesig, örtlich**	loh*kahl, hee*zikh, ertlikh
lock	**das Schloss**	shloss
lock (to)	**schließen**	*shleessen*
long	**lang**	lang
look at (to)	**ansehen**	*an-zay*en
look for (to)	**suchen**	*zookhen*
like (to)	**aussehen**	*ows-zay*en
loose	**los(e)**	lohs(er)
lorry	**der Lastwagen**	*last-vah*gun
lose (to)	**verlieren**	fair*leeren*
lost property office	**das Fundbüro**	*foont-*buiroh
lot	**viel**	feel
loud	**laut**	lowt
love (to)	**lieben**	*lee*ben
lovely	**schön**	shern
low	**niedrig**	*need*rikh
luggage	**das Gepäck**	gu*peck*
lunch	**das Mittagessen**	*mit-*tahg-essen

M

mad	**verrückt**	fair-*ruickt*
magazine	**die Zeitschrift**	*tsite*-shrift
maid	**das (Dienst-) Mädchen**	(deenst-) *mayt*-khen
mail	**die Post**	post
main street	**die Hauptstraße**	*howpt-strahss*er
make (to)	**machen**	makhen
make-up	**das Make-up**	make-up
male *adj.*	**männlich**	menlikh
man	**der Mann**	man
manage (to)	**auskommen**	*ows-kom*men
manager	**der Leiter**	*lyter*
manicure	**die Maniküre**	manee*kuir*er
many	**viel(e)**	feel(er)
map	**die Karte**	karter
market	**der Markt**	markt
married	**verheiratet**	fair-*hy*-rahtet
Mass	**die Messe**	messer
massage	**die Massage**	mass*ah*jer
match *to strike*	**das Streichholz**	*strykh*-holts
sport	**das Spiel**	shpeel
material	**der Stoff**	shtof
matinée	**die Matinee**	mateen*ay*

mattress	**die Matratze**	ma*tratt*ser
me	**mich, mir**	mikh, meer
meal	**die Mahlzeit**	*mahl*-tsite
measurements	**die Maße**	masser
meet (to)	**treffen**	*tref*fen
memory stick	**der Memorystick**	memory-stick
mend (to)	**reparieren**	repah*reeren*
mess	**die Unordnung**	*oon-ord*noong
message	**die Nachricht**	*nahkh*-rikht
metal	**das Metall**	may*tahl*
middle	**die Mitte**	mitter
middle-aged	**in mittlerem Alter**	in *mitl*erem *alt*er
middle class	**die Mittelklasse**	*mit*tel-klasser
mild	**mild**	milt
mine *pron.*	**mein**	mine
minute	**die Minute**	mee*noot*er
mirror	**der Spiegel**	*shpee*gul
Miss	**Fräulein**	*froy*line
miss (to)	**verpassen**	fair*passen*
mistake	**der Fehler**	failer
mix (to)	**(ver)mischen**	(fair)*mishen*
mixed	**gemischt**	gu*misht*
mobile phone	**das Handy**	handy
modern	**modern**	moh*dairn*

moment	**der Augenblick**	*ow*gun-blick
money	**das Geld**	gelt
month	**der Monat**	*moh*naht
monument	**das Denkmal**	*denk*mahl
moon	**der Mond**	mohnt
more	**mehr**	mair
mosque	**die Moschee**	mo*shay*
most	**meist, die meisten**	myst, *my*sten
mother	**die Mutter**	*moo*tter
motor boat	**das Motorboot**	moh*tor*-boht
motor cycle	**das Motorrad**	moh*tor*-raht
motor racing	**das Autorennen**	*ow*toh-rennen
motorway	**die Autobahn**	*ow*toh-bahn
mountain	**der Berg**	bairg
mouthwash	**das Mundwasser**	*moont-vasser*
Mr	**Herr**	hair
Mrs	**Frau**	frow
much	**viel**	feel
museum	**das Museum**	moo*zay*oom
music	**die Musik**	moo*zeek*
muslim	**der Moslem**	moslem
must (to have to)	**müssen**	*mui*ssen
my	**mein, meine**	mine, miner
myself	**mich**	mikh

N

nail	**der Nagel**	*nah*gul
nailbrush	**die Nagelbürste**	*nah*gul-*buir*ster
nailfile	**die Nagelfeile**	*nah*gul-*fy*ler
nail polish	**der Nagellack**	*nah*gul-lack
name	**der Name**	*nah*mer
napkin	**die Serviette**	zairvee-*yet*ter
nappy	**die Windel**	vindel
narrow	**schmal**	shmahl
natural	**natürlich**	na*tuir*likh
near	**in der Nähe von . . .**	in dair *nay*er fon . . .
nearly	**fast**	fast
necessary	**notwendig**	*noht*vendikh
necklace	**die (Hals-) Kette**	(hals-) ketter
need (to)	**brauchen**	*browkh*en
needle	**die Nadel**	*nah*del
nephew	**der Neffe**	neffer
net	**das Netz**	nets
never	**nie, niemals**	nee, neemahls
new	**neu**	noy
news	**die Nachrichten**	*nahkh*-rikhten
newspaper	**die Zeitung**	*tsite*-oong

New Zealand	Neuseeland	noy-*zeh*land
New Zealander	der Neuseeländer, die Neuseeländerin	noy-*zay*lender, noy-*zay*lenderin
next	nächst	naikhst
nice	nett	net
niece	die Nichte	nikhter
night	die Nacht	nahkht
nightclub	der Nachtklub	*nahkht*-kloob
nightdress	das Nachthemd	*nahkht*-hemt
nobody	niemand	*nee*mant
noisy	lärmend	*lair*ment
none	keine, keinen	kiner, kinen
north	der Norden	norden
not	nicht	nikht
(bank) note	der Geldschein	*gelt*-shine
notebook	das Notizbuch	noh*tits*-bookh
nothing	nichts	nikhts
notice	die Notiz	noh*tits*
notice (to)	bemerken	bu*mair*ken
novel	der Roman	roh*mahn*
now	jetzt	yetst
number	die Nummer, Zahl	noommer/tsahl
nylon	das Nylon	nuilon

O

occasion	**die Gelegenheit**	gu*lay*gunhite
occupation	**der Beruf**	bur*oof*
occupied	**besetzt**	bu*zetst*
ocean	**das Meer**	mayer
odd *not even*	**ungerade**	*oon*-gurahder
strange	**sonderbar**	zonderbar
of	**von**	fon
off	**ab**	ap
offer	**das Angebot**	*an*-guboht
offer (to)	**anbieten**	*an*-beeten
office	**das Büro**	buiroh
officer/official	**der Beamte, die Beamtin**	bu-*am*ter, bu-*am*tin
officer *military*	**der Offizier**	offits-*yer*
official *adj.*	**offiziell**	offits-*yel*
often	**oft**	oft
oily	**fettig**	*fe*ttikh
ointment	**die Salbe**	zalber
OK	**OK/in Ordnung**	oh-kay/in *ord*noong
old	**alt**	alt
on	**auf, an**	owf, an
once	**einmal**	*ine*-mahl
online	**online**	online

only	**nur**	noor
open (to)	**öffnen**	*erf*nen
open(ed)	**geöffnet**	gu-*erf*net
opening	**die Öffnung**	*erf*noong
opera	**die Oper**	*oh*per
opportunity	**die Gelegenheit**	gu*layg*unhite
opposite	**gegenüber-liegend**	*gayg*un-*ui*ber-leegunt
or	**oder**	*oh*der
orchestra	**das Orchester**	or*kes*ter
order (to)	**bestellen**	bu-*shtel*len
ordinary	**gewöhnlich**	guv*ern*likh
other	**ander**	*an*der
otherwise	**sonst**	zonst
our/ours	**unser**	*oon*zer
out	**aus**	ows
out of order	**außer Betrieb**	*ows*ser bu*treep*
outside	**draußen**	*drow*ssen
over *above, across*	**über**	*ui*ber
finished	**fertig/zu Ende**	*fair*tikh/tsoo *en*der
over there	**da drüben**	dah *drui*ben
overcoat	**der Mantel**	*man*tel
overnight	**über Nacht**	*ui*ber nahkht
owe (to)	**schulden**	*shool*den
owner	**der Besitzer**	bu*zit*ser

P

pack (to)	**packen**	packen
packet	**das Paket**	pa*kayt*
page	**die Seite**	ziter
pain	**der Schmerz**	shmairts
paint (to)	**malen**	mahlen
painting	**das Gemälde**	gu*mel*der
pair	**das Paar**	pahr
palace	**der Palast**	pa*last*
pale	**blass**	blass
panties	**der Schlüpfer**	*shluip*fer
paper	**das Papier**	pa*peer*
parcel	**das Paket**	pa*kayt*
park	**der Park**	park
park (to)	**parken**	parken
parking meter	**die Parkuhr**	*park*-oor
parking ticket	**der Parkschein**	*park*-shine
parliament	**das Parlament**	parlah*ment*
part	**der Teil**	tile
party	**die Gesellschaft**	gu*zel*shaft
pass (to)	**vorbeigehen**	for-*by*-*gay*en
passenger	**der Passagier**	passa*jeer*
passport	**der Pass**	pass

past *noun*	**die Vergangenheit**	fair*gang*-en-hite
path	**der Pfad**	pfaht
patient	**der Patient**	pats-*yent*
pavement	**der Bürgersteig**	*buir*gur-shtyg
pay (to)	**bezahlen**	bu-*tsahl*en
peak	**der Gipfel**	gipfel
peace	**der Frieden**	freeden
pearl	**die Perle**	pairler
pebble	**der Kiesel**	keezel
pedal	**das Pedal**	pe*dahl*
pedestrian	**der Fußgänger**	*foos*-geng-er
pedestrian crossing	**der Fußgängerübergang**	*foos*-geng-er-*uiber*-gang
pedestrian precinct	**die Fußgängerzone**	*foos*-geng-er-tsohner
pen	**die Feder**	*fay*der
pencil	**der Bleistift**	*bly*-shtift
penknife	**das Federmesser**	*fay*der-messer
pensioner	**der Rentner**	rentner
people	**die Leute**	*loy*ter
perfect	**tadellos**	*tah*del-lohs
per (person)	**pro (Person)**	pro (pair*zohn*)
performance	**die Aufführung, Vorstellung**	*owf*-fuiroong, *for*-*shtel*loong
perfume	**das Parfüm**	par*fuim*
perhaps	**vielleicht**	feel-*lykht*

perishable	**leicht verderblich**	lykht *fairdair*blikh
permit	**die Erlaubnis**	air*low*bnis
permit (to)	**erlauben**	air*low*ben
person	**die Person**	pair*zohn*
personal	**persönlich**	pair*zern*likh
petrol	**das Benzin**	bent*seen*
petrol station	**die Tankstelle**	*tank-shtel*ler
photograph	**das Foto**	fohtoh
photographer	**der Fotograf**	fohtoh-*grahf*
piano	**das Klavier**	kla*veer*
pick (to) *choose*	**aussuchen**	*ows-zook*hen
gather	**pflücken**	pfluicken
picnic	**das Picknick**	peek-neek
piece	**das Stück**	shtuick
pier	**die Landungsbrücke**	*land*oongs-*bruic*ker
pillow	**das Kopfkissen**	*kopf*-kissen
pin	**die Stecknadel**	*shteck-nah*del
(safety) pin	**die Sicherheitsnadel**	*zikh*er-hites-*nah*del
pipe	**die Pfeife**	pfifer
place	**der Ort**	ort
plain	**einfach**	*ine*-fakh
plan	**der Plan**	plahn
plant	**die Pflanze**	pflantser
plastic	**die plastik**	*plas*tik

plate	**der Teller**	teller
platform	**der Bahnsteig**	*bahn*-shtyg
play	**das Schauspiel**	*show*-shpeel
play (to)	**spielen**	*shpee*len
player	**der Spieler**	*shpee*ler
please	**bitte**	bitter
plenty	**die Menge**	meng-er
pliers	**die Zange** (sing.)	tsang-er
plug *bath*	**der Stopfen**	shtopfen
electric	**der Stecker**	*shteck*er
pocket	**die Tasche**	tasher
point	**der Punkt**	poonkt
poisonous	**giftig**	giftikh
policeman	**der Polizist**	pohlit*sist*
police station	**die Polizeiwache**	pohlit*sy*-vakher
political	**politisch**	pohl*i*tish
politician	**der Politiker**	pohl*i*tikher
politics	**die Politik**	pohl*i*tik
pollution	**die Umweltver-schmutzung**	*oom*velt-fairs*hmoot*soong
poor	**arm**	arm
popular	**populär**	pohpoo*lair*
porcelain	**das Porzellan**	portsel-*lahn*
port	**der Hafen**	hahfen

possible	**möglich**	*merk*likh
post (to)	**einstecken, aufgeben**	*ine*-shtecken, *owf-gay*ben
post box	**der Briefkasten**	*breef*-kasten
postcard	**die Postkarte**	*post*-karter
postman	**der Briefträger**	*breef-tray*gur
post office	**die Post**	post
postpone (to)	**zurückstellen**	tsoo-*ruick-shtel*len
pound	**das Pfund**	pfoont
powder	**der Puder**	*pood*er
prefer (to)	**vorziehen**	*for*-tsee-yen
pregnant	**schwanger**	shvang-er
prepare (to)	**vorbereiten**	*for*-bu-*ry*ten
present *gift*	**das Geschenk**	gu-*shenk*
press (to)	**bügeln, plätten**	buigeln, pletten
pretty	**hübsch**	huipsh
price	**der Preis**	price
priest	**der Priester**	preester
print	**der (Ab-) Druck**	(*ap*-) drook
print (to)	**(ab)drucken**	(*ap*)drooken
private	**privat, persönlich**	priv*aht*, pair*zern*likh
problem	**das Problem**	prob*laym*
profession	**der Beruf**	bu*roof*
programme	**das Programm**	proh*gram*

promise	**das Versprechen**	fair*shprekh*en
promise (to)	**versprechen**	fair*shprekh*en
prompt	**sofortig**	zoh*fort*ikh
Protestant	**der Protestant**	protes*tant*
provide (to)	**besorgen**	bu*zorg*un
public	**öffentlich**	*erf*entlikh
public holiday	**Feiertag**	*fyer*-tahg
pull (to)	**ziehen**	*tsee*-yen
pump	**die Pumpe**	*poomp*er
pure	**rein**	rine
purse	**das Portemonnaie, die Geldbörse**	portmon*nay*, *gelt-berr*ser
push (to)	**stoßen**	*shtohss*en
put (to)	**stellen**	*shtell*en
pyjamas	**der Schlafanzug**	*shlahf*-antsoog

Q

quality	**die Qualität**	k-vali*tayt*
quantity	**die Quantität**	k-vanti*tayt*
quarter	**das Viertel**	*feer*tel
queen	**die Königin**	*kern*eegin
question	**die Frage**	*frahg*ur
queue	**die Schlange**	shlang-er

queue (to)	**Schlange stehen**	shlang-er *shtay*en
quick(ly)	**schnell**	shnell
quiet(ly)	**ruhig**	roo-ikh
quilt	**das Federbett**	*fay*der-bet
quite	**ganz**	gants

R

race	**das Rennen**	rennen
race course	**die Rennbahn**	*renn*-bahn
radiator	**der Heizkörper**	*hites-ker*per
radio	**das Radio**	*rah*deeyoh
railway	**die Eisenbahn**	*eye*-zen-bahn
rain	**der Regen**	*ray*gun
rain (to)	**regnen**	*rayg*nen
rainbow	**der Regenbogen**	*ray*gun-bohgun
raincoat	**der Regenmantel**	*ray*gun-*man*tel
rare	**rar**	rahr
rather	**ziemlich**	*tseem*likh
raw	**roh**	roh
razor	**der Rasierapparat**	razeer-appa*raht*
razor blade	**die Rasierklinge**	razeer-kling-er
reach (to)	**reichen**	*rykh*en
read (to)	**lesen**	*lay*zen

ready	**bereit**	*burite*
real	**wahr**	vahr
really	**wirklich**	*veer*klikh
reason	**der Grund**	groont
receipt	**die Quittung**	*k-vitoong*
receive (to)	**bekommen**	bu*kommen*
recent	**neu**	noy
recipe	**das Rezept**	ray*tsept*
recognize (to)	**erkennen**	air*kennen*
recommend (to)	**empfehlen**	emp*faylen*
record	**der Rekord**	*rekord*
refreshments	**die Erfrischungen**	air*frish*oong-en
refrigerator	**der Kühlschrank**	*kuil*-shrank
regards	**die Grüße**	*gruisser*
register (to)	**(Gepäck) aufgeben, einschreiben**	(gu*peck*) owf-*gay*ben, *ine*-shry*ben*
relative	**der/die Verwandte**	fair*vandt*er
religion	**die Religion**	raylig-*yon*
remember (to)	**sich erinnern**	zikh air*inn*ern
rent	**die Miete**	*meeter*
rent (to)	**mieten, leihen**	*meet*en, *ly*-en
repair (to)	**reparieren**	repah*reeren*
repeat (to)	**wiederholen**	*veeder*-*hohl*en
reply (to)	**antworten**	*ant*vorten

reservation	**die Reservierung**	rezair*veer*oong
reserve (to)	**reservieren**	rezair*veer*en
restaurant	**das Restaurant**	restor-*rant*
restaurant car	**der Speisewagen**	shpyzer-*vah*gun
return (to) *go back*	**zurückkehren**	tsoo-*ruick*-kairen
give back	**zurückgeben**	tsoo-*ruick*-*gay*ben
reward	**die Belohnung**	bu*lohn*oong
ribbon	**das Band**	bant
rich	**reich**	rykh
ride	**die Fahrt**	fahrt
ride (to)	**reiten**	*ry*ten
right *opp. left*	**rechts**	rekhts
opp. wrong	**richtig**	*rikh*-tikh
ring	**der Ring**	ring
ripe	**reif**	rife
rise (to)	**sich erheben**	zikh air*hay*ben
get up	**aufstehen**	*owf-shtay*en
river	**der Fluss**	flooss
road	**die Straße**	*strah*sser
rock	**der Felsen**	felzen
roll (to)	**rollen**	*rol*-len
roof	**das Dach**	dakh
room	**das Zimmer**	tsimmer
rope	**das Seil**	zile

rotten	**faul**	fowl
rough	**rauh, grob**	row, grohp
round	**rund**	roont
rowing boat	**das Ruderboot**	*rooder*-boht
rubber	**das Gummi**	*goom*mee
rubbish	**der Abfall**	*ap*-fal
rude	**unhöflich**	*oon*-herflikh
ruins	**die Ruine**	roo-*weener*
rule (to)	**beherrschen**	bu*hair*shen
run (to)	**laufen**	*low*fen

S

sad	**traurig**	*trow*rikh
saddle	**der Sattel**	*zattel*
safe	**sicher**	*zikher*
sailor(s)	**der Seemann (die Seeleute)**	*zay*-man (*zay-loy*ter)
sale *clearance*	**der Ausverkauf**	*ows*-fairkowf
(for) sale	**verkäuflich**	fair*koy*flikh
salesman	**die Verkäufer**	fair*koy*fer
saleswoman	**der Verkäuferin**	fair*koy*ferin
salt water	**das Salzwasser**	*zalts-vass*er
same	**der-, die-, dasselbe**	dair-, dee-, das-*zel*ber

sand	**der Sand**	zant
sandal	**die Sandale**	zan*dahl*er
sanitary towel	**die Binde**	bin-der
satisfactory	**befriedigend**	bu*free*digunt
save (to)	**retten**	*ret*ten
say (to)	**sagen**	*zahg*un
scald (to)	**verbrühen**	fair*brui*-en
scarf	**der Schal**	shahl
scenery	**die Landschaft**	*lant*-shaft
school	**die Schule**	shooler
scissors	**die Schere**	shairer
Scot	**der Schotte, die Schottin**	*shot*ter, *shot*tin
Scotland	**Schottland**	*shot*-lant
Scottish	**schottisch**	*shot*tish
scratch (to)	**kratzen**	*krat*sen
screw	**die Schraube**	*shrow*ber
screwdriver	**der Schraubenzieher**	*shrow*ben-tsee-yer
sculpture	**die Skulptur**	skoolp*toor*
sea	**das Meer, die See**	mayer, zay
sea food	**die Meeresfrüchte**	*may*eres-*fruikh*ter
seasickness	**die Seekrankheit**	*zay*-krank-hite
season	**die Jahreszeit**	*yahr*es-tsite

seat	**der Platz**	plats
seat belt	**der Sicherheitsgurt**	*zikher*-hites-goort
second	**zweite**	tsviter
second-hand	**zweite Hand**	tsviter hant
see (to)	**sehen**	*zayen*
seem (to)	**scheinen**	shinen
sell (to)	**verkaufen**	fair*kowfen*
send (to)	**schicken**	shicken
separate *adj.*	**getrennt**	gu*trent*
serious	**ernst**	airnst
serve (to)	**bedienen**	bu*deenen*
service *in a shop*	**die Bedienung**	bu*deenoong*
church	**der Gottesdienst**	*gottes*-deenst
several	**mehrere**	*mayrerer*
sew (to)	**nähen**	*nayen*
shade *colour*	**der Farbton**	*farb*-tohn
shade/shadow	**der Schatten**	shatten
shallow	**flach**	flakh
shampoo	**das Schampoo**	*sham*poh
shape	**die Form**	form
share (to)	**teilen**	*tylen*
sharp	**scharf**	sharf
shave (to)	**rasieren**	rah*zeeren*

shaving brush	der Rasierpinsel	rahzeer-pinzel
shaving cream	die Rasiercreme	rahzeer-kraymer
she	sie	zee
sheet	das Bettlaken	bet-lahken
shell	die Muschel	mooshel
shelter	die Unterkunft	oonter-koonft
shine (to)	scheinen	shinen
shingle	der Kiesel	keezel
ship	das Schiff	shif
shipping line	die Schiff-Fahrtsgesellschaft	shif-fahrts-guzelshaft
shirt	das Hemd	hemt
shock	der Stoß	shtohs
shoe	der Schuh	shoo
shoelace	der Schnürsenkel	shnuir-zenkel
shoe polish	die Schuhwichse	shoo-vikhser
shop	der Laden, das Geschäft	lahden, gusheft
shopping centre	das Einkaufszentrum	ine-kowfs-tsentroom
shore	das Ufer, die Küste	oofer, kuister
short	kurz	koorts
shorts	die Shorts	shorts
show	die Vorstellung	for-shtelloong

show (to)	**zeigen**	*tsy*gun
shower	**die Dusche**	*doo*sher
shut (to)	**schließen**	*shlee*ssen
closed	**geschlossen**	gu-*shlo*ssen
side	**die Seite**	*zi*ter
sights	**die Sehenswürdigkeiten**	*zay*ens-*vuir*dikh-kiten
sightseeing	**die Besichtigung von Sehenswürdigkeiten**	bu*zikh*tigoong von *zay*ens-*vuir*dikh-kiten
sign	**das Zeichen**	*tsykh*en
sign (to)	**unterschreiben**	*oonter-shry*ben
signpost	**der Wegweiser**	*vek*-vizer
silver	**das Silber**	*zil*ber
simple	**einfach**	*ine*-fakh
since	**seit**	*zi*te
sing (to)	**singen**	*zing*-en
single	**einzig, einzeln**	*ine*-tsig, *ine*-tseln
single room	**das Einzelzimmer**	*ine*-tsel-tsimmer
sister	**die Schwester**	*shvest*er
sit (to)	**sitzen**	*zit*sen
sit down (to)	**sich setzen**	zikh *zet*sen
size	**die Größe**	*grer*ser
skating	**Schlittschuh laufen**	*shlit*-shoo-*low*fen
skid (to)	**rutschen**	*root*shen

skiing	das Skilaufen	*shee-low*fen
skirt	der Rock	rock
sky	der Himmel	himmel
sleep (to)	schlafen	shlahfen
sleeper	der Schlafwagen	*shlahf-vahg*un
sleeping bag	der Schlafsack	*shlahf*-zack
sleeve	der Ärmel	*airmel*
slice	die Schnitte	shnitter
slip	der Unterrock	*oonter*-rock
slipper	der Hausschuh	*hows*-shoo
slowly	langsam	*lang*zam
small	klein	kline
smart	schick	shick
smell	der Geruch	*gurookh*
smell (to)	riechen	*reekh*en
smile (to)	lächeln	lekheln
smoke (to)	rauchen	*rowkh*en
no smoking	rauchen verboten	*rowkh*en fair*bohten*
snack	der Imbiss	*imbiss*
snow	der Schnee	shnay
snow (to)	schneien	*shny*-en
so	so	zoh
soap	die Seife	*zyfer*

soap powder	**das Seifenpulver**	*zy*fen-poolfer
sober	**nüchtern**	*nuikh*tern
sock	**die Socke**	zocker
socket *electrical*	**die Steckdose**	*shteck-dohz*er
soft	**weich**	vykh
sold	**verkauft**	fair*kowft*
sole *shoe*	**die Sohle**	*zohl*er
solid	**fest**	fest
some	**einige, etwas**	*ine*-igur, etvas
somebody	**jemand**	*yay*mant
somehow	**irgendwie**	*eer*gunt-vee
something	**etwas**	etvas
sometimes	**manchmal**	*mankh*mahl
somewhere	**irgendwo**	*eer*gunt-voh
son	**der Sohn**	zohn
son et lumière show	**die Ton- und Lichtshow**	tohn- oont likht-show
song	**das Lied**	leet
soon	**bald**	balt
sort	**die Art**	art
sound	**der Laut**	lowt
sour	**sauer**	*zow*er
south	**der Süden**	*zui*den
souvenir	**das Andenken**	*an*denken

space	der Raum	rowm
spanner	der Schraubenschlüssel	*shrow*ben-*shluis*sel
spare	Ersatz-, Reserve-	airzats-, re*zair*ver-
speak (to)	sprechen	shprekhen
speciality	die Spezialität	shpay-tsee-yali*tayt*
spectacles	die Brille (*sing.*)	*bri*ller
speed	die Geschwindigkeit	gush*vin*dikh-kite
speed limit	die Geschwindig-keitsgrenze	gush*vin*dikh-kites-grentser
spend (to)	ausgeben	*ows-gay*ben
spoon	der Löffel	*ler*fel
sport	der Sport	shport
sprain (to)	verstauchen	fair-*shtowkh*en
spring *water*	die Quelle	k-*vel*ler
square *shape*	viereckig	*feer*-ekikh
in a town	der Platz	plats
square metre	der Quadratmeter	k-vad*raht-may*ter
stable	der Stall	shtal
stage	die Bühne	buiner
stain	der Fleck	fleck
stained	beschmutzt	bu-*shmootst*
stairs	die Treppe	*trep*per
stale	schal	shahl

stalls	**das Parkett**	par*ket*
stamp	**die Briefmarke**	*breef*-marker
stand (to)	**stehen**	*shtay*en
star	**der Stern**	shtairn
start (to)	**anfangen**	*an*-fang-en
(main) station	**der (Haupt-) Bahnhof**	(*howpt*-) *bahn*-hohf
stay (to)	**bleiben**	*bly*ben
step	**der Schritt**	shrit
steward	**der Steward, Flugbegleiter**	*shtoo*-art, floog-bug*ly*ter
stewardess	**die Stewardess, Flugbegleiterin**	*shtoo*-ardess, *floog*-bug*ly*terin
stick	**der Stock**	shtock
stiff	**starr**	shtar
still *not moving*	**still**	shtil
time	**noch**	nokh
sting	**der Stich**	stikh
stolen	**gestohlen**	gu-*shtoh*len
stone	**der Stein**	shtine
stool	**der Stuhl, Hocker**	shtool, hocker
stop (to)	**(an)halten**	(*an*)halten
storm	**der Sturm**	shtoorm
stove	**der Ofen**	ohfen
straight	**gerade**	gu*rah*der

straight on	**geradeaus**	*gurahder-ows*
strange	**sonderbar**	*zonder*bar
strap	**der Riemen**	*reemen*
stream	**der Bach**	bakh
street	**die Straße**	*strahs*ser
stretch (to)	**(aus)strecken**	*(ows)*shtrecken
string	**die Schnur**	shnoor
strong	**stark**	shtark
student	**der Student**	shtoo*dent*
stung (to be)	**gestochen werden**	gu-*shtokhen vair*den
style	**der Stil**	shteel
suburb	**der Vorort**	*for*-ort
subway	**die Unterführung**	*oonter*-fuiroong
such	**solch**	solkh
suede	**das Wildleder**	*vilt-lay*der
sugar	**der Zucker**	*tsoo*ker
suggestion	**der Vorschlag**	for-*shlahg*
suit *men*	**der Anzug**	*ant*soog
women	**das Kostüm**	kostuim
suitcase	**der (Hand-) Koffer**	*(hant-)* koffer
sun	**die Sonne**	*zon*ner
sunbathe (to)	**sonnenbaden**	*zonnen-bah*den
sunburn	**der Sonnenbrand**	*zonnen*-brant
sunglasses	**die Sonnenbrille** (*sing.*)	*zonnen-bril*ler

sunhat	der Sonnenhut	*zonn*en-hoot
sunny	sonnig	*zonn*ikh
sunshade	der Sonnenschirm	*zonn*en-sheerm
supermarket	der Supermarkt	*zoop*er-markt
supper	das Abendessen	*ah*bent-essen
sure	sicher	*zikh*er
surgery	das Sprechzimmer	*shprekh*-tsimmer
surgery hours	die Sprechstunde	*shprekh*-shtoonder
surprise	die Überraschung	uiber-*rash*oong
surprise (to)	überraschen	uiber-*rash*en
sweater	der Pullover	pool*ohv*air
sweet	süß	zuis
sweets	die Bonbons	bonbons
swell (to)	anschwellen	*an*-shvellen
swim (to)	schwimmen	*shvim*men
swimming pool	das Schwimmbad	shvimbaht
swings	die Schaukel, Wippe	*show*kel, vipper
Swiss	schweizerisch	*shvyt*serish
Swiss man/woman	der Schweizer, die Schweizerin	*shvyt*ser, *shvyt*serin
switch *electrical*	der (Licht-) Schalter	(*likht*-) shalter
Switzerland	die Schweiz	shvites
swollen	angeschwollen	*an*-gu-*shvoll*en
synagogue	die Synagoge	zuinah-*gohg*ur

T

table	**der Tisch**	tish
tablecloth	**das Tischtuch**	*tish*-tookh
tablet	**die Tablette**	ta*blet*ter
tailor	**der Schneider**	*shny*der
take (to)	**nehmen**	*nay*men
talk (to)	**reden**	*ray*den
tall	**groß**	grohs
tampon	**das Tampon**	tampon
tank	**der Tank**	tank
tap	**der Wasserhahn**	*vasser*-hahn
taste	**der Geschmack**	gu-*shmack*
taste (to)	**schmecken**	shmecken
tax	**die Steuer**	*stoyer*
taxi	**das Taxi**	taxi
taxi rank	**der Taxistand**	taxi-shtant
teach (to)	**lehren**	*lay*ren
tear	**der Riss**	riss
tear (to)	**(zer)reißen**	(tsair)*ryssen*
telephone	**das Telefon**	tele*fohn*
telephone (to)	**telefonieren**	telefohn*neer*en
telephone call	**der Anruf**	*an*-roof
telephone directory	**das Telefonbuch**	tele*fohn*-bookh

telephone number	**die Telefonnummer**	tele*fohn*-noommer
telephone operator	**der Telefonist, die Telefonistin**	tele*fohn*ist, tele*fohn*istin
television	**das Fernsehen**	*fairn-zay*en
tell (to)	**erzählen**	air*tsay*len
temperature	**die Temperatur**	tempera*toor*
temple	**der Tempel**	*tempel*
temporary	**vorläufig, vorübergehend**	*for-loy*fikh, *for-ui*ber-*gay*ent
tennis	**das Tennis**	*tennis*
tent	**das Zelt**	tselt
tent peg	**der Zeltpflock**	*tselt*-pflock
tent pole	**der Zeltmast**	*tselt*-mast
terrace	**die Terrasse**	tair*rasser*
text message	**die Textnachricht**	*text*-nahkh-rikht
than	**als**	als
that	**jener, jene, jenes**	*yay*ner, *yay*ner, *yay*nes
the	**der, die, das**	dair, dee, das
theatre	**das Theater**	tay*ahter*
their(s)	**ihr, ihre**	eer, eerer
them	**sie, ihnen**	zee, eenen
then	**dann**	dan
there	**da, dort**	dah, dort
there is	**es ist/gibt**	es ist/geebt

there are	**es sind/gibt**	es zint/geebt
thermometer	**das Thermometer**	tairmoh-*mayt*er
these	**diese**	deezer
they	**sie**	zee
thick	**dick**	dick
thief	**der Dieb**	deeb
thin	**dünn**	duin
thing	**das Ding, die Sache**	ding, zakher
think (to)	**denken**	denken
thirsty	**durstig**	*door*stikh
this	**dieser, -e, -es**	deezair, deezer, deezez
those	**jene**	*yay*ner
though	**obwohl**	op*vohl*
thread	**der Faden**	*fah*den
through	**durch**	doorkh
throughout	**während**	*vair*ent
throw (to)	**werfen**	*vair*fen
thunderstorm	**das Gewitter**	guvitter
ticket	**die Karte**	karter
tide	**die Gezeiten** (*pl.*)	gu-*tsite*-en
tie *clothing*	**der Schlips**	shlips
sport	**der Gleichstand**	*glykh*-shtant
tight	**eng**	aing

tights	die Strumpfhose	shtroompf-hohzer
time	die Zeit	tsite
timetable	der Fahrplan	fahr-plahn
tin	die Dose	dohzer
tin opener	der Dosenöffner	dohzen-erfner
tip	das Trinkgeld	trinkgelt
tip (to)	ein Trinkgeld geben	ine trinkgelt gayben
tired	müde	muider
tissues	die Papiertücher	papeer-tuikher
to	zu, nach	tsoo, nahkh
tobacco	der Tabak	taback
tobacco pouch	der Tabaksbeutel	tabacks-boytel
together	zusammen	tsoo-zammen
toilet	die Toilette	twahletter
toilet paper	das Toilettenpapier	twahletten-papeer
toll	die Maut	mowt
too also	auch	owkh
too (much, many)	zu (viel, viele)	tsoo (feel, feeler)
toothbrush	die Zahnbürste	tsahn-buirster
toothpaste	die Zahnpasta	tsahn-pasta
toothpick	der Zahnstocher	tsahn-shtokher
top	das obere Ende	ohberer ender
torch	die Taschenlampe	tashen-lamper

torn	zerrissen	tsair-*rissen*
touch (to)	berühren	bu*ruiren*
tough	hart, zäh	hart, tsay
tour	die (Rund-) Reise	(*roont-*) *ryzer*
tourist	der Tourist	too*rist*
tourist office	das Verkehrsamt, die Touristeninformation	fair*kairs*-amt, tooristen-informats-*yon*
towards	gegen	*gay*gun
towel	das Handtuch	hant-tookh
tower	der Turm	toorm
town	die Stadt	shtat
town hall	das Rathaus	*raht*-hows
toy	das Spielzeug	*shpeel*-tsoyg
traffic	der Verkehr	fair*kair*
traffic jam	der Verkehrsstau	fair*kairs*-shtow
traffic lights	die Verkehrsampeln	fair*kairs-ampeln*
trailer	der Anhänger	*an*heng-er
train	der Zug	tsoog
trainers	die Sportschuhe	*shport*-shoo-wer
tram	die Straßenbahn (S-Bahn)	*shtrahssen*-bahn (*es*-bahn)
transfer (to)	übertragen	uiber-*trahgun*
travel	umbuchen	*oom-book*hen

transit	der Durchgang	*doorkh*-gang
translate (to)	übersetzen	*ui*ber-zetsen
travel (to)	reisen	*ryzen*
travel agency	das Reisebüro	*ryzer-buiroh*
traveller's cheque	der Reisescheck	*ryzer*-sheck
treat (to)	behandeln	bu*handeln*
treatment	die Behandlung	bu*hant*loong
tree	der Baum	bowm
trip	der Ausflug	*ows*-floog
trouble	die Mühe	mui-er
trousers	die Hose (*sing.*)	*hohzer*
true	wahr	vahr
trunk	der Koffer	koffer
trunks *swimming*	die Badehose (*sing.*)	*bahder-hohzer*
truth	die Wahrheit	*vahr*hite
try (to)	versuchen	fair*zookhen*
try on (to)	anprobieren	*an*-prohbeeren
tunnel	der Tunnel	*toonel*
turn (to)	umdrehen	*oom*-drayen
turning	die Biegung	*bee*goong
tweezers	die Pinzette (*sing.*)	pint*setter*
twin-bedded room	das Zweibettzimmer	*tsvy*-bet-tsimmer
twisted	verrenkt	fair-*renkt*

U

ugly	**hässlich**	*hess*lik
UK	**Großbritannien**	grohs-brit*tan*-yen
umbrella	**der Regenschirm**	*ray*gun-sheerm
(beach) umbrella	**der Sonnenschirm**	*zonnen*-sheerm
uncle	**der Onkel**	*onk*el
uncomfortable	**unbequem**	*oon*-bu-*k-vaym*
unconscious	**ohnmächtig**	*ohn-mekh*tikh
under(neath)	**unter**	*oonter*
underground	**die U-Bahn**	oo-bahn
underpants	**die Unterhose**	*oonter-hohzer*
understand (to)	**verstehen**	fair*shtayen*
underwater fishing	**Unterwasserfischen**	*oonter-vasser-*fishen
underwear	**die Unterwäsche**	*oonter*-vesher
university	**die Universität**	oonee*vairseetayt*
unpack (to)	**auspacken**	*ows*-packen
until	**bis**	bis
unusual	**ungewöhnlich**	*oon*-guvernlikh
up	**auf**	owf
upstairs	**oben**	*ohben*
urgent	**dringend**	*dring*-ent
us	**uns**	oons

USA (United States of America)	**die USA (Vereinigten Staaten von Amerika)**	oo-ess-ah (fair-*ry*nigten *shtah*ten fon a*mair*eekah)
use (to)	**brauchen**	*browkh*en
useful	**brauchbar**	*browkh*bar
useless	**unbrauchbar**	*oon-browkh*bar
usual	**gewöhnlich**	guv*ern*likh

V

vacancies	**Zimmer frei**	tsimmer fry
vacant	**frei**	fry
vacation	**die Ferien**	*fair*ee-yen
valid	**gültig**	*guil*tikh
valley	**das Tal**	tahl
valuable	**wertvoll**	*vairt*fol
value	**der Wert**	vairt
vase	**die Vase**	*vah*zer
VAT	**MWS (Mehrwertsteuer)**	em-vee-ess (*mair*-vairt-*shtoy*er)
vegetable	**das Gemüse**	ge*muiz*er
vegetarian	**der Vegetarier**	vegay*tah*ree-yer
ventilation	**die Ventilation**	ventilahts-*yon*
very	**sehr**	zair
vest	**das Unterhemd**	*oon*ter-hemt

view	**der Blick**	blick
villa	**die Villa**	vee*lah*
village	**das Dorf**	dorf
violin	**die Geige**	*gy*gur
visa	**das Visum**	*vee*zoom
visibility	**die Sicht (-barkeit)**	*sikht* (-barkite)
visit	**der Besuch**	bu*zookh*
visit (to)	**besuchen**	bu*zookh*en
voice	**die Stimme**	shtimmer
voltage	**die Spannung**	*shpann*oong
voucher	**der Gutschein**	*goot*-shine

W

wait (to)	**warten**	*var*ten
waiter	**der Kellner**	*kell*ner
waiting room	**der Warteraum**	*varter*-rowm
waitress	**die Kellnerin**	*kell*nerin
wake (to)	**aufwachen**	*owf*-vakhen
Wales	**Wales**	vayls
walk	**der Spaziergang**	shpats*eer*-gang
walk (to)	**spazierengehen**	shpats*eeren-gay*en
wall *inside*	**die Wand**	vant
outside	**die Mauer**	*mouw*er

wallet	**die Brieftasche**	*breef*-tasher
want (to)	**wollen**	vollen
wardrobe	**der Kleiderschrank**	*klyder*-shrank
warm	**warm**	varm
wash (to)	**waschen**	vashen
washbasin	**das Waschbecken**	*vash*-becken
waste	**der Abfall**	*ap*-fal
waste (to)	**verschwenden**	fair*shvenden*
watch	**die Armbanduhr**	*arm*bant-oor
water	**das Wasser**	*vasser*
waterfall	**der Wasserfall**	*vasser*-fal
water skiing	**das Wasserskilaufen**	*vasser*-*shee*-*low*fen
waterproof	**wasserdicht**	*vasser*dikht
wave	**die Welle**	veller
way	**der Weg**	vayg
we	**wir**	veer
wear (to)	**tragen**	*trah*gun
weather	**das Wetter**	*vet*ter
weather forecast	**die Wettervorhersage**	*vet*ter-for-hairz*ah*gur
wedding ring	**der Ehering**	*ayer*-ring
week	**die Woche**	*vokher*
weekend	**das Wochenende**	*vokh*en-ender
weigh (to)	**wiegen**	veegun

weight	**das Gewicht**	gu*veekht*
welcome	**willkommen**	vil-*kommen*
well	**gut**	goot
Welsh	**walisisch**	va*leez*ish
Welsh *man/woman*	**der Waliser, die Waliserin**	va*leez*er, va*leez*erin
west	**der Westen**	vesten
wet	**nass**	nass
what?	**was?**	vas
wheel	**das Rad**	raht
when?	**wann?**	van
where?	**wo?**	voh
whether	**ob**	op
which?	**welcher, welche, welches?**	*velkh*er, *velkh*er, *velkh*es
while	**während**	*vair*ent
who?	**wer?**	vair
whole	**ganz**	gants
whose?	**wessen?**	vessen
why?	**warum?**	vah*room*
wide	**weit**	vite
widow	**die Witwe**	*veet*ver
widower	**der Witwer**	*veet*vair
wife	**die Frau**	frow

wild	**wild**	vilt
win (to)	**gewinnen**	guvinnen
wind	**der Wind**	vint
window	**das Fenster**	*fenster*
wing	**der Flügel**	fluigel
wire	**der Draht**	draht
wish (to)	**wünschen**	*vuinshen*
with	**mit**	mit
without	**ohne**	ohner
woman	**die Frau**	frow
wood *trees*	**der Wald**	valt
timber	**das Holz**	holts
wool	**die Wolle**	voller
word	**das Wort**	vort
work	**die Arbeit**	*arbite*
work (to)	**arbeiten**	*arbiten*
worry (to)	**(sich) beunruhigen**	(zikh) bu-*oon*-roo-igun
worse	**schlechter**	*shlekh*ter
worth (to be)	**wert sein**	vairt zine
wrap (to)	**wickeln**	vickeln
write (to)	**schreiben**	*shry*ben
writing paper	**das Schreibpapier**	*shryb*-pa*peer*
wrong	**falsch**	falsh

Y

yacht	**die Jacht**	yakht
year	**das Jahr**	yahr
yet	**noch**	nokh
you	**Sie, du** (familiar)	zee, doo
young	**jung**	yoong
your	**Ihr, dein**	eer, dine
youth hostel	**die Jugendherberge**	*yoo*gunt-*hair*bairger

Z

zip	**der Reißverschluss**	*rice*-fairs*hlooss*
zoo	**der Zoo**	tsoh

INDEX